T0295769

THE IMPACT OF FOREIGN-OWNED COMPANIES ON HOST ECONOMIES

A COMPUTABLE GENERAL EQUILIBRIUM APPROACH

ECONOMIC ISSUES, PROBLEMS AND PERSPECTIVES

Additional books in this series can be found on Nova's website under the Series tab.

Additional E-books in this series can be found on Nova's website under the E-book tab.

ECONOMIC ISSUES, PROBLEMS AND PERSPECTIVES

THE IMPACT OF FOREIGN-OWNED COMPANIES ON HOST ECONOMIES

A COMPUTABLE GENERAL EQUILIBRIUM APPROACH

CONCEPCIÓN LATORRE

Nova Science Publishers, Inc.
New York

NOTICE TO THE READER

The Publisher has taken reasonable care in the preparation of this book, but makes no expressed or implied warranty of any kind and assumes no responsibility for any errors or omissions. No liability is assumed for incidental or consequential damages in connection with or arising out of information contained in this book. The Publisher shall not be liable for any special, consequential, or exemplary damages resulting, in whole or in part, from the readers' use of, or reliance upon, this material.

Independent verification should be sought for any data, advice or recommendations contained in this book. In addition, no responsibility is assumed by the publisher for any injury and/or damage to persons or property arising from any methods, products, instructions, ideas or otherwise contained in this publication.

This publication is designed to provide accurate and authoritative information with regard to the subject matter covered herein. It is sold with the clear understanding that the Publisher is not engaged in rendering legal or any other professional services. If legal or any other expert assistance is required, the services of a competent person should be sought. FROM A DECLARATION OF PARTICIPANTS JOINTLY ADOPTED BY A COMMITTEE OF THE AMERICAN BAR ASSOCIATION AND A COMMITTEE OF PUBLISHERS.

Additional color graphics may be available in the e-book version of this book.

LIBRARY OF CONGRESS CATALOGING-IN-PUBLICATION DATA

The impact of foreign-owned companies on host economies / Concepción Latorre.
    p. cm.
  Includes index.
  ISBN 978-1-62100-847-7 (Softcover)
  1. Business enterprises, Foreign. 2. International business enterprises.
3. Investments, Foreign. I. Title.
  HD2755.5.L374 2009
  338.8'8--dc22
                            2010002311

Published by Nova Science Publishers, Inc. ✛ *New York*

DEDICATION

To my parents,
Inmaculada C. and Rafael

CONTENTS

"(...) the great strength of our theory of international trade is its general-equilibrium approach. If one is to integrate the multinational into the theory of international trade, one needs to turn to a general-equilibrium framework."

(Markusen, 2002, p. 77)

PREFACE

The aim of the book is analysing the macro and microeconomic effects on a host economy of the entry of foreign-owned companies (i.e., multinational enterprises, henceforth, MNEs). There is some controversy regarding the impact of MNEs, as can be seen in the active antiglobalisation movements. Therefore, we offer a thorough and up-to-date review of the literature analysing what is known about MNEs nowadays.

In addition, we also make use of an applied methodology, namely, computable general equilibrium (CGE) simulations, to provide quantitative outcomes and not just qualitative intuitions regarding how MNEs affect economies. CGE models are widely used across international institutions such as the IMF, World Bank, European Commission, to name a few, as well as in the academic literature. We provide a detailed explanation about how this type of model works. As the world becomes increasingly integrated, more accurate results on the magnitude of the impact on GDP, trade and welfare (at the aggregate level), as well as production, labour demand, prices, imports and exports (across sectors) can be very useful. CGEs are suitable to derive those results, but very few of them have considered the presence of MNEs. Thus, the CGE model with MNEs presented in this book offers a rather new approach to study the effects of MNEs.

The structure of the book is as follows. Chapter 1 offers an introduction where the central concepts are defined, the relevance of MNEs and FDI flows in the world economy are highlighted and some considerations regarding the methodological approach are made. Chapter 2 develops a comprehensive and up-to-date review of the theoretical and empirical literature on MNEs. The CGE model is explained in detail in Chapter 3. We have expanded a publicly available CGE model to include MNEs. This is the GTAP model (Hertel,

1997), which is designed to make use of a database of the world economy. We have introduced MNEs in the model in such a manner that OECD (2007) data on the activities of MNEs could be used, as the latter are absent in the GTAP database. By doing this we overcome the problem of obtaining data for general equilibrium simulations considering MNEs – all these data are also publicly available –, which has been partly the reason why most applied trade models have not included the role of MNEs during decades. Thus, although the empirical analysis is applied to the Czech Republic -a country that has received many MNEs in the last few years- the model can be applied to other countries as well. The simulations of the impact of MNEs considering economy-wide effects are performed in Chapters 4 and 5.

The conclusion seems of relevance. Profit repatriation matters. The mere entry of MNEs leads to small increases in GDP and welfare, which are likely to be offset when profit repatriation is above a certain threshold level. For the Czech economy profit repatriation beyond 50 and 60 percent of the income generated by the entry of MNEs would result in a fall of GDP and welfare, respectively. Thus, we point to the importance of an aspect that few previous studied have analysed.

FOREWORD

Holger Görg

Multinational enterprises are important players in the globalised world economy. The *United Nations World Investment Report 2008* reports that there are roughly 79,000 multinationals that control almost 800,000 foreign subsidiaries world-wide. In 2006, foreign direct investment stocks amounted to around $ 12,8 trillion – roughly comparable to the gross domestic product of the Eurozone.

Multinationals can bring important economic stimuli for host economies. They bring in new technology, new capital, create jobs, import and export, among many other things. Governments around the globe try actively to attract multinationals to locate in their country, assuming that these companies bring large benefits. Yet, when it comes to empirically verifying whether such positive effects on host countries actually exist, and what there magnitude may be, one quickly realizes that not much is known. The evidence that is out there generally focuses on a small aspect of the whole picture – for example, establishing whether multinationals pay higher or lower wages than domestic firms – while completely neglecting any other potential benefits for the host country.

This book by Concepción Latorre provides a fresh new perspective on examining how multinationals affect host countries. She uses a Computable General Equilibrium (CGE) model, which sheds light on the impact multinational companies have on aggregate macroeconomic and sectoral variables. Thus the study covers their macroeconomic impact on variables such as GDP, wages, rental rate of capital, consumer prices, exports, imports and welfare. Regarding sectoral variables the study considers production, prices, intermediate costs, value added, exports and imports at a highly disaggregated sectoral level. The study is based on a comprehensive and up-to-date review of the main theoretical strands on foreign direct investment and multinationals, together with an assessment of the existing empirical evidence available on some of their effects on host economies.

The CGE model that is developed is applied to the Czech Republic, a country with very high presence of foreign multinationals. Given the general nature of the model, this study could also be applied to other countries, which make the set up and empirical results not only extremely illuminating but also of very high practical relevance.

Thus, this is a very worthwhile read not only for students and researchers interested in multinational enterprises and CGE modelling, but also for policy makers interested in seriously assessing the potential effects multinationals can have on their host economies.

Kiel, June 2009

Holger Görg

ACKNOWLEDGMENTS

I would like to express a sincere gratitude to many who have helped me in different ways to arrive where I am now.

First of all, I would like to thank my big family. They have helped me to concentrate on my work with great generosity. My parents, Inma and Rafael, deserve a very special mention, as they have been particularly close and encouraging. My brother, Rafael, also deserves a special mention. His joy and sense of humour are a proof of a nice way of giving strength to others.

I am highly indebted to my PhD supervisors, Oscar Bajo-Rubio and Antonio Gómez-Plana. They have devoted their time and experience with magnanimity to this research which is now updated and published. They have always been available and willing to suggest new inputs, ideas and improvements. How many Friday afternoons and evenings I have met Oscar to work on this! How many trips to Navarre to work intense days with Antonio! They have saved no efforts at all. They have taught me not only economics but rigour and depth in research. Working with them has also been a lesson of intellectual and human integrity.

I would like to thank in a very particular way Professors José Molero and Mikel Buesa. They opened the doors of academic research and teaching, which was, and still is, like a dream for me. I am also very grateful to Professor Rafael Myro for continuously expanding my horizons and academic projects.

I would like to thank other people, of the Department of Applied Economics II at the University Complutense of Madrid and other places, who have helped at different stages of this book. In particular, Professors Jose Carlos Fariñas, Rafael Salas and Jose Luis García Delgado, as well as Carmen Díaz-Roldán.

During my stays in other universities many persons offered valuable advice and help. Those are the cases of those working in the University of Manchester: Paul Madden, Rabah Amir, Keith Blackburn and Marcia Wall. More recently, the people from the University of Nottingham, particularly: Holger Görg, Adam Blake, Geoff Reed, Ben Ferrett, Bob Hine, Jennifer Siggers and, last but, certainly not least, María Montero.

I would also like to thank the staff of the libraries of the Faculty of Economics and the School of Statistics of the University Complutense of Madrid, in particular, Carmen Antón (Director of the Statistics Library) and Plácido Sandía, whose high efficiency and kindness made the work much easier.

Finally, I would like to thank my good friends, who know who they are, for their interest and support.

Madrid, July 2009
Concepción Latorre

ABSTRACT

The aim of this book is analysing the impact on a host economy of the entry of foreign-owned companies or multinational enterprises (MNEs). It provides an up-to-date, comprehensive synthesis and evaluation of the existing literature on multinational firms and foreign direct investment. It further, offers a new perspective on the issue by means of a a computable general equilibrium (CGE) approach, through a version of the Global Trade Analysis Project (GTAP) model extended to incorporate MNEs. We have paid a special attention to a mostly neglected aspect of the effects of MNEs, namely, profit repatriation. The empirical analysis is applied to the case of the Czech Republic, a country that has received substantial inflows of foreign direct investment in the last few years.

Keywords: Foreign-owned companies, foreign direct investment, computable general equilibrium, profit repatriation, host economies

JEL Classification: C68, F21, F23

Chapter 1

INTRODUCTION

ABSTRACT

This is an introductory chapter in which the central concepts in the book, namely, Foreign Direct Investment or FDI, Foreign-owned companies or Multinational Enterprises (MNEs) and Fragmentation, are defined in detail. It also offers data on the relevance of MNEs and FDI flows in the world economy, particularly, in Eastern Europe, the area to which the analysis is applied. Some considerations are made regarding the methodological approach used in the book: the Computable General Equilibrium (CGE) technique. It finally, offers the structure of the book explaining the contents of each of its chapters.

During decades most applied trade models have not considered the presence of foreign-owned companies (i.e., multinational enterprises, MNEs, henceforth). This absence seems to be, at least partly, due to data constraints on their activities. But also, at the theoretical level, it is probably fair to say that the introduction of MNEs has posed an important challenge to trade models for a long time (Markusen, 2002).

It is clear, however, that MNEs are behind many trade flows. In this respect, the World Investment Report (UNCTAD, 2000) reports two relevant figures. First, one-third of the volume of world trade is accounted by transactions in which multinationals firms are in one of the two sides of the exchange. Second, another third of the volume of world trade is intra-firm trade (i.e. trade within the MNEs, either between the parent and the subsidiary or between affiliates). Can we, then, expect to deal with trade in a correct manner with models which do not include MNEs?

The main objective of this book is to extend the GTAP model (Hertel, 1997) to include MNEs in it. GTAP stands for Global Trade Analysis Project. This is the name of a team of researchers working at Purdue University in Indiana (USA) on computable general equilibrium (CGE) models, which allow for the use of a unique database of the world economy for general equilibrium simulations, namely, the GTAP database (Dimaranan, 2007). The model, together with the database, offer great possibilities for the analysis of trade flows, as will be clearer in Chapters 3 to 5. Thus, our aim is to extend a model which deals carefully with trade to incorporate MNEs. Furthermore, we have worked in this extension in such a manner that the publicly available OECD (2007) data for the activities of MNEs can be used. This is because the GTAP database, despite its richness, does not contemplate MNEs.

On the other hand, there is some controversy regarding the impact of MNEs on host economies, as can be seen in the active antiglobalisation movements. This has attracted our attention to this issue as well. CGE simulations yield quantitative outcomes and not just qualitative intuitions regarding how MNEs would affect economies. As the world becomes increasingly integrated, more accurate results on the magnitude of the impact on GDP, trade and welfare (at the aggregate level), as well as production, labour demand, prices, imports and exports (across sectors) can be very useful. We have chosen to adopt this approach thinking that it offers a new perspective into the analysis of the effects of MNEs that may provide well grounded insights.

Our analysis has been applied to the Czech Republic. There are several reasons for choosing this country which are related to two main ideas: 1) the presence of MNEs in the Czech Republic is prominent and, 2) from a practical perspective, we have particularly good data regarding their operations there.

Some comments are in order with respect to the first point above. The demise of central planning in Eastern Europe opened these markets for the operations of MNEs. The region as a whole has received a very important amount of FDI inflows (Latorre, 2002). What is more, the Czech Republic clearly stands out in the area. It has been the top recipient of FDI flows when measured in per capita terms. It, further, ranks second in terms of cumulative FDI inflows, after Poland. Why is this so? There are several reasons why the amount of FDI inflows has been so important in this country.

First, the Czech Republic was one of the first countries expected to join the European Union (EU), which happened in 2004. The experience shows that FDI inflows have in general increased at the time of a country's integration with the EU; see, e.g., Bajo-Rubio and Torres (2001) for the case of Spain, and Baldwin et al. (1996) for the accession of Austria, Finland and Sweden. But the magnitude of FDI inflows in the Czech Republic has surpassed those previous experiences (Latorre, 2002).

Second, privatisation processes attracted foreign investors (UNCTAD, 2001; EBRD, 2001). In general, for the transition economies not all the FDI flows have been related to privatisation processes (Kalotay and Hunya, 2000). At the beginning, foreign investors were excluded from them, since the governments preferred domestic investors. But the Czech Republic seems to be an exception as foreign investors could participate in privatisation earlier than in other countries. Although the data available invite to a prudent attitude regarding their interpretation, for the years 1992 to 1997 most of FDI inflows into the Czech Republic were related to privatisations. By 1998, only 20 per cent of the State property in the Czech Republic was still in public hands. As will be clearer later, large amounts of FDI flows arrived after that year, so that they might be unrelated to privatisations (Kalotay and Hunya, 2000).

Third, there are fears that FDI going to the Czech Republic may be related with the fall in FDI received by other areas, such as the European periphery (Buch et al., 2003; Lorentowicz et al., 2002), or may be even a result of disinvestments or delocalisation processes, i.e., a reduction of the capital owned by foreign MNEs, in those areas (Fernández-Otheo and Myro, 2003; Fernández-Otheo, Martín and Myro, 2004). This remains an open question which deserves more empirical research.

Finally, there are some other factors that make the Czech Republic an attractive location for FDI, such as its particular situation in Central Europe, good endowments of human capital (OECD, 2001; Marin, 2004), a most advanced position in its way to a market economy (which reduces uncertainties and provides better future expectations for investment), or high level of per capita GDP as compared to other "first wave" Eastern European countries.

On the other hand, regarding the second point above, for this country we have the most comprehensive data on FDI and MNEs among transition economies. Because of its coverage of a wide range of variables, it has one of the best and most updated datasets among the countries for which the OECD offers information. Additionally, the Czech National Bank has also been collecting data on MNEs that broaden the scope covered by the OECD. It offers higher sectoral detail, which allows for a further level of sectoral disaggregation. And, moreover, it supplies some rich statistics about the external transactions of MNEs that are lacking in the OECD database (OECD, 2007); this gives a better perspective than that available for any other country, enhancing the possibilities of the analysis.

The rest of this chapter consists of four more sections. In section 1, we define in detail the central concepts in this study. Section 2 highlights the relevance of MNEs and FDI flows in the world economy nowadays, particularly, in the area to which our analysis is applied. Section 3 makes some considerations regarding the methodological approach used in this book. The last section offers the structure of the book explaining the contents of each of its chapters.

1. DELIMITING CONCEPTS

As mentioned above, this book analyses the effects of *multinational enterprises* (MNEs) on host, or receiving, economies. These effects arise, on the one hand, through *foreign direct investment* (FDI) flows and, on the other hand, from MNEs' operations themselves. Given the central role of these two concepts (MNEs and FDI) in this study, it is worth devoting some time to delimit what they involve.

FDI and MNEs are two sides of the same phenomenon of firms' internationalisation. Therefore, they are related concepts. However, each concept gives a particular angle and conveys complementary aspects of that phenomenon. In other words, data on FDI (flows or stocks) offer complementary information to those contained in data on MNEs' activities (their production and contribution to value added, their employment, their expenditures on R&D, …).

1.1. Foreign Direct Investment

What are FDI flows? They are a type of capital flow characterised, in principle, by a long-term vocation and the purpose of establishing or controlling a firm abroad. In this sense, they are opposed to short-term capital movements, such as portfolio investments.

The classical definition of FDI is that of the IMF (1993): FDI is an inter-company debt transaction in which one of the parties needs to own at least 10 percent of the other's party equity. Several explanations seem useful here. On the one hand, it is worth noting that the 10 percent threshold is rather arbitrary.

The degree of influence is not measured exactly by the percentage of common stock held by the foreign investor (Lipsey, 2003). It is also of relevance to differentiate between different types of affiliates, i.e., foreign controlled plants. There is some ambiguity in the literature, but basically there are two types of affiliates: 1) "subsidiaries" or MOFAs (majority-owned foreign affiliates), which are more than 50 percent owned by the direct investor, and 2) "associates" which are owned between 10 and 50 percent by their parents. By contrast, it is standard to refer to the controlling firm as "parent firm".

On the other hand, a clarification regarding what "debt transactions" are in the definition above is also useful. These "debt transactions" (and consequently, FDI flows) can take three different forms: 1) *equity capital*, which comprises non-resident investment in the equity of a company and all shares in subsidiaries and associates; 2) *reinvested earnings*, which consists of the direct investor's share (in proportion to direct equity participation) of earnings not distributed as dividends; and 3) *other capital* which covers the borrowing and lending of funds between direct investors and their subsidiaries and associates.

FDI is related to the macroeconomic side of MNEs, whereas MNEs data are more related to the microeconomic side (Markusen, 2002). Regarding the former, there are two main channels by which FDI may affect macroeconomic variables: 1) through its effects in the balance of payments (which may entail an impact on savings in the economy); and 2) through its impact on the capital stock of the economies. We will analyse this in depth in the following chapter.

1.2. The Foreign-Owned Company or Multinational Enterprise

FDI consequences go beyond financial transactions and capital stock variations. The essence of FDI is that is related to "a particular type of firm going abroad", i.e., the MNE. What are the peculiarities of this type of firms? Most authors put emphasis on the *superiority of the assets hold by the MNE*, compared to assets owned by firms that are not MNEs. Many of these assets are intangible (brand name, reputation, skills, experience, management, engineering and marketing techniques, …). Indeed, MNEs tend to be firms in which the value of intangible assets is large relative to its market value (Markusen, 2002). Further, some of these MNEs' assets have a "public good" character, in the sense that they can be spread geographically in a non-rival way and at no cost (Barba Navaretti and Venables, 2004, chapter 1). This "public good" character is a source of firm level economies of scale that gives the firm incentives to expand and create new plants.

These *specific assets* seem to be crucial in explaining the reasons why FDI is undertaken. One should therefore realise that each FDI flow is different in the sense that it is attached to a specific firm which brings with it a unique bundle of factors and abilities. Therefore, "an (FDI) inflow is not simply offset by an outflow. (…) Equal direct investment from France to Germany and Germany to France do not simply cancel each other out; there has been an addition to the stock of French skills producing in Germany and an addition to German skills producing in France" (Lipsey, 2003, p. 309).

Consistent with the peculiarities of MNEs assets, only a small fraction of firms engages in FDI, and these firms are larger and more productive than exporting firms, which in turn, are also more productive and larger than firms with no foreign operations (Helpman et al., 2004; Helpman, 2006). However, through its impact on employment, production, R&D and trade, among others, the small number of MNEs may exert an important influence on the economic restructuring of countries and industries.

Also consistent with the intangibility of their assets and with their public good nature, MNEs tend to be more present in some sectors. These are characterised by the production of technically complex or differentiated products, and/or by a large number of nonproduction workers (skilled labour, managers), and/or high levels of R&D expenditures over sales (Barba Navaretti and Venables, 2004; Markusen, 1995, 2002).

These characteristics of MNEs give an idea of their peculiarity and of their relative superiority in terms of efficiency and productivity, compared to domestic firms. This will also be developed in length in the following chapter. At the moment, we want to go more deeply into the relationship between FDI and MNEs.

1.3. The Relationship between Foreign Direct Investment and Multinationals

It is an initial FDI flow which generates a MNE. But as we said before the 10 percent threshold of foreign ownership established by the IMF may or may not be enough to exert control on the firm whose shares have been acquired. Consequently, by relying only on FDI inward data one may overestimate or underestimate the importance of MNEs firms in the host economy.

On the other hand, after the MNEs are set up, their activities may or may not be related with FDI flows. Sometimes, MNEs, once established, do not have recourse to their parents or other affiliates of the group financial resources (i.e. FDI flows do not take place any longer), because they borrow in the local markets of the host economy. This implies that a MNE or foreign affiliate can be economically important even when it does not obtain its funds from its parent firm. In other words, MNEs may be very active in the host economy (in terms of increasing their production, employing a rising share of workers, etc.) without this being reflected in an increase of FDI flows. In this case, the use of FDI inward data on flows may underestimate MNEs' importance for that economy.

Note, however, that data on the activities of MNEs, such as their weight on employment, value added, production, exports and imports..., are rather scarce. This contrasts with the availability of data on FDI, for which there are long time series at hand. There exists data on samples of MNEs, and many econometric studies are based on those samples, but then one may well face problems with representativeness. National statistics should, in principle, overcome these problems of representativeness. However, except for trade data, they are still anchored in a system of "national" variables, in which there is no information regarding which part of the variable is domestic and which is foreign, e.g., production by domestic firms versus production by foreign firms (OECD, 2005). As mentioned above, the OECD has been since recently gathering data of MNEs but they are not still available for many countries and the series are rather short (OECD, 2005, 2007). Our model tries to offer a way in which these data from the OECD can be used and exploited in a general equilibrium framework.

1.4. Fragmentation

The discussion above has noted that data on FDI and MNEs are complementary. It remains to explain the relationship between FDI and an interesting phenomenon which is growing in importance and attracting a lot of attention, namely, *fragmentation*. This term designates the process by which firms split geographically their production process into separate parts. It implies that there is a *geographic separation* of activities involved in production. The term, however, is a bit vague because it may denote geographic fragmentation within the same country as well as across borders (the latter could be called international fragmentation). It is also a bit vague because the fragmentation of production may take place within the same firm (i.e. internally, in different plants of the same firm, a process usually denoted "insourcing") or through plants outside the firm (i.e. under arm's-length contracts[1] with independent suppliers, or "outsourcing"). Helpman (2006) has noted that MNEs play a central role in the growing fragmentation of production, within and across national borders. This deserves some explanation.

The concept of MNE involves that at least some production processes undertaken abroad are kept internal to the firm (we will come back to this in the review of the theoretical literature in Chapter 2). The essence of the MNE is this *internalisation* process. However, this does not exclude other processes related to the MNE's production from being done through arm's-length contracts. When the latter take place MNEs are involved in fragmentation that is not only *geographical* but also *organisational*, in the sense that some of their processes are performed by independent producers.

Some MNEs decide to keep all the processes internal to them, e.g., Intel Corporation, which assembles its microchips in wholly-owned affiliates in China, Costa Rica, Malaysia and Philippines, according to the 2002 edition of the *World Investment Report* (UNCTAD, several years). In this case, Intel Corporation has sent FDI flows to install plants in those countries. Therefore, this process of fragmentation involves FDI flows. But when fragmentation is not only geographical but also organizational, no FDI flows will take place as a result of that process of fragmentation. This is the case of some operations of Nike, in particular, of those operations in which this MNE subcontracts that manufacturing of its products to independent producers in Thailand, Indonesia, Cambodia and Vietnam (Donaghu and Barff, 1990). As Nike did not invest to create the plants of those independent producers this process of fragmentation is not associated with FDI flows.

Thus, we can see that sometimes the process of international fragmentation is associated with FDI, but others not. Therefore, FDI data are not comprehensive when measuring this process; they will understate its importance. In the same line, fragmentation is related to some MNEs data on production, employment, etc., but it is also related to the data on production

---

[1] Arm's-length contracts denote a "contractual relationship between two independent firms, e.g. licensing agreements, subcontracting agreements, agency agreements, franchising agreements" (Barba Navaretti and Venables, 2004, p. 299). Note also that different terms related to several ways of undertaking fragmentation appear in the literature, and that they are not always univocal. Footnote 5 in Chapter 2 explains a widespread notation.

and employment of "independent producers" that are not affiliates of MNEs. Looking within MNEs alone does not give the full perspective on what is happening in the international disintegration of the production process (Feenstra, 1998).

In this study, we concentrate only on the effects of the type of fragmentation that takes place *within* the MNE. We focus on fragmentation that is done by wholly-owned affiliates and which is linked to FDI flows (e.g., the Intel case before). The effects of fragmentation, in the manner of the Nike case just mentioned, arise more from trade data and have a vague, probably inexistent, relationship with FDI.

2. MULTINATIONALS AND FOREIGN DIRECT INVESTMENT FLOWS IN THE WORLD ECONOMY

MNEs are central players in today's worldwide economic organisation. The OECD (2007) offers some data on the share of MNEs over the whole economy for a few countries. Table 1 shows their shares on employment, value-added and R&D. There is, of course, considerable variation across countries. This ranks from the minor weight of MNEs in Japan to their more important presence in small economies such as Hungary and the Czech Republic. However, looking at the average one sees they account for a considerable part of employment (13%), value added (19%) and R&D (31%).

The OECD (2004, 2007) increases the scope of countries and variables covered when dealing with data of MNEs in manufactures. Table 2 offers some indicators for manufacturing sectors in OECD countries. As can be seen, the share on employment and value added increases considerably with respect to their value for the whole economy. MNEs account for nearly one-fourth of the employment and around one-third of the value added, turnover and R&D expenditures in manufacturing in these OECD host economies. These averages, again, hide considerable variation across countries.

The data shown in the tables cover the years to which the analyses in Chapters 4 and 5 are applied. More recent data on the activities of MNEs and FDI flows can be found in OECD (2009a and 2009b), respectively. Furthermore, Eurostat offers two databases with information on the activities of foreign-owned companies (Eurostat, 2009a and 2009b). The data from Eurostat are, however, somewhat less regular in the years and variables covered than the ones in the OECD. Although, as noted above, the availability of data on MNEs differs considerably depending on the country studied.

Table 1. Percentage weight of MNEs on employment, value added, and R&D, 2001 (or latest year available)

	% Employment	% Value added	%R&D
Australia	12.3	20.8	n.a.
Finland	14.1	13.6	14.2
Hungary	27.6	39.1	39.2
Italy	6.4	11.7	33.0
Japan	0.4	0.6	3.9
Netherlands	10.8	15.0	19.6
Sweden	13.3	25.9	38.2
United Kingdom	10.6	16.1	39.4
Czech Republic	20.7	27.2	61.0
Average	12.9	18.9	31.1

Source: OECD (2007).
Notes: n.a.stands for not available.

Table 2. Percentage weight of MNEs on employment, value added, R&D, and turnover in manufacturing, 2001 (or latest year available)

	% Employment	% Value added	% R&D	% Turnover
Australia	22.7	34.5	45.4	n.a.
Czech Republic	30.3	41.4	59.0	45.5
Denmark	10.2	11.5	n.a.	12.0
Finland	17.2	15.8	13.1	16.2
France	30.8	35.8	21.4	35.9
Germany	16.6	n.a.	25.6	24.4
Hungary	43.6	54.5	78.0	71.6
Ireland	49.2	86.7	74.2	78.0
Italy	13.8	17.1	37.3	22.3
Japan	0.8	1.2	3.8	2.6
Luxemburgo	41.4	n.a.	n.a.	52.9
Netherlands	21.0	30.8	22.2	35.3
Norway	23.1	31.2	n.a.	29.7
Poland	24.1	n.a.	11.9	38.9
Portugal	8.6	15.5	49.1	15.6
Spain	16.4	24.8	42.6	28.5
Sweden	32.5	43.0	41.2	39.3
Turkey	7.0	18.6	12.7	14.7
United Kingdom	20.4	26.8	31.5	36.1
United States	13.1	n.a.	19.0	25.0
Average	22.14	30.57	34.6	32.9

Sources: OECD (2004, 2007).
Notes: n.a.stands for not available.

The weight of MNEs on R&D is remarkable. It is a sign of the importance of MNEs as promoters of technological innovation and progress (Bajo-Rubio and Díaz-Roldán, 2002; Romer, 1993). This is related to the above mentioned characteristic of MNEs bringing with them new technologies, ideas and other intangible assets, which means an important channel through which they influence host economies. Although given its "intangible" character it is difficult to be measured as will be seen in Chapter 2.

On the other hand, the relationship between MNEs and the external sector of the economies is also of great relevance. In some countries, the volume of sales of their affiliates abroad has exceeded the country's total exports. This is the case of the United States, Japan and Finland (Barba Navaretti and Venables, 2004, chapter 1). This is something to note because the decision to install plants abroad, *a priori*, involves a much more complex process than exporting. Why do firms, then, prefer to serve foreign markets through MNEs rather than through exports? Why is FDI more important for these companies? This is something we will analyse in the review of the literature in the next chapter.

In line with the idea of the bigger complexity of installing plants abroad, for the world, as a whole, the volume of aggregate trade flows is much greater than FDI flows. But, as we will also see in detail, trade and FDI are often complementary. In fact, as already noted, MNEs are behind many trade flows, which in many cases is a sign of the strong link between MNEs and the so called process of fragmentation of production (Helpman, 2006) that was mentioned earlier.

Additionally, we know that the presence of MNEs keeps growing and growing in magnitude. The growth of sales by foreign affiliates has expanded much faster than exports and GDP from 1985 onwards according to the 2002 edition of the *World Investment Report* (UNCTAD, several years). This contrasts with the previous trend, when these variables followed similar growth rates. In parallel, FDI flows have experienced an enormous growth since the end of World War II. This growth accelerated in the 1980s and 1990s (Lipsey, 2003).

From a different perspective, as we mentioned above, the demise of central planning in Eastern Europe has opened new markets (UNCTAD, 2001), also broadening the scope for the activities of MNEs. This has attracted our attention to the role of MNEs in that region. Figure 1 offers the evolution of FDI flows for ten of the transition economies. In particular, for a group that has been called the CEEC10 (Central and Eastern European Countries), which comprises the ten economies that are already EU members (the Czech

Republic, Hungary, Poland, the Slovak Republic, Slovenia, Estonia, Latvia, Lithuania, Bulgaria and Romania). These economies have attracted most of the flows accruing to transition economies. The CEEC10 experienced a 25 percent annual average growth of gross FDI inflows in the period 1992-2004. This increase is higher than that in China (19 percent) or in the world as a whole (16 percent), according to data from the UNCTAD (several years). Furthermore, in 2001, when the world FDI flows remarkably fell, inflows to these countries did not decrease (UNCTAD, 2002). On the other hand, as can be seen in Figure 1, most of these flows are concentrated in three of them, i.e., Poland, the Czech Republic and Hungary.

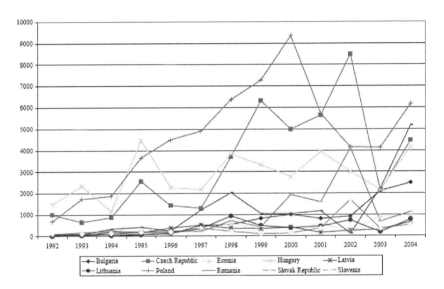

Source: UNCTAD (several years).

Figure 1. Gross FDI inflows into CEEC10, 1992-2004.

We explained in the previous section that FDI should be complemented, whenever possible, with data on MNEs' activities if one wants to evaluate MNEs' effects in an appropriate manner. A specific example from transition economies can be given. If we look at the data from MNEs' activities we will see that FDI and MNEs' weight on the economy do not run parallel. MNEs' activities have been permanently increasing during the period for which there is data available in the Czech Republic, Poland and in Hungary. This is shown in Table 3 which gives the evolution of the MNEs' employment in these three economies which already form part of the OECD; a similar picture would be found for value added and sales. The table presents the increases in employment in absolute terms, together with its percentage increase with respect to the previous year as well as its growing weight on the national total.

More details on the nature of FDI into the CEEC10 area are presented elsewhere (Latorre, 2002). Here, we concentrate on the effects of FDI on host economies. Our aim is to build a model that enables us to analyse the differential impact of FDI and MNEs accruing to the different sectors of the host economy, both at the sectoral and aggregate level. We turn now to the methodological approach used for this purpose.

**Table 3. MNEs weight on employment in Hungary,
Poland and the Czech Republic, 1995-2002**

	1997	1998	1999	2000	2001	2002
CZECH REP.						
Thousands	253.0	304.0	357.0	543.5	659.5	683.2
% increase		20.2	17.4	52.2	21.3	3.6
% on total	7.2	9	11	17	20.7	21.7
HUNGARY						
Thousands	543.0	580.7	584.0	609.9	615.8	580.6
% increase		6.9	0.6	4.4	1.0	-5.7
% on total	26	27.2	27.4	27.8	27.6	26.1
POLAND						
Thousands	416.3	497.3	590.7	648.3	655.4	715.9
% increase		19.4	18.8	9.7	1.1	9.2
% on total	7.6	9.2	11.9	13.8	14.7	16.6

Source: OECD (2007)
Note: for the Czech Republic there is a break in the series in the year 1999, when the criteria for collecting the data changed so that the values for the periods 1997-1999 and 2000-2002 are not strictly comparable.

3. WHY A GENERAL EQUILIBRIUM APPROACH?

Until very recently, the study of MNEs effects on host countries has mainly been undertaken using econometric techniques and a good deal of descriptive studies. These analyses have provided fruitful results. As we will see in our review of the literature in Chapter 2, there is a vast array of important contributions along these lines. However, these econometric and descriptive analyses constitute a body of research that is fragmented into separate parts according to the study of particular effects of MNEs. In other words, these approaches have provided dispersed contributions and different "strands" in the study of MNEs depending on the effect analysed. Thus, there is a literature on the effects of MNEs on wages, a literature on FDI spillovers over domestic firms' productivity, a different one on the relationship between trade and FDI, as well as, probably, fewer contributions analysing other types of effects. Facing these different strands one may find it difficult to compare the weight of the different effects of MNEs and have a good approximation to their relative importance. The use of a general equilibrium framework allows us to concentrate in a number of effects arising from the presence of MNEs, and derive their economy-wide impact in a unified framework. This will help us to shed some light on which forces prevail among all those that MNEs unleash in the host economy.

Our approach is based on a neoclassical *computable general equilibrium* (CGE) model, which incorporates real data into a rigorous theoretical framework. As explained in Shoven and Whalley (1984, 1992), neoclassical CGEs are based on the Arrow-Debreu general equilibrium model (as developed in Arrow and Hahn, 1971), with some potential extensions. The interactions among economic agents are, therefore, presented as a system of equations derived from microeconomic optimisation theory. The model covers the behaviour of households, firms and the government in the economy. These microeconomic optimisation decisions are embedded in a framework representing national accounts identities. In other words, the model also rests on the usual progression of the circular flow of the economy: production, income distribution, and domestic and foreign demand. Following that representation, it describes the equilibrium conditions in goods and factor markets, as well as in the foreign sector. Our model presents a modern formulation of the Arrow-Debreu approach using GAMS (General Algebraic Modeling System) software (Markusen, 2002; Rutherford, 2005; Gómez-Plana, 2005), as will be explained in Chapter 3.

CGE models share with the input-output methodology the fact of including intersectoral links in the analysis. Nevertheless, CGE models can use more flexible forms to model links than the fixed coefficient structure of the input-output framework. Thus, CGE is a methodology that allows dealing with many economic sectors taking into account the linkages among them (Dawkins et al., 2001) and "assessing who gains and who loses", i.e., which sectors are better or worse off after a shock (Shoven and Whalley, 1984, p. 1008).

The treatment of intersectoral links seems very relevant when one looks at the weight of intermediates in cost structures across sectors in the economy. The GTAP database allows us to obtain an approximation to the structure of production across sectors in the world economy. At a 20-sector aggregation level, which is also used in our empirical application for the Czech Republic, Figure 2 shows the distribution of value added and intermediates on gross output. It is clear that intermediates are very important for production in all sectors in the economy. In manufactures, intermediates weight more that 60 per cent of total gross output. In the rest of sectors their importance is smaller, but in general, well above 35 per cent. Figure 3 offers a higher level of disaggregation of the same data shown in Figure 2. It shows the weight of labour and capital (which form value added) together with the weight of imported and domestic intermediates on gross output. If one is to identify the particular impact of MNEs accruing to different sectors in the economy, as well as the pattern of adjustments across sectors, considering intermediate links seems crucial. We are very interested in this aspect, because we want to capture those different sectoral effects.

The idea that equivalent FDI inflows may have very different impacts depending on the sector to which they are directed has been stressed by other authors (Smarzynska, 2004; Barba Navaretti and Venables, 2004, chapter 7). In contrast with the econometric approach of these latter studies, we offer an alternative methodology, which seems appropriate to analyse this issue. Further, as we have data available for MNEs acting in services sectors we offer results for the impact of FDI in services, whereas the econometric literature has mainly focused on its effects in manufactures. On the other hand, there is a growing interest in MNEs' presence in services sectors. This is due to the fact that in the last two decades their presence in those sectors has increased considerably, parallel to the decline of MNEs in the primary sector. In fact, within the world total FDI inward stocks (i.e. the accumulated inward FDI gross flows through time), 50.3 percent was in services sectors, while 46.6% was in manufactures in 2001, the rest being in the primary sector (Barba Navaretti and Venables, 2004, chapter 1). Additionally, CGE modeling does not only offer a great flexibility regarding the number of sectors, but also in the number of households, factors of production and countries included in the analysis (Gómez-Plana, 2005). Ours will be a two-factor, two-region model with a representative household, and extensions are possible.

Notes: Author's own elaboration from Dimanaran (2007). The definitions of the sectors follow the ISIC Rev 3 Classification.
Figure 2. Weight of value added and intermediates on gross output in the world economy, 2001.

Sector	% Value Added	% Intermediates
01/05 Agriculture, hunting and fishing	55.3	44.7
10/14 Mining and quarrying	54.4	45.6
15/16 Food, beverages and tobacco	29.4	70.6
17/19 Textiles, wearing apparel, leather, footwear	30.1	69.9
20 Wood and wood products, except furniture	35.5	64.5
21/22 Paper; printing, publishing and recorded media	39.4	60.6
23 Petroleum	6.6	93.4
24/25 Chemicals, rubber and plastics	31.4	68.6
26 Non-metallic mineral products	36.8	63.2
27/28 Basic and fabricated metal products	29.7	70.3
34 Motor vehicles	24.3	75.7
35 Other transport equipment	36.0	64.0
30/33 Electronics	31.2	68.8
29 Machinery and equipment n.e.c.	38.4	61.6
36/37 Furniture, manufacturing n.e.c.	38.0	62.0
40/45 Electricity, gas and water supply; construction	44.9	55.1
50/55 Trade, repair; hotels and restaurants	60.7	39.3
60/64 Transport, Storage and Communication	50.2	49.8
65/74 Finance, insurance, real estate, business activities	65.4	34.6
75-79 NACE Other services	67.8	32.2

Figure 3 is a horizontal stacked bar chart showing the weight of inputs on gross output in the world economy, 2001. Legend: □ % Labour, ☒ % Capital, ☐ % Domestic Intermediates, □ % Imported Intermediates.

Sector	% Labour	% Capital	% Domestic Intermediates	% Imported Intermediates
01/05 Agriculture, hunting and fishing	27.1	28.2	40.1	4.7
10/14 Mining and quarrying	11.4	43.1	38.7	6.9
15/16 Food, beverages and tobacco	13.3	16.2	61.7	8.8
17/19 Textiles, wearing apparel, leather, footwear	18.5	11.6	54.4	15.5
20 Wood and wood products, except furniture	21.0	14.5	53.5	11.0
21/22 Paper; printing, publishing and recorded media	23.7	15.8	50.9	9.6
23 Petroleum	2.2	14.4	52.2	41.2
24/25 Chemicals, rubber and plastics	16.5	14.9	53.5	15.1
26 Non-metallic mineral products	20.5	16.3	54.9	8.3
27/28 Basic and fabricated metal products	19.4	10.3	58.2	12.1
34 Motor vehicles	16.7	7.6	58.8	17.0
35 Other transport equipment	26.0	10.0	49.7	14.3
30/33 Electronics	19.0	12.1	44.3	24.5
29 Machinery and equipment n.e.c.	25.3	13.1	46.9	14.7
36/37 Furniture, manufacturing n.e.c.	20.5	17.4	47.3	14.7
40/45 Electricity, gas and water supply; construction	26.5	18.5	48.3	6.8
50/55 Trade, repair; hotels and restaurants	38.1	22.5	35.8	3.5
60/64 Transport, Storage and Communication	27.4	22.7	42.4	7.5
65/74 Finance, insurance, real estate, business activities	24.0	41.3	32.2	2.5
75-79 NACE Other services	52.1	15.7	28.7	3.5

Notes: see Figure 2.

Figure 3. Weight of inputs on gross output in the world economy, 2001.

Unlike an input-output analysis which concentrates mainly on the production side of the economy, a general equilibrium framework takes also into account the demand side. Further, CGE modeling allows the evaluation of consumers' welfare, "one issue that is missing from the discussion of effects of foreign direct investment (FDI), a strange omission from a literature dominated by economists (…)" (Lipsey, 2002, p. 60).

Due to its very nature, CGE models consider the interaction between goods and factor markets. This seems particularly important in order to assess MNEs' effects; as Markusen says: "(...) general-equilibrium interactions between goods and factor markets are key to interesting results" (Markusen, 2002, p. 129); "(There are) general equilibrium factor-market effects that do not arise in a partial equilibrium model" (Markusen, 2002, p. 91).

A CGE model further yields macroeconomic predictions stemming from its microeconomic aggregation. It has been asserted that the potential of CGE models lies in their ability to integrate micro and macro elements (Devarajan and Robinson, 2005). This means that CGE models can measure the impact over the whole economy of a change in a particular sector or in a particular variable (Scarf and Shoven, 1984), or of several changes or policy measures taking place simultaneously (Devarajan and Robinson, 2005). This integration of micro and macroeconomic aspects provides a richer framework in which both FDI and MNEs, the two complementary sides of the phenomenon of firms' internationalisation, are simultaneously taken into account in the analysis.

This comprehensive approach to the economy demands a model of considerable dimension (i.e. dozens of equations to be solved simultaneously), which cannot be solved analytically (Markusen, 2002). This is why we use a *computable* general equilibrium. As Markusen writes: "The most interesting questions simply cannot be asked in a small-dimension model capable of an analytical solution" (Markusen, 2002, p. 129).

4. STRUCTURE OF THE BOOK

The structure of this book is as follows. We begin with a review of the theoretical and empirical literature on MNEs and FDI in Chapter 2. The model is explained in detail in Chapter 3. The simulations of the impact of MNEs on host economies considering economy-wide effects are performed in Chapters 4 and 5. In this latter respect, we have concentrated on two main types of simulations. The first one (Chapter 4) deals with the impact of a higher involvement of MNEs in some particular sectors of the Czech economy. The MNEs present in those sectors receive a higher amount of capital to produce using their own "specific" technology. By contrast, in Chapter 5 the simulation combines the impact of the increase in the capital stock available for MNEs with the effect of profit repatriation, i.e., when the MNEs send back to their home country the remuneration of the increased capital stock that their entry brings about. In other words, in the simulation in Chapter 5, the impact of profit repatriation is added to the effects of MNEs already analysed in the previous chapter. This offers a benchmark with respect to which the effects of profit repatriation can be better analysed.

Note that, all along this study, and in addition to the aggregate results, we also focus on the differential impacts of MNEs across sectors, which may be of special interest for the policy- maker, and which are absent in many studies on the effects of MNEs.

Chapter 2

A REVIEW OF THE LITERATURE

ABSTRACT

This chapter provides an up-to-date, comprehensive synthesis and evaluation of the existing literature on multinationals (MNEs) and foreign direct investment (FDI). It covers both theoretical and empirical studies. On the theoretical side, it offers a chronological description of the main strands since the earliest perfect competition studies from the 1960s till new recent contributions such as the Knowledge-capital model, heterogeneous firms models and those on internalisation issues. Unlike most previous reviews it combines several insights showing their inconsistencies and complementarities. On the empirical side, it concentrates on the effects of MNEs and FDI on host economies, given their controversy. It reviews their impact on savings, the current account, foreign trade, the capital stock, domestic firms' productivity, market structure, wages and GDP growth. Furthermore, a new perspective on this issue is offered, by reviewing the available computable general equilibrium models that include MNEs and FDI. Once this latter literature has been presented, the main characteristics of the model proposed in this book can be better analysed, an aspect to which we turn in the final section of the Chapter.

1. INTRODUCTION

The study of the multinational enterprise (MNE) and foreign direct investment (FDI) is a young discipline. Most analyses begun in the 1960s, a period in which FDI was experiencing an enormous growth, which attracted economists' attention. This was not, however, the first moment in which FDI had grown dramatically. Baldwin and Martin (1999) describe two waves of globalisation which are related to a rise in FDI flows, among other aspects. The first wave had taken place in the period 1820-1914, and was characterised by North to South FDI in primary product sectors and railroads. The second wage initialised in the 1960s and still continues nowadays, involving FDI mainly among developed nations with a focus on manufacturing, services and outsourcing. What caused such remarkable growth of FDI in the past? What is causing it nowadays? Which are its consequences?

The study of MNEs and FDI has been a fertile research topic. A number of authors have devoted their efforts to review the literature; see Agarwal (1980), Graham (1992), Markusen (1995), Blomström and Kokko (1997), Lipsey (2002), Barba Navaretti and Venables (2004), Feenstra (2004), Helpman (2006), Caves (2007), Greenaway and Kneller (2007) and Antràs and Rossi-Hansberg (2008), to name a few. This chapter offers an up-to-date, comprehensive synthesis and evaluation of the existing literature covering both theoretical and empirical studies. Unlike most previous reviews it combines several insights showing their inconsistencies and complementarities. Furthermore, the chapter also presents a new perspective, which is absent in previous reviews, by describing the available computable general equilibrium models that include MNEs and DFI.

On the theoretical side, it offers a chronological description of the main theoretical strands. In particular, we show that some of the earlier studies provided enlightening ideas, which are now being developed through more formal and sophisticated analyses, such as Markusen's (2002) "knowledge-capital model", or the recent studies on heterogeneous firms and internalisation issues. We do not focus on a particular strand of the literature but combine the insights from contractual and technological theories of the MNE.

On the empirical side, the effects of MNEs have been very much debated, and there is still some controversy regarding their impact on host economies, as can be seen in the active antiglobalisation movements. Therefore, we take a look to the empirical studies on this matter. We find that this is a very fragmented area of the literature, in which there are dispersed contributions and different strands according to the particular effect of MNEs analysed. Thus, there is literature on their impact on wages, a different literature on their effects on foreign trade, another one on productivity, on market structure, and so on. Apart from the idea that MNEs are more productive and pay higher wages than domestic firms, the empirical studies seem rather inconclusive regarding many of their effects on the host economies. Can we see which economic forces prevail among the several simultaneous ones that MNEs unleash in a host economy? Facing such a fragmented literature, it seems difficult to obtain an economy-wide evaluation of their impact. Therefore, this chapter also looks at a less known and nascent empirical line of research which appears suitable for this type of analysis, namely, computable general equilibrium (CGE) models. A, still small number of CGE models have recently included the activities of MNEs. By reviewing them we offer a new perspective to grasp the effects of MNEs, which conveys a novelty in the available surveys on MNEs and FDI.

In our approach to the vast array of empirical and theoretical studies on MNEs and FDI we have three main targets in mind: i) to identify some important elements characterising MNEs and FDI flows in order to include them in our model; ii) to show that the empirical literature on the effects of MNEs is to a certain extent somewhat inconclusive, which justifies more efforts and the introduction of new methodologies, such as computable general equilibrium (CGE) models, in their analysis; iii) to review the few CGE models still available in this area, as well as putting ours in perspective.

To this end, this chapter is divided into three basic parts. The first one (section 2) reviews the most remarkable contributions on the theoretical side. Thus, it successively reviews the perfect competition approaches from the 1960s, which treated FDI as a mere capital movement (section 2.1); the imperfect competition approaches from the 1970s, in which some aspects of MNEs were added to FDI modeling (section 2.2); the imperfect competition approaches that appeared from the 1980s onwards, which differentiate between vertical and horizontal MNEs, including the "knowledge capital model" (section 2.3); the heterogeneous firms models in the 2000s (section 2.4); and finishes with some recent contributions on internalisation issues (section 2.5). Section 3 goes on with the review of empirical studies. In its first part (section 3.1) we present some characteristics for which applied studies have found rather robust evidence. Next (in section 3.2), we show some results on the impact of MNEs on savings (section 3.2.1), the current account (section 3.2.2), the capital stock (section 3.2.3), foreign trade (section 3.2.4), domestic firms' productivity (3.2.5), market structure (3.2.6), wages (3.2.7) and GDP growth (3.2.8). Section 4 reviews the available CGE models (section 4.1); so that the main characteristics of the model proposed in this book can be better analysed (section 4.2). The main conclusions are presented in section 5. A review of the theoretical strands and the CGE literature, but not of the empirical literature, can also be found in Latorre (2009).

2. Theoretical Literature on Multinational Firms and Foreign Direct Investment

2.1. Perfect Competition Approaches (1960s): Foreign Direct Investment as a Capital Movement

The first formalisations of FDI tended to model it as capital (i.e., a production factor) moving across countries. This idea was a logical extension of the traditional theory of investment responding to differences in the expected rates of return on capital. This view, therefore, predicted that FDI would go from capital abundant countries (where its return was low) to capital scarce countries (where its return was high). Two early theoretical contributions in this line are Mundell (1957) and MacDougall (1960).

Mundell (1957) analysed the effects of factor movements in a 2-sector, 2-countries and 2-factors (2×2×2) Heckscher-Ohlin model. Under this framework, unless factor endowments differences between the two countries are extreme, so that the factor price equalisation theorem does not hold, product and factor prices remain unchanged after a capital inflow. On the contrary, with extreme factor endowments differences, countries would specialise in the production of the good which is a relatively heavy user of the more abundant and, therefore, cheaper factor of production in each country, thus, excluding factor price equalisation. Another outcome stemming from his model is that the capital inflow reduces imports, i.e., trade and capital movements are found to be substitutes. This is why his contribution has been summarised in the idea that "trade in factors is a substitute for trade in goods".

The suggestion that capital flows do not have any effect on factor prices, obtained in a Heckscher-Ohlin model, is a rather surprising result. In fact, adding the assumption of specific factors to a simple (2×2×2) Heckscher-Ohlin model considerably changes the outcomes, as capital inflows do affect factor rewards and give rise to cross-hauled FDI flows, i.e., there will be two-way flows between pairs of countries (Jones, 1971; Neary, 1978; Caves, 2007). This is a nice characteristic which matches the empirical evidence of most developed countries simultaneously sending and receiving FDI inflows.

Rather than analysing factor movements, as in Mundell (1957), MacDougall (1960) focuses on the simplest case of a capital inflow into a one-sector economy. FDI inflows in this setting lower the capital rent in the receiving economy, but also increase labour productivity. The latter effect predominates, increasing welfare for the receiving economy.

Some findings from the models above, such as two-way flows of direct investment, or the potential substitution between trade and FDI are genuine intuitions. However, this theory does not seem to be convincing as an explanation of FDI. The bulk of FDI flows originates in (and is directed to) developed economies, which should be capital abundant (Barba Navaretti and Venables, 2004, chapter 1; Markusen, 2002; UNCTAD, several years). In fact, the share of developing economies in world gross FDI flows has usually been around 20-25 percent since the 1970s onwards (Barba Navaretti and Venables, 2004, chapter 1). Furthermore, only a small number of developing economies receive these FDI inflows in the last years, e.g., China accounts for nearly one-quarter of the total, and a few economies in Asia and Latin America account for the rest, whereas flows going to Africa are nearly negligible (Barba Navaretti and Venables, 2004, chapter 1; UNCTAD, several years). This means that capital does not go to high return locations, i.e., developing countries with low capital endowments. Nevertheless, data problems may lead to defend that this theory still holds because it was tested using inappropriate variables. On the one hand, there are many problems to calculate the correct rate of return. Empirical analysis usually relies on profits calculated from an accounting point of view which differ from those derived from economic criteria. This is so because MNEs use transfer prices for transactions between the parent and subsidiaries to make profits arise in countries with the most favourable tax environment, among other reasons. On the other hand, Yeaple (2003a) maintains that aggregation biases might be behind the empirical outcome that FDI is not related to differences in capital endowments (and, consequently, on the rate of return of capital) across countries.

In the 1960s and 1970s some economists worked on the empirical relationship between FDI, the rate of return and risk (Agarwal, 1980). The so called *portfolio theory* predicts a positive relation of FDI with respect to the rate of return and a negative one with respect to risk. Portfolio diversification may help to reduce the total risk involved, i.e., a firm can reduce risks by undertaking projects in more than one country. However, the portfolio theory is an extension of a vision of FDI as capital movements. In this sense, it is still incomplete. We see clearly nowadays, that the essence of FDI is that is related to a particular type of firms' production abroad. Each firm has a unique bundle of factors, competencies and procedures which get transferred to foreign operations when FDI occurs. Therefore, FDI is best thought of as movements of firms, rather than simple movements of capital (Graham, 1992; Barba Navaretti and Venables, 2004, chapter 11). This idea had appeared earlier.

Indeed, some authors abandoned the emphasis on FDI as capital movements and turn their attention to the MNE.

2.2. Imperfect Competition Approaches (1970s): Adding Some Aspects of Multinationals

The theories discussed above are based on the assumption of perfect competition in domestic factor and/or product markets. They belong to the traditional trade theory that has dominated for decades, based on competitive, constant-returns models. Hymer's (1976) work showed that the idea of FDI as a simple capital movement responding to rates of return (with or without risk) did not match the real characteristics of MNEs' activities. His pioneering analysis was in his PhD Dissertation, which dates back to 1960, but was published much later, in 1976. The consequences of his contribution were and still are very important. He drew attention to the MNE, in particular, to the type of assets the MNE owned and to the difficulty of transferring those assets -due to *market imperfections*-. Two main types of market imperfections are relevant. One arises from MNEs' advantages with respect to firms with no foreign operations (the differentiation between firm types -MNEs versus domestic- violates the assumptions of perfect competition); and the other is due to transaction costs. Let us briefly review both in turn.

First, MNEs have some advantages compared to local firms. When establishing plants in a foreign country MNEs have some disadvantages compared with local firms (e.g., ignorance of customers' preferences, legal system, institutional framework and the cost of operating away from the parent company). If, despite these disadvantages, MNEs decide to establish plants abroad, they must possess some advantages to which existing or potential local competitors have no access and that more than compensate the disadvantages. Second, the concept of transaction costs. Transaction costs arise from the difficulties of using the market to organise transactions (e.g., it is hard to design a contract between the firm and its suppliers that contemplates all the circumstances that may arise in the future), therefore the firms' internal procedures are better suited than markets to organise transactions. This point will be further developed later on.

A different approach to FDI is the product-cycle theory (Vernon, 1966). This theory gave useful explanations for the expansion of US MNEs after World War II. It explains FDI as a reaction to the threat of losing markets as a product matures, and as a search of cheaper factor costs to face competition.

Its essence is that most products follow a similar life cycle. In a first stage, the product appears as an innovation which is sold locally in the same country where it is produced (the US). This is so in order to facilitate satisfying local demand while having an efficient coordination between research, development and production units. In a second stage, the product begins to be exported (to Western Europe). In a third stage, some competitors arise in Europe. If conditions are favourable the firm will establish foreign subsidiaries there to face the increased competition and it may also establish subsidiaries in less developed countries to have access to cheaper labour costs to enhance its competitiveness.

By that time, Hirsch (1976) worked on the circumstances which influence a firm's decision on whether using exports or FDI to serve the foreign market. His model takes into account the costs of managing production abroad as well as the asset specificity of the capital owned by MNEs in a simple but complete framework. Other studies, this time empirically oriented, worked on the effects of tariffs on FDI and on the predominance of MNEs in industries characterised by differentiated output and more highly educated employees. Thus, we find some authors that were already using modern approaches to FDI, anticipating those of the 1980s. Before moving on to that period, though, we have to devote some attention to the important work of Dunning.

The analysis of Hymer (1976) was given an important step forward by Dunning's work (1977a, 1979, 2000). Dunning put together already existing elements in a coherent and unified framework. He provided a triad of conditions necessary for a firm to become a MNE. These three conditions constitute the basis of the eclectic or OLI paradigm, where OLI stands for "ownership, location, internalisation". Ownership means the sort of advantages that MNEs should have, in the same line pointed out in Hymer's contribution. Location gives the idea that for a MNE to establish a new plant in a foreign country, this country must have some advantages compared to the home country of the MNE. These advantages may be cheaper factors of production, better access to natural resources, a bigger market, and so on. Finally, the internalisation idea had also been noted by Hymer when he dealt with transaction costs. It may be more beneficial for a firm to exploit its ownership advantages within its subsidiaries than to sell or license them to other independent firms.

The central concepts of the OLI paradigm have been also introduced in a dynamic framework known as the Investment Development Path. This concept relates the inward and outward direct investment position of countries with their corresponding stages of development (Dunning, 1981; Dunning and

Narula, 1996). It suggests that countries tend to go through five main stages of development. Each of the stages links the GNP level with the net outward investment position (NOI), i.e., the difference between outward and inward FDI stocks. Less developed countries, which are in stages one and two, have a negative NOI. In stage three, the NOI increases strongly. In stage four, the NOI becomes positive and keeps growing. Finally, at stage five there is a balance between outward and inward FDI, so that the NOI oscillates around zero. Developed countries are usually between stages three and five. This approach suggests that the NOI position is related to the OLI conditions of the local firms, emphasising that the government is critical in influencing the role of MNEs in a country's economy. Indeed, locational and ownership advantages are influenced by government' policies. It also emphasizes that the stages of development depend on other complex socio/political/economic factors.

2.3. Imperfect Competition Since the 1980s: Vertical Versus Horizontal Multinationals

We have already alluded to the emergence of the importance of some aspects related to the firm in the framework of the analysis of FDI. This had also been the case in trade theories. Indeed, trade theories had begun to incorporate important elements of the industrial organisation literature, such as imperfect competition, economies of scale and product differentiation starting at Krugman (1979, 1980) and Helpman (1981). Clearly, this new approach, which is sometimes called "new trade theory", was a considerable improvement in trade models; reviews of this literature can be found in Bajo-Rubio (1991) and Krugman (1995). Triggered by the empirical observation of intra-industry trade (i.e. trade within the MNEs, either between the parent and the subsidiary or between affiliates), it delivered theoretical models able to resemble this form of trade. What is more, it further provided a framework in which MNEs could better integrate into the trade theory. Imperfect competition, economies of scale and differentiated products are more in accordance with Hymer's enlightening ideas regarding the nature of the MNE.

A new literature on MNEs has risen from this perspective. It is an approach that deals primarily with the incentives, or determinants, for FDI to arise. Taking a microeconomic perspective, the theory relies on location and ownership determinants, according to Dunning's terminology. Location advantages are related to the host country (factor prices, factor endowments, and distance measured as transport costs). Ownership advantages are captured from technological aspects of the firm, such as economies of scale, R&D efforts and transport costs. In what follows we will highlight some remarkable contributions stemming from this line of research.

Within this approach some studies concentrate on the analysis of horizontal MNEs or FDI, whereas others do the same on the vertical side of the phenomenon. Vertical MNEs are those which geographically separate each stage of the production process according to relative cost advantages. They, therefore, look for low-cost inputs and supply their output to other subsidiaries of the MNE through intra-firm exports. The link between vertical MNEs and intra-firm trade should not be overlooked, particularly because intra-firm trade, in turn, accounts for a relevant and increasingly growing part of international trade (Hanson et al., 2005). Horizontal MNEs are those producing roughly the same product in different locations in order to gain an easier access to the host market, i.e. they are mainly interested in sales in the foreign country.

Let us begin with the studies on vertical MNEs. They deal primarily with the following question: why do firms sometimes break the production process across borders rather than keeping all stages in the home country? A pioneering model was that of Helpman (1984). He extended a 2×2×2 Heckscher-Ohlin model to include MNEs with monopolistic competition and differentiated products. In his model the incentive for vertical MNEs to arise stems from factor price differences across countries. Helpman showed that by splitting production processes with different input requirements MNEs can exploit cross-country differences in factor prices by shifting activities to the cheapest locations. In the presence of factor price differences across countries, firms have an incentive to geographically separate capital-intensive production of intangible assets (headquarters services, for example) from the more labour-intensive production of goods.

Therefore, the sort of MNEs described by Helpman, the vertical MNEs, tends to be more prevalent when there are differences in relative factor endowments among countries. Furthermore, in the case of vertical MNEs, FDI and trade are complements: "the larger the difference in relative factor endowments the larger is the volume of trade" (Helpman, 1984, p. 467). In addition, the introduction of MNEs increases the possibilities of FDI leading to the elimination of international factor price differences.

Zhang and Markusen (1999) offer a (2×2×2) model of vertical MNEs in a Cournot oligopoly incorporating transport costs that were absent in Helpman (1984). Their model predicts a positive relationship between the size of the host country and the number of vertical multinationals. There is a minimum threshold size below which no FDI takes place. The reason for this lies in transport costs and economies of scale. All production that cannot be sold in the host country market will have to be shipped back to the parent's country, which entails paying for transport costs. If trade costs and economies of scale are low then the host country size is not so important, though. The model also suggests the need for a minimum threshold of skilled labour in the host country where fragmentation takes place. Below that minimum FDI is discouraged. Furthermore, when MNEs arise, their more skilled-labour intensive technologies lead to a more skilled labour-intensive production in both countries. This pushes up the real wage of this factor of production in both countries.

What about the horizontal approach? This is concerned with the question: why do firms decide to serve foreign markets through FDI rather than simply exporting? This is not a recent question (see, e.g., Hirsch (1976)), and we have nowadays a better idea regarding its answer. Markusen (1984) includes the analysis of this decision in a general equilibrium trade model with imperfect competition. Brainard's (1993, 1997) work is also an outstanding contribution. Her main findings are that firms choose horizontal FDI versus exporting when the gains from avoiding trade costs outweigh the costs of maintaining productive capacity in multiple markets, i.e. the so called *proximity-concentration trade off*. More technically, horizontal MNEs are more likely to arise when: 1) firm-level scale economies of scale are high, 2) plant-level scale economies of scale are low, and 3) trade costs are high. She tested her predictions empirically obtaining robust support for them.

Markusen and Venables (1998, 2000) offer two models of MNEs that also support the predictions of Brainard's analysis. Their novelty lies in their well-grounded outcome regarding two other determinants of the emergence of horizontal MNEs (and the corresponding impact on the pattern of trade and factor prices): countries' size and factor endowments. Horizontal FDI flows are increasing in countries similarities in size, as measured by GDP, and factor endowments; i.e., the more similar in GDP and factor endowments two countries are, the more FDI will take place between them. The logic is simple. When countries are very different, MNEs derive their disadvantage from having to locate costly additional "capacity" in a "disadvantaged" country (i.e., the one in which sales are smaller, factor costs are higher, and/or factor productivity is smaller). MNEs, therefore, cannot compete against single-plant national firms settled in an "advantaged" country, which serve the "disadvantaged" countries by exports. Note this outcome is just the opposite to that offered by models of vertical MNEs. Furthermore, these two models deliver a strong prediction regarding the relationship between trade and horizontal MNEs. When countries have a similar size and factor endowments, trade tends to go down and MNEs tend to increase, as horizontal MNEs compete and displace national firms and trade. Thus, trade and horizontal FDI are substitutes, again the opposite relationship compared to that predicted by vertical MNEs models.

Another important contribution is Markusen's "knowledge-capital model", developed in Markusen (1997; 2002, chapters 7 and 8). This is a 2-country, 2-factor, 2-good model in which both vertical and horizontal MNEs are included simultaneously. This means a step forward in MNEs' modeling, which is of particular relevance given the empirical importance of both types of flows (Helpman, 2006). Markusen is, further, one of the few authors, to the best of our knowledge, that offers a detailed study regarding the welfare effects of MNEs to which we turn now[1].

Markusen maintains that MNEs may benefit both countries in his model. However, it is the larger one that loses if indeed one country loses. This is the country in which MNEs' headquarters are, so he concludes that in contrast to some conventional arguments, it is generally the host economies that are ensured of gains and the parent countries that could lose from investment liberalisation. Markusen also looks at the effects on a host economy of trade liberalisation, investment liberalisation, and simultaneous investment and trade liberalisation. This perspective allows him to show that the host economies' welfare is highest under full liberalisation (investment and trade liberalisation). He notes that the "knowledge-capital model" resembles a "pro-skilled labour bias", which is an important factor in making results go against the logic of traditional theory. The "pro-skilled labour bias" means that the effects of MNEs' emergence are analogous to a change to a more skilled-labour intensive technology in the world in general. In other words, MNEs make both countries specialise in more labour-skilled technologies than before MNEs' arrivals. An important consequence can be drawn from the skilled labour bias. If a factor of production loses from MNEs' emergence it will be unskilled labour. This finding is consistent with the results of Zhang and Markusen (1999).

---

[1] A deeper analysis of the rich contributions of his book is available in Latorre (2004).

Within this framework of location and ownership advantages, a line of research incorporates R&D decisions into theoretical models of the MNE. MNEs are generally characterised by a strong effort in R&D activities. However, the intangible nature of many of these assets makes it difficult to incorporate them into theoretical (and empirical) models. An interesting answer to this is offered by Sanna-Randaccio and Veugelers (2003, 2007). Their theoretical model analyses the costs and benefits of undertaking R&D activities in a subsidiary of the MNE versus keeping those activities within the headquarters. The empirical evidence on this shows that R&D activities are mostly done in the headquarters, however we also have evidence that subsidiaries are increasing the scope of this sort of activities (Sanna-Randaccio and Veugelers, 2003). The authors obtain two important conclusions. First, the more technologically advanced the host economy is, the more likely it will benefit from the presence of foreign subsidiaries performing R&D activities. Second, the potential harmful effects of MNEs are likely to diminish if they are not direct competitors in the same market of the local firm. In other words, vertical (or inter-industry) relationships between foreign and local firms (i.e., backward and forward linkages) are more beneficial than horizontal (or intra-industry) ones.

2.4. FIRM HETEROGENEITY MODELS IN THE 2000S

As noted above, in the 1980s, the "new trade models" had introduced monopolistic competition and product differentiation. In so doing, they resembled a sort of within-industry heterogeneity, because each firm produced a different variety of a good. Further, a new source of welfare gains arose from the presence of economies of scale and several varieties, since foreign trade could make more varieties available for consumers. However, in these models, all exporting firms were treated as having similar productivity levels, size and participation in trade[2]. What is more, these models predicted that all firms would export. Empirical data are at odds with this sort of symmetry assumptions. Throughout the 1990s better firm-level data made clearer that only a small fraction of firms within an industry export, and that exporters are

---

[2] These models still assumed a "representative firm", at least within each industry. Even MNEs had also the same productivity and size as exporters, although their trade patterns could be different to those of exporters.

larger and more productive than non-exporters. The evidence supporting that the causality runs from higher productivity to exports and not vice versa (Bernard et al., 2007a; Greenaway and Kneller, 2007).

Melitz (2003) and Bernard et al. (2003) offer two pioneering trade models of exporting versus non-exporting firms, which resemble these features of the data. The former has been particularly influential and transmits the idea that more dispersion in productivity raises the share of exporting firms in domestic output. Both models, though, include fixed costs of exporting and productivity differences across firms within the same industry, which were absent in most models of the "new trade" literature and are key ingredients for the results. This "Firm heterogeneity models" predict that trade liberalisation or a fall in transportation costs lead to higher average industry productivity, because the more productive firms survive and grow, whereas the lower-productivity non-exporting firms may more easily contract production or exit. Thus, in this type of models, within-industry reallocation of activity is possible. The old theoretical models predicted that trade costs could raise welfare through specialisation across industries and countries according to comparative advantage. An additional source of welfare emerges now because trade increases output and employment in high-productivity exporting firms within an industry, which is a force pulling up average productivity. This latter welfare gain seems to be more sizeable than across-industry reallocations (Bernard et al., 2007a)[3].

Helpman et al. (2004) extend Melitz's (2003) model to include MNEs, analysing the decision to open a subsidiary abroad. Their model is consistent with the above noted conclusions of the models of Brainard and Markusen and Venables on horizontal FDI, which is the type of MNEs that all these models consider. However, the addition of intra-industry firm heterogeneity leads these authors to derive that the sales of foreign affiliates relative to exports are larger in sectors with more firm heterogeneity in productivity, the latter being proxied by firms' sales or size. Furthermore, they obtain strong support for this result in a cross-section of industries using a regression analogous to that in Brainard (1997). Heterogeneity, therefore, arises as an important factor to explain not only trade patterns but also MNEs' behaviour. In their model, exporting involves lower fixed costs than FDI activities, while FDI involves lower variable costs than exporting. MNEs are the most productive firms,

---

[3] Two recent remarkable trade models along these lines, which do not include MNEs, are Bernard et al. (2007b) and Helpman et al. (2007).

followed by exporters which are, in turn, more productive than firms serving only the domestic market. These assumptions are confirmed by their empirical evidence.

The relationship between firm efficiency and three modes of foreign market distinction access, namely, exports, greenfield investments, and mergers and acquisitions (M&A) is analysed by Nocke and Yeaple (2007). Note that the difference between two FDI types (greenfield and M&A) is absent in Helpman et al. (2004). Their findings suggest that, in industries where the source of firm heterogeneity is due to the internationally mobile factors (such as R&D intensive technologies), firms involved in both M&A and greenfield FDI investments are more efficient than exporters. By contrast, in industries where the source of firm heterogeneity is not internationally mobile (such as firm marketing expertise), firms undertaking greenfield FDI are more efficient than exporters but those engaging in cross-border M&A are less efficient than exporters; this latter result would contradict the prediction of Helpman et al. (2004). Accordingly, "the common procedure of pooling industries in regression analysis is inappropriate as the mapping from firm characteristics to mode choices differs qualitatively across industries" (Nocke and Yeaple, 2007, p. 378). Note that this assertion supports the focus of this book on the differential impact of MNEs across sectors.

Grossman et al. (2006) provide a model in which MNEs may undertake complex strategies in which horizontal and vertical FDI are simultaneous. Contrary to Markusen's (2002) "knowledge capital model", this does not mean vertical and horizontal MNEs interacting, but that the same firm can undertake both vertical and horizontal (i.e., complex) strategies simultaneously. Grossman et al. (2006) follow Yeaple's (2003b) model of complex strategies and are also inspired by Ekholm et al. (2007) model of export platform FDI. Indeed, they extend Yeaple's (2003b) framework by including heterogeneous firms following Melitz (2003). Their outcomes are in accordance with the productivity sorting of Helpman et al. (2004), with MNEs, exporting and domestic firms exhibiting decreasing levels of productivities, respectively. Their model suggest that not only cross-country differences in costs are important for the complex strategies of MNEs to arise, as in Yeaple (2003b) and Ekholm et al. (2007), but that within industry firm heterogeneity, which is absent in the latter, plays an important role in determining the different strategies of MNEs. In fact, the introduction of firm heterogeneity allows Grossman et al. (2006) to abandon Yeaple's (2003) sort of "symmetric producers" outcome, by which all MNEs within an industry end up developing the same type of complex strategy, which is at odds with the empirical evidence. Through heterogeneity Grossman et al. (2006) also depart from the determinism in Ekholm et al. (2007), which establishes that intermediate goods, which may be assembled in any county, must always be produced where the headquarters are.

Aw and Lee (2008) follow Grossman et al. (2006), but instead of analysing complex strategies between two rich countries in the North and one in the South, they construct a 3-country model in which heterogeneous firms of a middle-income country choose between exporting or sending MNEs to a high-income or a low-income country. Using data from Taiwanese electronics firms they also find that the firms sending FDI are more productive than the ones that export. Their original contribution is that MNEs which invest only in the rich country (US) are more productive than those investing only in the poor country (China), which seems due to the higher fixed costs of investment in the rich country compared to those in the poor one.

These latter "3-country models" on "complex strategies" are of particular interest, at least for two important reasons. First, because they deal with the role of "origin and destination" of trade and FDI. This point may be quite influential for results and is frequently overlooked in theoretical and empirical analyses. Second, because they consider the possibility of firms producing different number of products for several destinations. They, therefore, can explain what seems to constitute the main part of trade, i.e. the extensive-margin, which is explained by both the number of destinations and the number of exported products (Bernard et al., 2007a).

Heterogeneity has brought trade and FDI models closer to reality by capturing the fact that within-industries different types of firms coexist (non-exporters, exporters, and different types of MNEs), which has led to abandon the "representative firm" assumption. Within-industry adjustments and new sources of welfare and growth have been identified. There seem to be still some challenges ahead, however. In particular, it seems that "heterogeneous firms" models are not so good at grasping the differences between vertical and horizontal differentiation in goods, while there is empirical evidence that prices within the product categories traded "vary substantially and systematically across countries" (Bernard et al., 2007a). Furthermore, to come closer and closer to reality, the already identified within-industry adjustments need to take a step further and consider the adjustments "within the firm" (Grossman et al., 2006). We turn to this point in the next section, which belongs to an area often called "contractual theories" of the multinational firm.

2.5. Recent Contributions on Internalisation Issues

The issue of internalisation, which is the center of the "contractual theories" of the MNE, covers a gap present in those theories more oriented to location and ownership advantages, i.e., the so called "technological theories", reviewed in sections 2.3 and 2.4[4]. The latter give an idea of the incentives to produce abroad but do not explain why foreign production of a MNE will occur *within* the firm's boundaries (i.e., within the MNE), rather than through arm's-length subcontracting (i.e., contracts with independent firms, a phenomenon known as foreign *outsourcing*)[5]. Furthermore, the interest on this subject goes beyond the area of firms' internal organisation. Why? Trade statistics seem to exhibit systematic patterns related with internalisation (i.e., the decision of foreign *insourcing* versus foreign *outsourcing* seems related with some firm, industry and country characteristics) and the reallocation of economics activities that these processes bring about may well impact macroeconomic aggregates (Antràs and Rossi-Hansberg, 2008). We showed in section 2.2 how internalisation issues were central in the analyses of Hymer and Dunning. However, there is a recent literature which has formalised internalisation including it in the framework of newer trade theories. We offer in the next paragraphs a brief overview of this literature.

Analysing internalisation decisions leads us to a world where the classical assumption of complete contracting is not possible. Let us explain this. When choosing between arm's-length subcontracting versus internalising, the MNE, as well as a national firm, faces a trade-off. On the one hand, if the firm decides to internalise its foreign operations it will have to pay the higher costs

---

[4] Following Coase's (1937) and Williamson's (1975, 1985) view, this consideration also holds for a neoclassical theory of the firm, i.e., a theory based purely on technological considerations.

[5] Our discussion uses the notation in Antràs and Helpman (2004). When a firm decides to keeps its operations, e.g., the production of intermediate inputs, within its boundaries, this internalisation or integration or insourcing may take place in the home country (vertical integration) or abroad (by which the firm becomes a MNEs and engages in intrafirm trade). When a firm decides to outsource the production of an input, it may buy it at home (domestic outsourcing) or abroad (arm's length trade or foreign outsourcing). Offshoring denotes the sourcing of inputs from foreign countries, both via arm's-length trade (international outsourcing) and via intrafirm trade (vertical FDI). Note that if a firm outsources one activity it is not internalising that activity, and that internalisation of activities undertaken abroad is necessary to become a MNE. However, it may be that a MNE is so because it has some activities internalised abroad while it outsources others. Therefore, the relationship between outsourcing and MNEs, as pointed out in Chapter 1, cannot be taken for granted.

involved in setting up and running a wholly owned plant in a foreign country; on the other hand, if the firm decides to outsource it will have to face some market failures affecting contractual relationships with local firms. Local firms tend to have more information about their market than a MNE has. If there were no contractual problems firms would decide to outsource activities to local suppliers in order to benefit from their experience. However, there are market failures arising from the difficulty of coordinating and controlling the actions of local firms through contracts. In most cases, the firm that outsources has to pay a high rent to local firms to ensure that the process "will work". This results in a reduction of the profits accruing to the firm that outsources, incentivating internalisation. How has this trade-off been formalised in the literature?

An issue frequently studied is the so called hold-up problem, which has two components. One is the difficulty of writing contracts covering all possible contingencies in the relationship between a firm and its external supplier. The other one is that the local supplier has to do some specific investments to produce the components demanded by the firm it serves, or from a different angle, that the goods he will produce for its customer are very specific, which makes it difficult to sell them to other customers. The local supplier knows that the contract will be incomplete, as well as the specificity of its production. He may fear that after having invested to produce the input for the firm, the contract then should have to be renegotiated as long as some contingencies uncovered have occurred. As the investments made by the local supplier are specific to that relationship he will be in a weak bargaining position. Under these circumstances, local suppliers are likely to underinvest, compared to what they would do if we were in a world of complete contracting. This inefficiency of suboptimal investment reduces the total return to outsourcing.

Ethier (1986) was the first one to analyse the hold-up problem in a context of MNEs' activities within a general equilibrium framework. According to his model, internalisation is more likely when the affiliates are in countries with small factor endowments differences. Note that this result contradicts the outcome of Helpman's (1984) model on vertical MNEs. This suggests that internalisation decisions may change the panorama offered by FDI models of technological theories. Incomplete contracts also arise from the difficulty of protecting intangible assets. Ethier and Markusen (1996) first formalised the case of transferring an intangible asset with superior knowledge embodied. In their model firms may choose among exporting, opening a subsidiary, or licensing their technology to an independent firm. If the knowledge is transferred to the licensee, the latter may set up its own plant and start competing with the original owner of the knowledge. To avoid this, the firm needs to design an optimal licensing contract. In this case, the contract should promise important rents to the local supplier to make defection unprofitable. But these high rents may be too costly to the firm, again incentivating internalisation. Their findings again suggest that similarities in relative factor endowments favour FDI over licensing, as in Ethier (1986).

In the two previous models, as happens in much of the literature on the theory of the firm, the choice of the firm to integrate seems independent of the decisions of other firms within the same industry. McLaren (2000) and Grossman and Helpman (2002) develop models considering the decision of firms to integrate suppliers, in which those decisions affect market conditions, thereby influencing other firms' decisions. Both models transmit the idea that vertical integration may be negative for the remaining non-integrated bilateral relationships, by thinning the market for inputs thereby worsening opportunism. Trade opening brings about an expansion of the market for inputs and thus favours firms' *outsourcing* over FDI.

So far, the models have neglected the costs of internalisation. They belong to the "transaction-cost approach" which considers the contractual problems among firms that are not integrated, but does not take into account the costs of intra-firm transactions (Antràs and Rossi-Hansberg, 2008). A more comprehensive approximation is the "property-rights approach" to internalisation, which includes both types of contractual frictions and is derived from the seminal paper of Grossman and Hart (1986). We review now some influential papers along this latter perspective.

Antràs (2003) has shown that R&D or capital intensity measures are the main determinants of the considerable variation of intrafirm trade across industries. He uses a general equilibrium model of international trade with monopolistic competition, increasing returns and product differentiation combined with insights from the property-rights approach. Simple R&D and capital intensity measures account for almost 75% of the cross-industry variation in the weight of intrafirm imports in total US imports. This implies that more complex goods (which are capital-intensive or research-intensive, e.g., chemicals) are more likely to be produced under vertical integration, thus, bringing about intrafirm trade. By contrast, simpler goods (labour-intensive, e.g., textiles) tend to be bought under contract, through outsourcing and, thus, involve arm's length trade. He derives a parallel result for countries. The share of intrafirm imports in total U.S. imports is larger the higher the capital-labour ratio of the exporting country (i.e., exports coming from capital-abundant countries, such as Switzerland, tend to take place between affiliated units of MNEs, whereas exports of capital-scarce countries, such as Egypt, occur mostly at arm's length). In a cross-section of countries he obtains robust support for the impact of capital abundance.

In brief, Antrás (2003) suggests that capital intensity (both at the country and industry level) is positively associated with internalisation. This is of particular interest, because his model does not consider the presence of important determinants of FDI, according to the technological approach to MNEs, such as, factor price differences across countries, nor a distinction between firm specific and plant specific economies of scale neither transport costs. Remember that factor price differences were the key for the emergence of vertical MNEs in Helpman (1984). Moreover, the rest of characteristics constituted the ingredients of Brainard's *proximity-concentration trade off*, which was also supported and expanded by Markusen and Venables (1998, 2000) and Markusen (2002), whose work also derived the importance of similarities in countries' sizes and factor endowments to explain horizontal FDI. Therefore, the importance of Antràs' (2003) theoretical model and its econometric robustness is that, without those "technological" characteristics, it gives new reasons for the prevalence of FDI among rich countries (versus FDI flows going from rich countries to poor ones). Furthermore, it describes an intrafirm trade pattern which matches the empirical evidence that "the well-known predominance of North-North trade in total trade is even more pronounced within the intrafirm component of trade" (Antràs, 2003, p. 1376).

Antràs and Helpman (2004) combine Antràs (2003) with firm heterogeneity à la Melitz (2003). The model has two countries, North and South. Final-good producers are based in the North, where they produce an input necessary for production called "headquarter services". Intermediate-input producers can be either in the North or in the South, variable costs being lower in the latter. Like in Antràs (2003), the relative intensity in the use of these two inputs (now termed differently, establishing "heaquarter" versus "component" intensive technologies) will be an important determinant of the choice between (home versus foreign) integration and outsourcing[6].

However, the prevalence of the different organizational forms depends in Antrás and Helpman (2004) on a wider range of characteristics than the above commented in Antràs (2003). These are: the wage gap between the North and

---

[6] Their model offers a richer framework for the choice between integration and outsourcing than the one in Grossman and Helpman (2002) who use a one-input general equilibrium framework without differences in firms productivity.

the South, the trading costs of intermediate inputs and the degree of productivity dispersion within a sector. Other two key determinants, which were already present in Antràs (2003), are the distribution of the bargaining power between the final-good producers and supplier of components[7] and the "headquarter intensity" of the technology (the latter being what Antràs (2003) identified as "capital intensity"). From the interaction of all these characteristics, four organizational forms are possible within an industry: integrating abroad, outsourcing abroad, integrating at home, outsourcing at home, where integrating abroad has the highest level of fixed costs and this sorting reveals their corresponding decreasing level of fixed costs, respectively. Even for alternative sortings of fixed costs, which they also study, the model still keeps the flavour of Antràs (2003) in predicting the prevalence of FDI in relative headquarter intensive sectors, whereas outsourcing dominates in those with lower headquarter intensity (i.e., components-intensive[8]).

The presence of heterogeneity now leads Antrás and Helpman (2004) to derive, that the share of intrafirm imports of components in total imports is higher in industries with higher productivity dispersion. As vertical integration abroad involves larger fixed costs than outsourcing abroad, the most productive firms, among those which are "headquarter" (or capital) intensive, will be in a better position to undertake vertical FDI. By contrast, both the widening of wage gap between the North and the South and a reduction of the trading costs of intermediate inputs, result in a reduction of the costs of foreign sourcing, which raises arm's-length trade rises relative to intrafirm trade. Why is the reduction in foreign sourcing biased to arm's length trade? On the one hand, in component-intensive industries integration is rare according to these models. Thus, the fall in South wages and transport costs favours outsourcing in the South over outsourcing in the North. On the other hand, for headquarter-

---

[7] The model keeps the features of Grossman and Hart (1986), by which final-good producers are able to appropriate higher fractions of revenue under integration than under outsourcing, with this fraction being higher when integration takes place in the North than in the South.

[8] The exact sorting pattern derived in Antrás and Helpman (2004), which is summarised in Figure 2 of their article, differs from the one derived by Grossman and Helpman (in press), which does not distinguish between component- and headquarter-intensive sectors but includes organizational structures that use managerial incentives. Notice that, Antrás and Helpman (2004) do not consider the empowerment of workers "(which) may also be an important determinant" (p. 570). *On the other hand,* Nunn and Trefler (2008) have found strong support for the role of headquarter-intensiv technologies and high productivity in predicting intrafirm trade.

intensive industries, the low productivity firms that outsource in the North are too far from productivity levels that make foreign sourcing profitable. But among the integrated producers in the North, the most productive are indifferent between integration in the North and outsourcing in South. Therefore the fall in wages and transport costs favours foreign outsourcing over integration in the North. These tendencies for a wider wage gap and lower trade costs seem to prevail empirically and, as commented by the authors, are in accordance with the still scarce empirical evidence suggesting that the growth of foreign outsourcing might have outpaced the growth of foreign intrafirm sourcing in the US and in the world trade flows.

Antràs (2005) uses a dynamic general equilibrium model that provides a theory for Vernon's product-cycle (1966) original one. He shows that firms from the rich North may find it profit maximising to shift production to the low-wage South after a time lag, due to incomplete contracts. More recently, Antràs and Helpman (2008) have extended the setting of Antràs and Helpman (2004) to include varying degrees of contractual frictions across both inputs and countries. The main question analysed in this paper is: How do improvements in contractibility affect the relative prevalence of the four possible organisational forms just mentioned above? In their model, an improvement in South's contracting institutions (logically) increases offshoring, but whether the expansion of offshoring is biased toward FDI or toward outsourcing depends on whether the easing of contractual frictions disproportionately affects headquarters services or intermediate inputs. In contrast with the transaction-costs literature, where any type of contractual improvement tends to favour outsourcing, in this property-rights approach better contractibility of headquarter services encourages outsourcing, while better contractibility of intermediate inputs encourages integration.

The property-rights approach from Grossman and Hart (1986) and adopted in Antràs (2003) and Antràs and Helpman (2004) suggests that in headquarter-intensive firms/industries it is important that the final good producer be highly incentivised. This is done through vertical integration, because final-good producers are able to appropriate higher fractions of revenue under integration than under outsourcing. In contrast, in component-intensive industries, it is important that the foreign supplier be highly incentivised, which is done by outsourcing. This offers an explanation for the puzzling result in Antràs & Helpman (2008) that more contractibility of the foreign supplier's inputs will typically lead to less outsourcing. As the supplier's share of noncontractible inputs falls, the party that requires relatively more incentives is the headquarters firm, which is achieved through vertical integration.

A firm faces a wider variety of possibilities between the two extremes of outsourcing and internalisation that we have so far considered. There is not much research on these intermediate varieties, though. A firm may, for instance, engage in different types of joint ventures, where this term denotes a situation in which "two or more entities have joint ownership of a firm and none is in the position to exert unilateral control of the firm" (Barba Navaretti and Venables, 2004, p. 300). A model of joint ventures (Rauch and Trindade, 2003) can allow us to show a final market failure. The model analyses the matching of firms, i.e., the difficulty for a firm to find the most suitable local supplier to the specific component or activity that the firm needs. The authors conclude that when the uncertainty about the right international partner diminishes, joint ventures lead to a greater integration of international labour markets than autarky. Furthermore, the lower this uncertainty the more the outcome from their model approaches the perfect capital mobility framework of the MacDougall's (1960) one-sector economy. This is again a nascent research topic which seems of great interest.

3. Empirical Literature on the Effects of Multinationals and Foreign Direct Investment

After reviewing the theoretical side of the literature we turn to empirical issues. In the first part of this section we deal with two characteristics of MNEs for which there is a rather strong empirical support. In the second part, we analyse a broader set of empirical aspects related to the effects of MNEs and FDI flows, for which the literature has found mixed results. As previously noted, this should encourage further efforts to better capture what the impact of MNEs and FDI may be.

3.1. Two Characteristics of Multinationals with a Rather Strong Empirical Support

3.1.1. Multinationals Are More Productive than Domestic Firms
The comparison with those firms that do not have foreign operations is clear: MNEs are much more productive. This outcome is obtained in studies

using either total factor productivity (Doms and Jensen, 1998; Evenett and Voicu, 2001; Lipsey, 2002) or labour productivity (Doms and Jensen, 1998; Djankov and Hoekman, 2000; Conyon et al., 2002; Helpman et al., 2004). This makes a lot of sense, because, as already mentioned, MNEs have "a very distinctive bundle of capabilities" (Barba Navaretti and Venables, 2004, p. 278), the "ownership advantages" on which the OLI paradigm is based (Dunning, 1977a, 1979, 2000).

An interesting taxonomy has been found. MNEs are larger and more productive than exporting firms, which in turn, are also larger and more productive than firms with no foreign operations (Helpman et al., 2004; Helpman, 2006; Greenaway and Kneller, 2007).

3.1.2. Multinationals Pay Higher Wages than Domestic Firms

Many studies support this conclusion (Agarwal, 1980; Aitken et al., 1996; Doms and Jensen, 1998; Djankov and Hoekman, 2000; Conyon et al., 2002; Brown et al., 2003; Barba Navaretti and Venables, 2004, chapter 7; Lipsey, 2002; Lipsey and Sjoholm, 2003, 2004; Huttunen, 2007). This result holds for MNEs operating in both developed and developing countries. The reasons for this, however, are not clear and there are many possible explanations:

1   Because MNEs tend to be more prevalent in sectors which employ a large number of nonproduction workers and have high levels of R&D (Molero and Buesa, 1993; Markusen 1995; Molero, 2000; Bajo-Rubio and López-Pueyo, 2002; Markusen, 2002, chapter 1; Barba Navaretti and Venables, 2004, chapter 1; Blonigen 2005). Accordingly, many of their employees receive higher wages, pulling average wages up.

2   MNEs usually are large firms (Molero, 2000; Barba Navaretti and Venables, 2004, chapter 1; Djankov and Hoekman (2000); Helpman et al., 2004; Helpman, 2006), and large firms, in general, tend to pay higher wages (Lipsey, 2002).

3   As MNEs carry with them a bunch of superior assets, this should raise labour productivity, ceteris paribus. Wages remunerating more productive labour experience a tendency to be higher, unless the MNE has considerable market power in the labour market. We know that market power in the labour market will diminish if MNEs are in urban areas because competition from other firms is likely to flatten their perceived labour supply (Brown et al., 2003). In this latter case, maybe higher wages are due to higher productivity.

4   MNEs can pay higher wages to avoid their employees to leave and
     work for other firms, thus transferring valuable MNEs' knowledge to
     other firms (e.g., Fosfuri et al., 2001).
5   It could also be the case that the labour hired by MNEs is more
     productive per se. MNEs may choose the best workers by paying
     them more than the rest of firms.

Several studies deal with this latter point. Conyon et al. (2002) use a
sample of firms in the United Kingdom, which have been acquired by
domestic or foreign firms. Their dataset contains firms' performance before
and after the change in ownership. This helps them to isolate the effect of
"foreign ownership". Interestingly, they find that labour productivity of firms
acquired by foreigners was lower than the labour productivity of the firms
acquired by domestic firms. This would suggest that MNEs were not choosing
firms with the best employees. Lipsey and Sjoholm (2004), after controlling
for the quality of labour, find a substantial wage premium in MNEs. However,
as they estimate the wage premium without fixed effects for individual
establishments, there may still be unmeasured characteristics (e.g., capital
intensity) of individual firms that are associated with both high wages and
foreign ownership. Therefore, there may be other factors accounting for the
differences in wages, apart from skill levels. In another study, which includes
establishment fixed effects, Lipsey and Sjoholm (2003) still obtain a wage
premium for workers in foreign firms. Huttunen (2007) has analysed the
effects of foreign acquisitions on wages of different skill groups using panel
data on Finnish establishments, which include plant-specific fixed effects and
more modern econometric techniques. Her results also indicate the existence
of a wage premium in foreign firms. This gives evidence for the idea that in
Finland higher wages in foreign firms are not due to the quality of the
workforce, but to foreign ownership itself.

3.2. Some Empirical Effects of Multinationals and Foreign Direct Investment

3.2.1. Foreign Direct Investment and Savings
This idea underlies in the national accounts identities. Current account
deficits necessarily imply that a country is investing above the level of its
national savings and has an internal final demand which is greater than its
national income. This is possible because the capital flows (e.g., FDI flows)

stemming from abroad are funding those expenses which go beyond the country's own possibilities.

FDI itself is one of the main components of the financial account of the balance of payments. The net effect of this component may be rather small and therefore have negligible impact on an economy. This is usually the case in developed countries, not only because their GDP size (and accordingly the volume of their transactions) renders the effect of FDI small, but also because they usually are FDI exporters and importers, so that the net effect of FDI tends to cancel out. Nevertheless, for smaller economies and those which are primarily FDI recipients (i.e., their FDI outflows are small) the impact of FDI may be of importance. In this latter case, FDI inflows may well contribute to alleviate current account deficits. They may take the role that Lipsey sees in capital flows: "International capital flows permit levels of domestic investment in a country to exceed the country's level of saving. That has been the case for the US for the past fifteen years and for most of the past 25 years. For rapidly growing economies, such as the US and Argentina in the 19th century, inflows of foreign investment permit faster growth, or growth with less sacrifice of current consumption, than could otherwise take place" (Lipsey, 1999, p. 307).

The relationship between FDI and savings in the host economy has not been directly tested, to the best of our knowledge. Krkoska (2001a) offers some evidence which may be associated to this issue for some transition economies. He finds some econometric evidence that macroeconomic vulnerability in the Czech Republic in 1997 was preceded by a growing gap between the current account deficit and FDI. He obtains the same result for other periods of macroeconomic vulnerability in Hungary and the Slovak Republic. This gap between the current account and FDI gives the clearest signal among the standard early warning indicators of macroeconomic vulnerability.

It is to note, however, that there is a certain degree of volatility in FDI inflows (even though volatility tends to be smaller for them compared to portfolio flows). This would imply, then, that the relationship between FDI and savings may vary depending on the year. This volatility, together with the small and net FDI recipient character needed for the positive impact of FDI on savings narrows the scope of countries in which it may take place. In other words, the relationship between FDI and savings seems to lack generality.

3.2.2. Multinationals and the Current Account

We have just discussed that FDI could compensate current account deficits and constitute a source of savings for a host economy. We want to note now, however, that the activities of MNEs could also have an important impact on the current account itself, whose magnitude may be larger than the effect of FDI net inflows.

MNEs affect the current account through its impact on: 1) capital rents (or profit repatriation); 2) the services balance (due to MNEs' imports or exports of services related with technology and other intangible assets such as use of patents, brands, etc); and 3) the trade balance (depending on the relative weight of MNEs' imports and exports). The net effect of all these forces is an empirical matter and, as happened with FDI inflows, may vary considerably from year to year.

Let us analyse first, the impact that MNEs may have on the rents balance (i.e., through profit repatriation). In some moment the MNE may begin to remit cumulative earnings to its parent (or another affiliate of the group). These earnings may be large compared to the initial injection of FDI inflows (Caves, 2007, chapter 9). In this case, MNEs may be contributing to current account deficits instead of helping to alleviate them.

Regarding point 2), often, we cannot have access to the shares of MNEs and domestic firms in imports of technology. This means that we cannot infer what their impact will be on this component of the current account.

Something similar applies to point 3). It is difficult to find information on the relative shares of MNEs and domestic firms on total imports and exports of goods, and consequently, whether MNEs' activities contribute to trade deficits or tend to alleviate them. This will be discussed in length in short.

All in all, the activities of MNEs either through FDI flows themselves or through their impact on the current account may have an impact on the level of savings available for an economy. Nevertheless, we do not have a priori any clear cut predictions on this.

3.2.3. Foreign Direct Investment and the
Capital Stock of the Host Economy

An important aspect of FDI is that it may have an impact on the capital stock. In this sense, paradoxically, the name of FDI is misleading (Graham, 1992). FDI does not necessarily imply an investment that increases the capital stock of the host (or receiving) economy, neither a decrease of the home (or sending) country (with regard to this latter case see the interesting article by Feldstein (1995)). The transaction may well be a merger or an acquisition, by which no capital is added. In this case, FDI involves a change in ownership and location of the firms, without any capital flows moving across countries. When FDI implies the creation or an increase in productive capacities (i.e., an increase in capital) it is called greenfield investment. The concept of brownfield investment is sometimes used to denote that FDI which does not increase production capacities.

The majority of FDI takes place through mergers and acquisitions rather than through greenfield investment. For the world as a whole, the share of FDI flows accounted by mergers and acquisitions has increased steadily from 66.3 percent in the mid 1980s, to 76.2 percent in the period 1998-2001 (Barba Navaretti and Venables, 2004, chapter 1).

Nevertheless, for the case of transition economies, empirical studies suggest that modeling FDI as a capital increase is appropriate. On the one hand, Schöllmann (2001) maintains that the weight of greenfield investment in flows accruing to transition economies is bigger than in flows going to developed countries. On the other hand, there are large amounts of obsolete capital stocks in these economies (Krkoska, 2001b; Lizal and Svegnar, 2002; Bornstein, 2001), so new firms entering those markets will have to replace the existing capital with some new one (Caves, 2007, Chapter 9). Therefore, their entry can be associated with increases in the capital stock. It is probably easier for MNEs than for national firms to undertake this effort in investment. Indeed, it has been found, in the case of the Czech Republic, that foreign investors exhibit the highest propensities to invest in gross capital formation (Lizal and Svegnar, 2002).

3.2.4. Multinationals and Foreign Trade

As mentioned earlier, it is not easy to find out whether MNEs tend to generate trade deficits or surpluses in the host economy. On the one hand, FDI inflows may reduce or increase imports received by the host country. There is evidence for both cases (Blomström and Kokko, 1997; Goldberg and Klein, 1999; Blonigen, 2001 and Swenson, 2003). Lipsey and Weiss (1981; 1984) find a positive relationship between FDI and imports but fail to consider endogeneity stemming from the characteristics of the host market. Bajo-Rubio and Montero-Muñoz (2001), having corrected for endogeneity, also find a positive relationship, while Gruber and Mutti (1991) using similar data to Lipsey and Weiss (1981) find an insignificant negative relationship between FDI and imports. On the other hand, more evidence exists regarding the idea that FDI inflows increase exports of the host economy (Blomström and Kokko, 1997; Lipsey, 2002; Greenaway and Kneller, 2007).

The relationship between FDI and trade is related to the predominance of vertical or horizontal MNEs. Recall that for the former trade and FDI are complementary whereas for the latter they are substitutes. Indeed, the findings in Blonigen (2001), Head and Ries (2001) and Swenson (2004) suggest that FDI increases imports of intermediate inputs from the host economy but decreases imports of finished products. Which type of MNEs prevails? Markusen states that: "the weight of empirical evidence suggests the dominance of horizontal motives for foreign production" (2002, p. 128). He defends this idea for the world, as a whole, because most FDI flows are among developed economies, which according to his view tend to be horizontal. However, Markusen himself also acknowledges (2002, p. 189) that "vertically integrated firms are important in some industries and surely important to some host countries".

Using data for inward and outward U.S. affiliate sales, Carr et al. (2001) obtain support for Markusen's knowledge capital model which considers the simultaneous presence of vertical and horizontal MNEs. However, with respect to their results, Blonigen et al. (2003) argue that there is some misspecification in the proxy for skill-labour differences that, when corrected, leads to econometric results that support the horizontal MNEs model. This would give less importance to the weight of vertical US MNEs. Nonetheless, in their reply, Carr et al. (2003) explain some flaws existing in the approach of Blonigen et al. (2003), such as the use of FDI stocks rather than MNE's data, which are the focus of the theory developed by Markusen.

Hanson et al. (2005) have obtained robust evidence for the importance of vertical US MNEs and argue that their results are at odds with those derived by Carr et al. (2001). They give a reason why they find strong evidence of vertical FDI. This is because they use micro-level data on foreign affiliates whereas previous work uses data that aggregates not just across the activities of a given affiliate but also across all affiliates.

3.2.5. Multinationals and Domestic Firms' Productivity

One of the most studied effects from FDI is that of spillovers, i.e., positive or negative externalities arising from the presence of MNEs. One type of externalities is the arrival of new or better products introduced by foreign affiliates from which consumers benefit. This aspect, however, has been generally neglected in the empirical industrial organisation literature of MNEs. By contrast, some computable general equilibrium models report that FDI inflows raise welfare by increasing the number of varieties available for consumers (e.g., Bchir et al., 2001, and Rutherford and Tarr, 2008). Other type of externalities is related to the more advanced techniques and know-how that MNEs bring with them. This may be transferred to domestic firms voluntarily (through the creation of linkages or licensing agreements with domestic firms) or involuntarily (through imitation or labour mobility). Many studies on spillovers have focused on whether this transference of new technologies from MNEs affects domestic firms' productivity. In this respect, the results are fairly ambiguous.

The studies on Eastern European countries –an area that has received a lot of attention in the last few years– seem quite eloquent. Djankov and Hoekman (2000) find a negative effect of the presence of MNEs on domestic firms acting within the same sector in the Czech Republic. Also for the Czech economy, Damijan et al. (2003) do not detect horizontal spillovers and finds negative spillovers for R&D intensive firms, whereas Kinoshita (2001) finds positive spillovers for those R&D intensive firms. In the rest of six transition economies which Damijan et al. (2003) also study, positive intra-industry effects were obtained only for Romania, but Konings (2001) finds negative spillovers for this same country. All these studies use the same methodology (panels), firm-level data and analyse a very similar period of time, 1992-1998, approximately.

Some other studies are also noteworthy given their particularly careful econometric approach. Aitken and Harrison (1999) find evidence for negative spillovers on domestic firms' productivity in Venezuela. FDI reduces the output of those firms, which makes them produce in less efficient points of their declining average cost curve, thus, reducing their productivity. Haskel et al. (2002) obtain evidence of positive horizontal spillovers in the United Kingdom. However, these positive spillovers do not seem to be large enough to justify the amount of money spent by the government to attract MNEs. Smarzynska (2004) finds positive spillovers through backward linkages and no evidence for horizontal or forward linkages in Lithuania. This suggests that vertical spillovers may be more likely than horizontal ones. These latter analyses, together with the ones covering a wider spectrum of studies (e.g., Görg and Greenaway, 2004; Barba Navaretti and Venables, 2004, chapter 7; Crespo and Fontoura, 2007) show a vague, and even negative, evidence of MNEs' effects on domestic firms' productivity.

3.2.6. Multinationals and Market Structure

Another important, and nearly under-researched, aspect is the effect of FDI on market structure. Theoretical predictions (Ferrett, 2004) are consistent with both a pro-competitive effect (i.e. they promote competition and reduce price-cost mark-ups) and a more concentrated structure (i.e. they "crowd out" (less efficient) domestic firms with the danger of turning the market into a more oligopolistic structure). Markusen and Venables (1998, 2000) and

Markusen (1997, 2002) show that the type of firms (MNEs versus domestic) which will prevail depends on the relative endowments and size of countries, of the level of transport costs, and of firm-level and plant-level economies of scale. Therefore, in the end, as happens with most effects of FDI, whether MNEs crowd out domestic firms or not, is an empirical matter. Empirical studies on this aspect, however, are scarce and particularly troubled with methodological problems (Barba Navaretti and Venables, 2004, chapter 7).

Co (2001) derives a complex interplay between previous levels of concentration, the type of FDI undertaken (i.e., greenfield versus non greenfield) and the timing of adjustments in the levels of concentration after the entry of MNEs in the US economy. Barrios et al. (2005) and Sembenelli and Siotis (2005) find that the pro-competitive effect first dominates but is gradually outweighed by positive externalities in Ireland and in non R&D intensive sectors in Spanish manufacturing, respectively. However, the latter authors find that in R&D intensive sectors positive spillovers result in an increase in margins after the entry of MNEs, thus leading to a more concentrated market structure.

There is a nascent literature on plants shutdowns which could be seen as related to this issue of market structure. However, so far, this literature has focused on the firms and plants characteristics associated with the shutdown decision and has not analysed the dynamics of the process. A recent outstanding contribution is Bernard and Jensen (2007) who find, with US data, that single-plant firms have higher probability of death than multiplant firms and MNEs. However, this is due to the fact that the latter type of firms are usually characterised as larger, older and more productive than domestic firms. When they control for these characteristics, plants belonging to multiplant firms and MNEs are more likely to close than single plant units. This line of research may give us some hints to analyse the effects of MNEs on market structure. It is not nationality itself which matters, but a comparison of firm and plant characteristics between incumbent firms and the MNEs which arrive.

3.2.7. Multinationals and Wages

We have seen that MNEs pay higher wages, but this result does not tell us about the effects of MNEs on average wages of the whole economy. In particular, MNEs' wages can be above domestic ones as a result of a negative effect caused by MNEs, e.g., the presence of MNEs causes a large fall in average wages, with a disproportionate negative effect on workers of domestic firms. There is empirical evidence, rather scarce, but still some evidence, of this type of effect. Aitken et al. (1996) find that FDI had a negative and significant effect on the average wages of workers employed by domestic firms in Venezuela, while for Mexico FDI had the same negative (although non significant) effect. Feenstra and Hanson (1996) show that MNEs increased the wage of skilled workers relative to unskilled ones in Mexico in the 1880s. These findings are consistent with the theoretical model they build and also with Markusen's (1997; 2002, chapters 7 and 8) knowledge-capital model. With a rich dataset Huttunen (2007) also obtains results in this line. She derives a clear causality indicating that foreign acquisitions themselves lead to higher wages in Finland, and that the increase in wages are higher the more educated workers are.

One may also look at the effect of MNEs' entry on average wages in a country or industry. Aitken et al. (1996) find that the wage increase for workers in foreign firms counteracted the negative effect for domestic workers in Venezuela, so that average wages increased in that country. Feliciano and Lipsey (1999) could not find a significant effect for the average wage in manufacturing in Mexico; but, for the rest of sectors, average wages increased. Indeed, Lipsey (2002, p. 34) summarises the scarce available evidence on the effect on average wages as positive in the sense that MNEs' entry increased them. All in all, this is still an area in which further research should be done, a task which would be facilitated by the availability of better data on labour' skills and their corresponding wages (Markusen, 2002, chapter 1).

3.2.8. Foreign Direct Investment and Economic Growth

MNEs often exhibit more advanced techniques and high levels of R&D expenditures, possess higher skills and experience, and so on. These characteristics lead to think about the role of MNEs as promoters of technological innovation and progress and, therefore, of economic growth. However, given the "intangible" nature of these assets it may be difficult to empirically grasp their impact on growth. What are the results of empirical studies? These studies have found that FDI increases growth when host economies characteristics point to the existence of an "absorptive capacity". What exactly constitutes that absorptive capacity varies. It may be related to a high income level (i.e., rich) countries (Blomström, Lipsey and Zejan, 1994), an open trade regime (Balasubramanyam et al., 1996), a highly educated workforce (Borensztein et al., 1998, Campos and Kinoshita, 2002) or well-developed financial markets (Alfaro et al., 2004; 2006).

An exception to this positive relationship is the study by Carkovic and Levine (2005). Using a panel for 72 economies over the period 1960-1995 they find no evidence that either the level of education, income, trade openness or the financial system development are critical for the effect of FDI on growth. Nor do FDI flows themselves impact on GDP growth, after controlling for endogeneity, country-specific effects and the inclusion of lagged dependent variables in the growth regression. However, using the same methodology in an analysis for a group of developed and homogeneous economies, Bajo-Rubio et al. (2008) have found a clear positive impact of FDI on growth. This latter analysis again shows that due to the presence of absorptive capacity, in this case, in the Spanish regions, FDI flows increase growth in them.

4. A REVIEW OF CGE MODELS THAT INCLUDE MULTINATIONALS

We turn now to the computable general equilibrium (CGE) models, which, as mentioned earlier, allow combining a set of effects arising from the presence of MNEs in a unified framework to obtain their overall impact. Note also that this technique offers not only the intuition on how the economy will adjust but also quantitative outcomes on aggregate variables, such as GDP and welfare, as well as on sectoral variables. Despite these advantages, there has been little previous work on FDI and MNEs in a CGE context. An overview of those few CGE models is presented (section 4.1). This will also permit us to put in perspective the characteristics of the model developed in this book (section 4.2).

4.1. Previous CGE Models

From a theoretical perspective CGE techniques have been used to perform analyses that do not rely on real data but on a range of simplified values for different variables of the model –the so called "numerical CGE models"–. This is the approach followed in Markusen and Venables (1998, 2000) and Markusen (1997; 2002, chapters 5 to 9), mentioned above, and, more recently, in Markusen et al. (2005). This latter methodology uses sophisticated theories (synthesised in a generous number of equations) for which computational methods greatly facilitate solving the model and establishing interesting taxonomies in solutions for different levels of the variables (e.g., the interaction of factor endowments and the size of the host and home countries, or different values for trade costs, with the absence or existence of MNEs or of different types of MNEs). These models tend to analyse real world problems for which data are difficult to be obtained by simplifying the dataset assumed. The inclusion of real data in such a rich theoretical framework constitutes a challenge for modellers.

The so called "empirical CGE models", by contrast, are based on data from real economies, which are embedded in a robust theoretical framework. Petri's (1997) paper is, to the best of our knowledge, the first empirical CGE model incorporating MNEs. He initialises a small number of papers mainly concerned with the effects of FDI liberalisation (i.e., the lowering of barriers to FDI), which is a central element in most trading agreements. The model is a 3-sector, 6-region perfect competition setting where FDI flows are allocated endogenously responding to the fall in investment barriers. The paper has the clear virtue of providing a framework in which regional agreements may be analysed. In particular, interesting results on the differential impact of alternative trade liberalisation policies are obtained. His analysis is applied to the APEC (Asia-Pacific Economic Cooperation) liberalisation process. For the World as a whole, trade and FDI liberalisation in the APEC area, produces a higher impact on welfare than restricting liberalisation to trade only (FDI liberalisation accounts for about one-third of the impact). At the regional level, however, FDI liberalisation may exert a greater impact than trade liberalisation.

Lee and van der Mensbrugghe (2001) introduce a small modification in Petri's model just dealing with the order of the nesting in the demand for goods. They also analyse the APEC liberalisation process and find that at the aggregate level trade and FDI are complementary. This also holds at the micro level for manufactures, but for the primary and services sectors the relationship is ambiguous. They explain these results suggesting the prevalence of vertical FDI in manufactures. By contrast, in the primary sector FDI would be less sensitive to changes in trade because foreign presence is usually reduced in order to secure national energy and natural resources. For services, FDI also seems to be unrelated with trade levels because FDI is the only way to make them available abroad (i.e., many services cannot be exported). Again the sectoral perspective arises as a source of contrasting results.

Also following the pioneering work of Petri (1997), the "FDI and Trade Analysis Project" (FTAP) model analyses the impact of liberalising FDI barriers in the services sectors in a 19-region 3-sector setting. The model is explained in length in Hanslow et al. (1999). In a latter variant, Verikios and

Zhang (2001a) introduce some more sectoral detail, by disaggregating the tertiary sector into six subsectors. Large-group monopolistic competition within a Dixit-Stiglitz framework is assumed, but, as the authors claim, these features do not seem to be important for their results. These features, however, imply symmetry across all type of firms, which does not allow differentiating between MNEs and national firms' technology. As in Petri (1997) and Lee and van der Mensbrugghe (2001), the impact of MNEs is derived from the removal or reduction of FDI barriers. Verikios and Zhang (2001b) concentrate on the impact of liberalisation in the telecommunications and financial services sectors in turn. FDI barriers are higher in this latter sector, thus, its liberalisation causes a greater reallocation of the world capital stock across regions via FDI. Developed regions, which had lower levels of protection, lose capital which accrues to developing regions. Both regions gain from liberalisation but developing ones gain more. This final result also holds for the liberalisation in telecommunications but it does not occur mainly via FDI allocations, but through different adjustments in the model. Interestingly, unlike the typical effects of removing barriers to goods trade, regions with initial higher services barriers (i.e. developing ones) experience the biggest increases in services output as a result of liberalisation.

Brown and Stern (2001) extend the Michigan Model of world production and trade to incorporate FDI and MNEs in a 18-region 3-sector framework. Their approach also relies on Petri's (1997) work but incorporates monopolistic competition following an earlier version of Markusen et al. (2005). They again derive the effects from MNEs by simulating a fall in barriers to FDI, while explaining in length the difficulties to evaluate their levels. The authors introduce some less common variables in the analysis, such as a risk premium on the rate of return of capital (which influences, probably, their contrasting result on this variable) and a form of profit repatriation (fixed at the 10 per cent level). They emphasise that capital flows are expected to have larger welfare impact than trade flows. For the economies receiving FDI flows, welfare, wages, the rate of return of capital, imports and exports will increase. At the sectoral level, they obtain that capital inflows lead to an expansion of output which is mainly generated by firms realising economies of scale.

Bchir et al. (2002) develop the MIRAGE model, which incorporates some interesting features such as careful calculations of tariff data, imperfect competition à la Cournot and dynamics. Regarding their treatment of FDI it should be stressed that they include FDI in a framework in which MNEs are absent. This means that they model FDI as mere capital flows crossing borders in response to different rates of return. Capital is the same no matter whether it belongs to MNEs or national firms. Furthermore, all firms are symmetric and there is no technological differentiation between MNEs and domestic firms. They simulate the impact of trade liberalisation between the European Union and its periphery. The presence of FDI flows is a source of gains for the periphery. There is an increase in capital profitability in that region, due to trade liberalisation, which attracts FDI flows. FDI inflows, in turn, increase the capital stock and the number of firms (and product varieties) in the periphery. This brings about an increase in wages of skilled and unskilled workers together with a decrease in the rate of return to capital, which lead to an increase in GDP and, to a lesser extent, in welfare compared to the results in which FDI flows are absent (as they also run the model without considering the presence of FDI flows).

Gilham (2005) builds a single-country dynamic CGE model in a Cournot framework. However, as in the model of Bchir et al. (2002), FDI is modelled as capital flows that do not accrue to the MNE but to the whole sector. The novelty of Gilham's model is that in those sectors capital is split into a foreign and national origin. In other words, capital appears in the production function with a further nest differentiating between a national and foreign part. Nevertheless, as in Bchir et al. (2002) this does not reflect a proper differentiation of national versus MNEs' technologies since it overlooks their different capital intensities or reliance on imported intermediates. Furthermore, the shares of domestic and foreign capital are based on complex calculations from rates of return.

Jensen et al. (2007) introduce FDI in order to analyse the impact of Russia's accession to the World Trade Organisation (WTO). The authors analyse the differential effects of tariff reform, improved market access, and reforms of FDI barriers in services sectors. They conclude that the presence of MNEs in services sectors is the source of largest gains to Russia, accounting for 70 per cent of the overall gains. Their model assumes large-group monopolistic competition within a Dixit-Stiglitz framework in a 35-sector setting, which allows them to impose symmetry. However, their symmetry assumption is *within firm types*, i.e., all MNEs have identical cost structures, and all domestic firms that operate have cost structures identical to other domestic firms. The key distinction lies in the fact that MNEs produce using both domestic and imported inputs whereas domestic firms produce using only domestic factors of production. This distinction is an important step forward in order to model MNEs as a "peculiar" type of firm, which is different to a domestic firm.

The results of their simulations show that the fall in barriers to MNEs in Russia increases their profitability in that region, leading to an increase in the number of MNEs operating in Russia. Despite the reduction in domestic services varieties, due to the increased competition from MNEs, there would be a net increase in varieties; and, importantly, additional services varieties reduce the cost of services in Russia, through a Dixit-Stiglitz-Ethier effect. Wages of both skilled and unskilled workers would increase. The authors estimate that liberalisation of FDI barriers would increase Russian consumption by 5,2 per cent, which, as mentioned above, constitutes approximately 70 per cent of the total gains.

An interesting variant of the model in Jensen et al.'s (2007) is Rutherford and Tarr (2008), who abandon the assumption of a representative agent by introducing a large number of households (up to 55,098). They also analyse the impact for income distribution in Russia, due to its accession to the WTO, showing that accession would be beneficial for 99.9 per cent of households.

After reviewing the CGE models which include MNEs, it is also worth commenting that some critiques have been raised against the CGE technique itself. Kehoe (2005) has emphasised the poor performance of some of them in predicting the effects of NAFTA. However, NAFTA CGE models have received much better evaluations (Burfisher et al., 2001) and, Kehoe, himself, has also recognised the good performance of other CGEs (Kehoe et al., 1995). McKitrick (1998) and Jorgenson (1984) have raised the point of using adequate elasticities and parameters. In particular, they suggest the recourse to econometric estimation in order to obtain elasticities, rather than taking their values from estimations for different countries and sectoral disaggregations. Hertel et al. (2007) offer a way to combine econometric analysis with CGEs, and note how this methodology has been applied to one of the most widely used database, namely, the Global Trade Analysis Project (GTAP). GTAP refers to a 57-sector 113-region 5-factor database and model of the world economy for general equilibrium simulations. As mentioned in Chapter 1, this is the base model and database which will be expanded to include MNEs in this book.

A further challenge emerges, although this time, only for the CGEs dealing with MNEs. In the light of the theoretical studies analysed earlier, the introduction of recent developments on within-industry heterogeneity, as well as "internalisation" issues seems of much interest. This, of course, is shared by other methodologies, as it still involves costly demands in terms of data and complexity. A pioneering CGE model of trade with firm heterogeneity following Mélitz (2003) is Zhai (2008), who does not include the role of

MNEs. In Zhai's (2008) model, firm heterogeneity offers a theoretically well-grounded way to capture variations in the extensive margin of trade flows. By contrast, the Armington assumption, which does not capture this extensive margin, underestimates both trade and welfare effects from trade liberalisation. Modeling heterogeneity, however, seems to involve important challenges such as reducing the sensitivity of results to the parameter of the dispersion of firms' productivity, the inclusion of firms' entry and exit, or better characterisations of the different levels of fixed costs.

4.2. The Model Proposed in this Book

With respect to the models analysed in the previous section, the major intended contributions of this book and of the analysis provided in Latorre et al., (2009) can be summarised in the following points:

a   *The way of modeling the impact of MNEs.* Most of the above models derive the impact of MNEs from a reduction of the barriers to FDI. However, as noted before, an accurate estimation of these barriers is difficult to be obtained, while being crucial to properly derive the effects of MNEs. On the contrary, our model is not based on calculations of the level of barriers to FDI in every sector, but on the assumption that FDI inflows lead to an increase in the capital stock of the host economy; an assumption that proves to be particularly realistic in the case of transition economies, as will be discussed in Chapter 4, whose analysis constitutes the objective of this book. The model also builds on contributions to the literature on FDI suggesting that MNEs should be incorporated into the analysis. Hence, as will be detailed later on, that capital entering the country as a result of FDI inflows does not only increase the capital available for production in the whole host economy (as in Bchir et al., 2002), but increases the capital available for MNEs, which are characterised by a particular pattern of production (such as a higher capital intensity and a higher utilization of imported intermediates than their domestic counterparts). The model, therefore, builds on the distinction between domestic and MNEs' activities for which fairly reliable information exists (OECD, 2007). As noted before, this distinction between national firms and MNEs becomes blurred in models that include imperfect competition (e.g., in the FTAP model or in Bchir et al.,

2002). Because of the presence of a symmetry assumption across all types of firms (i.e., domestic and MNEs), a proper characterisation of MNEs seems to be absent.

b   *Expanding a well-known and tested CGE model.* Our model is an extension of a well-known CGE model to incorporate MNEs, namely, the GTAP model (Hertel, 1997), which implies a lower cost of entry to understand the model for other CGE modelers. Also, this is a model which is continuously used and checked by many CGE modelers around the world, therefore providing a rich empirical literature that makes up a framework in which the results can be better analysed. In addition, the GTAP model allows for different levels of regional and sectoral disaggregation following the utilization of the already mentioned database for the world economy, the GTAP database version 6 (Dimaranan, 2007). Finally, the model is flexible enough to accommodate a number of possible extensions, already undertaken in the existing literature (such as trade liberalisation, changes in taxation, and so on), as well as to incorporate publicly available data on the activities of MNEs (OECD, 2007). By contrast, the empirical data used by most of the models above rely to an important extent on activities of particular research teams (see Hanslow et al., 1999; Verikios and Zhang, 2001a, 2001b; Bchir et al., 2002; Jensen et al., 2007, Rutherford and Tarr, 2008), which makes significantly more difficult comparing the results from different models.

c   *A broader sectoral coverage.* Most of the above models have concentrated on the effects of MNEs in services sectors. The focus in this book, however, is fairly different since we are interested in analysing the differential impact of the activities of MNEs across both manufacturing and services sectors. Also, our model provides a higher disaggregating level (i.e., 20 sectors) than most of the models including MNEs, as well as many standard CGE models without MNEs.

d   *Using "algebraic GAMS".* In general, the models above that include either imperfect competition and/or dynamics (e.g., Jensen et al., 2007) use GAMS/MPSGE in order to solve the model. This is a software package where the modeller does not need to specify all the model equations because the software calculates them internally. This may have its advantages (e.g., programming is less error-prone) but we have opted for building a model using "algebraic GAMS", which makes the code more accessible to researchers (Chapter 3 offers a complete list and description of all the model equations). In addition to this, "algebraic GAMS" allows the use of different types of algorithms to solve the model (i.e., algorithms for non-linear programming (NLP) models together with those for mixed complementarity programming (MCP) models). By contrast, MPSGE is constrained to the use of MCP algorithms.

e   *A special attention to profit repatriation*. Finally, our model explicitly considers the effects of MNEs on the host economy, with a particular attention to the issue of profit repatriation, a mostly neglected aspect in the literature. Data from the latest UNCTAD's *World Investment Report* suggest that, by and large, since the mid-1990s, MNEs tend to repatriate more than 50 percent of the total income they generate. As an important result, we obtain that the effects of profit repatriation seem to be quite relevant, even leading to reductions in GDP levels.

5. CONCLUSIONS

In this chapter we have presented a comprehensive, up-to-date and "all-in-one" review of the main theoretical strands on FDI and MNEs. The earliest analyses, which appeared in the 1960s tended to model FDI as capital crossing borders in perfect competition settings. The work of Hymer drew attention to the idea that FDI flows were better understood as related with a particular type of firm, the MNE, which owned some sort of superior or special assets. The introduction of a different type of firm broke the assumption of homogenous producers and goods and led to imperfect competition as a framework for the analysis of MNEs. On the other hand, the need to transfer superior assets across borders by MNEs introduced transaction costs in the analysis, which lies behind the possibility of internalisation versus establishing contracts with independent suppliers. The analysis of Hymer was given an important step further by Dunning's OLI paradigm.

Later on, ownership and location advantages have been formalised in theoretical models of vertical and horizontal MNEs in the context of an industrial organisation approach. Many earlier intuitions were translated into formal models. New and powerful computational methods, have allowed theories to incorporate a great deal of relationships and specifications. This allows playing with simulations of different levels of factor endowments, size, trade costs and types of MNEs, among others, to establish interesting taxonomies in solutions. The "heterogeneous firms" literature has pushed further these efforts, by introducing into formal models the empirical fact that within an industry many types of firms coexist (non-exporters, exporters and different types of MNEs). Heterogeneous firms models are able to resemble the intra-industry reallocation of economic activity, as more productive firms grow and less productive ones contract or exit. They also reflect that a MNE may undertake a mixture of vertical and horizontal strategies, combining production of different types of goods directed to, or stemming from, several origins and destination countries.

The most recent developments introduce heterogeneity into internalisation models of FDI, in order to analyse a more complete picture of internationalisation strategies, including outsourcing, which may well be shaping not only trade and FDI patterns but also economic aggregates. As we have shown, the issue of internalisation conveys an important insight which introduces its own influences on FDI and trade patterns, sometimes contradicting those of more "technological" characterisations of MNEs. It seems that a complete theory of MNEs would gain much by integrating the complementarities of both perspectives (i.e., contractual and technological theories). The introduction of these recent perspectives also constitutes a challenge for empirical methodologies.

On the empirical side, we have shown some characteristics of MNEs for which the literature has found strong support, i.e., the higher levels of productivity and wages in MNEs compared to domestic firms. There are, however, other areas, such as their effects on host economies, for which the evidence is rather inconclusive and, sometimes, troubled with methodological aspects. There is mixed evidence on whether they lead to an increase in imports for the host economies while more support exists to the idea that they increase their exports. With respect to spillovers, some may find it counterintuitive, but the superior assets that MNEs hold do not generally lead to positive externalities for the host economies, e.g., an increase in the productivity of domestic firms, and there even exists some evidence on negative spillovers. At the macro level, however, many studies confirm a positive impact on GDP growth when host economies exhibit the so called "absorptive capacity". However, their impact on savings and the current account is not clear *a priori*. Much work still needs to be undertaken to grasp the effects of MNEs on market structure, as research is still scant in this area. All in all, the need for further empirical research on the effects of MNEs seems justified.

In what means a novel feature of this review of the literature, we have analysed the available CGE models that introduce MNEs. These tend to support the idea that the arrival of this type of firms results in higher (both skilled and unskilled) average wage levels in the host economy, as well as, increases in GDP, welfare and foreign trade. It remains to be analysed, the role of profit repatriation, which is an important objective of this book. As will be seen in the next chapters, profit repatriation may counteract and, even if repatriation were above a certain threshold, completely offset, the positive impact on GDP and welfare. It is the simultaneous interplay of all the forces that MNEs unleash which is important to get better approximations to their real impact on host economies. What is more, the CGE approach offers not only the intuition on how the economy adjusts but also quantitative evaluations of the impact of MNEs on both sectoral and aggregate variables, which may be of help for the policy maker when designing FDI attraction policies.

Finally, we have put the model presented in this book (a shorter version for which is available in Latorre et al., 2009) in perspective with respect to the still small number of CGEs that include MNEs. We have adopted a different approach to analyse the effects of MNEs as compared to most previous CGE models. That is, we do not simulate the impact of MNEs through a reduction of the barriers to FDI, which are difficult to be properly estimated. We rely instead on the assumption that FDI inflows lead to an increase in the capital stock of the host economy, which seems to be particularly realistic in the case of transition economies. Also, following the theoretical and empirical contributions, that highlight the peculiar characteristics of the MNEs, these increases in the capital stock take place within the MNEs, which are characterised by a different production technology as compared to domestic firms. Therefore, the model also rests on the technological distinction between domestic firms and MNEs', which, in turn, is based on fairly reliable data (OECD, 2007).

Our model explicitly analyses the effects of MNEs on the host economy, with a particular attention to the mostly neglected aspect of profit repatriation. It is an extension of a well known CGE model, i.e., the GTAP model (Hertel, 1997) within which a great deal of CGE empirical analysis has already been undertaken. This provides a rich framework of previous results, a continuous robustness check of the model itself, and several possibilities for future extensions. Our 20-sector disaggregating level is higher than that used in the majority of CGE models including (and also in many of those which do not include) MNEs. On the other hand, we do not focus just on the effects of MNEs in the services sectors as most CGE analyses have done. We want to analyse in turn the differential impact of MNEs across both manufactures and services sectors. Our model allows for the use of publicly available data, from both the activities of MNEs (OECD, 2007) and the GTAP database on the world economy (Dimaranan, 2007), which are flexible enough to accommodate different regional and sectoral disaggregating levels. So, in contrast with many previous CGE models of MNEs, we are not confined to a particular setting for which a team of researchers has obtained the data needed. Neither are we confined to a particular formulation of the model equations (i.e., the MCP formulation), because the use of "algebraic GAMS", instead of GAMS/MPSGE, allows using different solvers for different model specifications.

Chapter 3

THE MODEL

ABSTRACT

This chapter explains how the GTAP model is extended to include MNEs in it. In so doing, it offers an interesting description of the GTAP model, which is presented in a more digestive and friendly way than the other few available alternatives. The chapter provides a detailed explanation of all the model's equations. A brief but complete overview of the model is presented in the final section. The Appendix, at the end of the chapter, lists all the endogenous and exogenous variables and parameters used in the model, together with their definition.

1. INTRODUCTION

The model built for our analysis is an extension of a 2-region, 2-factor, 20-sector version of the Global Trade Analysis Project (GTAP) model (Hertel, 1997). The GTAP model is a static computable general equilibrium (CGE) model of the world, which allows the evaluation of medium term impacts of different shocks. In its mathematical form, the model is a system of non-linear equations, derived from microeconomic optimisation and national accounts identities.

This model allows using a unique database of the world economy for general equilibrium simulations, namely, the GTAP database (Dimaranan, 2007). Hertel (1997) offers a thorough explanation of the model and the database. The setup of Hertel's model is, however, adapted to the use of a particular software program called GEMPACK. In that program equations appear in the less common "linearised" form. Rutherford and Paltsev (2000) and Rutherford (2005) have developed an equivalent mathematical formulation to that provided by Hertel (1997) for a different software named GAMS. Their model allows the use of the GTAP database. We have, therefore, chosen to follow Rutherford's (2005) setting of the GTAP model, i.e. a version called GTAP6inGAMS, and use GAMS in our simulations.

The standard version of GTAP does not consider the presence of multinational enterprises (MNEs). As mentioned earlier the CGE literature has followed till very recently an approach in which MNEs were absent. Our extension of the GTAP model considers a host region (which, as will be seen in the next chapter, is the Czech Republic) in which MNEs are introduced and a ROW region in which, by contrast, MNEs are absent, due to lack of data.

By and large, two main departures from the GTAP standard model arise from the presence of MNEs. On the one hand, each good in the economy will be produced not only by domestic firms but also by MNEs. On the other hand, capital, as a factor of production, can be now foreign or domestic. In other words, the capital stock in the host country can be owned either by domestic firms or by MNEs. We turn now to a more detailed explanation on how to introduce MNEs in CGE models. We further offer an explanation of the GTAP6inGAMS version of the GTAP model (Rutherford, 2005).

In the next section we provide a detailed explanation of the model's equations. An overview of the model is presented in the final section.

2. EQUATIONS OF THE MODEL

Rutherford's version of GTAP draws on Mathiesen's (1985) setup of an Arrow-Debreu general equilibrium. Mathiesen showed that a general equilibrium could be defined using just three types of equations, namely, those defining zero profits, those on market clearing together with equations defining income balance conditions. Mathiesen's "shortcut" facilitates the computational implementation of the model.

The model equations derived from microeconomic optimisation use a dual approach (Dixit and Norman, 1980), i.e., production activities face the standard minimisation problem:

$$\min_{v} \{w'.v \, / \, g(v) = x\}$$

where w is a vector of input prices, v a vector of factor inputs, and x a scalar denoting output related to the inputs by a production function g. This optimal behaviour offers the way of adjustment to shocks introduced in the model. It is also consistent with the macroeconomic framework embedded in national accounts identities which has to be satisfied.

Before explaining the model equations some notation hints are useful:

1   We preserve *GTAP's notation* wherever possible.

2   *Indices*: i and j denote *sectors and commodities*, $(i, j = 1,...,n)$; r and s denote *regions*, which may be either the rest of the world (ROW) or the economy hosting MNEs (H), i.e., $r,s = ROW, H$; and f denotes *factors of production*, which may be either labour (L) or capital (K), i.e., $f = L,K$. An o superscript stands for *origin* of production according to the three type of firms existing in the model. Firms may be national (N) or MNEs (F) in the country hosting MNEs, or domestic (D) in the region in which MNEs are absent, i.e., { $o = N,F,D$, where $o = N,F$ if $r = H$ and $o = D$ if $r = ROW$ }. For example, as in GTAP, dfm_{Ljr} is the total demand for labour in the jth sector of region r; whereas dfm_{LjH}^{N}, dfm_{LjH}^{F}, dfm_{LjRow}^{D} and dfm_{Ljr}^{o} are, respectively, the demand for labour by national firms in the host economy, the demand for labour by MNEs in the host economy, the demand for labour by domestic firms in ROW, or any of the three, in the jth sector of region r. Note that $dfm_{LjRow}^{D} = dfm_{LjRow}$ and that $dfm_{LjH} = dfm_{LjH}^{N} + dfm_{LjH}^{F}$.

3   In contexts where two commodity subscripts are used (e.g., demand for intermediates among sectors), the first one refers to the producing industry of a commodity, and the second one to the consuming industry. For example, as in GTAP, $vdfm_{ijr}$ is the demand for good i to be used as an intermediate in the sector j of region r. In contexts where two regional subscripts are required (e.g., imports), the first one refers to the origin of a trade flow, and the second one to the destination. For example, $vxmd_{isr}$ is the amount of physical units of exports of the good i from region s to region r (or imports of good i in r coming from s).

4   Often the model uses both a variable and a parameter which is the initial value of that variable (i.e., its value in the benchmark). In that case, following GTAP, their notation is exactly the same, except for the first letter which will be *d* for variables (in most cases indicating demand) and *v* for parameters (indicating value, i.e., the initial value). For example, vfm_{Ljr} represents the benchmark labour demand in sector *j* of region *r*, while the above mentioned dfm_{Ljr} is the corresponding demand.

5   Equations with an asterisk reflect that they are either an addition, or have been modified with respect to the GTAP standard version.

The Appendix at the end of the chapter lists all the endogenous and exogenous variables and parameters used in the model, together with their definition.

2.1. Production

In contrast with the GTAP version, in the region hosting MNEs, the final price of each good *i* , and the good itself, is not the result of the production of a representative firm. In this model, for that region, good *i* is a composite of the production of a representative firm for national firms *and* of a representative firm for MNEs. This is shown in the discontinuous lines of the top nest of Figure 1. This figure resembles the production tree of the region hosting MNEs. The discontinuous lines imply an extension of the standard GTAP model. For the region in which MNEs are absent the GTAP's production structure is preserved, though.

The production of all types of firms in the model is based on the same nested technology of domestic and imported intermediate inputs, capital and labour. Starting from the top, the second level in Figure 1 begins a series of nestings which resemble the above mentioned structure of production – analogous for national, MNEs, and domestic firms–. The second level nest is a Leontief aggregation of value added and an intermediates' composite. Value added, in turn, is a CES composite of capital and labour. The intermediates' composite is a bit more complicated. It is obtained from a Leontief aggregation of CES composites of intermediates.

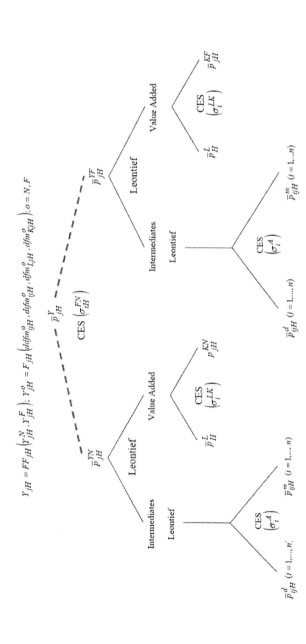

Figure 1. Production tree in the host region.

In other words, all intermediates are aggregated through a Leontief form in order to obtain an intermediates' composite. At the same time, each intermediate i results from a CES nest which specifies its foreign or domestic origin (lowest nests in Figure 1). These latter CES nests account for the fact that intermediates used by firms may be purchased domestically or imported, or a combination of the two. Further, these CES nests introduce greater flexibility in the use of intermediates than the one just relying on a Leontief combination with no CES choice of origin (Shoven and Whalley, 1992, chapter 1). This is an interesting feature of the GTAP model which thus extends the nesting structure further than usual.

In accordance with the above described structure of production, MNEs, national and domestic firms face the same optimisation problem. For all firms the objective is cost minimisation subject to the technical constraints embedded in the production tree, as usual in the dual approach. Taking into account that $difm_{ijr}^{o}$, $ddfm_{ijr}^{o}$ are the demands for the ith imported intermediate and for the ith domestically purchased intermediate to be used in the o-type firms of sector j^{th} in region r, respectively, and that dfm_{Ljr}^{o} and dfm_{Kjr}^{o} are the demands for labour and capital by the o-type firms in sector j in region r, the optimisation problem reads:

$$\min_{difm_{ijr}^{o},ddfm_{ijr}^{o},dfm_{Ljr}^{o},dfm_{Kjr}^{o}} \left(\bar{p}_r^{L}\, dfm_{Ljr}^{o}\right)+\left(\bar{p}_{jr}^{Ko}\, dfm_{Kjr}^{o}\right)+$$

$$+ \sum_i \left[\left(\bar{p}_{ijr}^{d}\, ddfm_{ijr}^{o}\right)+\left(\bar{p}_{ijr}^{m}\, difm_{ijr}^{o}\right)\right]$$

$$\text{s.t.}\quad F_{jr}\left(ddfm_{ijr}^{o},difm_{ijr}^{o},dfm_{Ljr}^{o},dfm_{Kjr}^{o}\right)=Y_{jr}^{o}$$

where $\bar{p}_r^{L}$ is the price of labour; $\bar{p}_{jr}^{Ko}$ is the price of capital in the o part of sector j; $\bar{p}_{ijr}^{d}$ is the price of the domestic intermediate i, to be used in sector j; and $\bar{p}_{ijr}^{m}$ is the price of the imported intermediate i, to be used in sector j. All these prices include *ad valorem* taxes. For domestic and imported intermediates *ad valorem* taxes differ across the sectors where they are used, i.e., intermediates coming from the same sector, say chemicals, exhibit different taxes according to whether they are used in Motor vehicles or in agriculture. They do not differ, however, according to whether they are used by the national or MNE part of each sector. By contrast, *ad valorem* taxes on labour and capital are the same in all sectors[1] (and in the national or MNE part of all sectors).

The unit costs functions are obtained from this firms' problem, and are then used in the zero profit conditions. Minimising firms' costs, thus, yields the unit cost functions for primary factors and for intermediate inputs, whose CES form are shown in equations (1*) and (2*), respectively:

$$cf_{fjr}^{O} = \left(\Sigma_f \, \theta_{fjr}^{O} \left(\overline{p}_{jr}^{fo} \right)^{\left(1-\sigma_j^{LK}\right)} \right)^{1\big/\left(1-\sigma_j^{LK}\right)} \tag{1*}$$

where θ_{fjr}^{o} is the share of factor f in value added in o-type firms in sector j of region r, $\overline{p}_{jr}^{fo}$ is the tax-inclusive price of factor f used by o-type firms in sector j of region r, and σ_j^{LK} is the elasticity of substitution between labour and capital; and:

$$ci_{ijr}^{O} = \left[\left(\theta_{dijr}^{O} \left(\overline{p}_{ijr}^{d} \right)^{\left(1-\sigma_i^{A}\right)} \right) + \left(\left(1-\theta_{dijr}^{O}\right) \left(\overline{p}_{ijr}^{m} \right)^{\left(1-\sigma_i^{A}\right)} \right) \right]^{1\big/\left(1-\sigma_i^{A}\right)} \tag{2*}$$

where θ_{dijr}^{o} is the share of the domestic intermediate input i, in total use of intermediate i, in o-type firm in sector j of region r, and σ_i^{A} is the elasticity of substitution between domestic and imported varieties (the so-called Armington elasticity; see below).

According to the Leontief technology that aggregates value added and intermediates in the production tree, we obtain a Leontief cost function of intermediates and primary factor inputs:

---

[1] The only exception is the tax on capital in agriculture which, contrary to the rest of the economy, is a subsidy.

$$c_{jr}^{yo} = \left(\sum_i \theta_{ijr}^o ci_{ijr}^o\right) + \left(\theta_{jr}^{fo} c_{fjr}^o\right) \qquad (3^*)$$

where θ_{ijr}^o and θ_{jr}^{fo} are the share of the ith intermediate input and value added in output, respectively.

The zero profit equation for o-type firms stems from equating the former Leontief costs' equation to the prices of commodities sold by firms, as follows:

$$c_{jr}^{yo} = p_{jr}^{Yo}(1 - t_{jr}^y) \qquad (4^*)$$

where, p_{jr}^{Yo} is the price of the good produced by o-type firms and t_{jr}^y is the subsidy rate on output, which is equal for both national firms and MNEs acting in the same sector.

The corresponding input demand functions exhibit a CES "calibrated share form", instead of the most common "coefficient form". The equivalence between both forms is explained in Böhringer et al. (2003) and Böhringer et al. (2005). In what follows demand functions will exhibit the "calibrated share form", which makes easier the computation of the model.

For domestic intermediate inputs their demand takes the form:

$$ddfm_{ijr}^o = vdfm_{ijr}^o \, Y_{jr}^o \left(\frac{ci_{ijr}^o}{\overline{p}_{ijr}^d}\right)^{\sigma_i^A} \qquad (5^*)$$

where $vdfm_{ijr}^o$ is the initial level of the demand for domestic intermediates from sector i to be used by o-type firms in sector j in region r, and Y_{jr}^o is one plus the percentage change in the output level. Percentage changes in the output level arise when a simulation is run, by comparing the initial value of production with respect to the one reached after the simulation. We will see that several variables in the model are presented in this form of "one plus the percentage change".

In a similar way, the demand for imported intermediate inputs is:

$$difm_{ijr}^{O} = vifm_{ijr}^{O}\ Y_{jr}^{O}\left(\left.ci_{ijr}^{O}\middle/\bar{p}_{ijr}^{m}\right.\right)^{\sigma_i^A} \qquad (6*)$$

Finally, the CES demand for primary factors is:

$$dfm_{fjr}^{O} = vfm_{fjr}^{O}\ Y_{jr}^{O}\left(\left.cf_{fjr}^{O}\middle/\bar{p}_{jr}^{fo}\right.\right)^{\sigma_i^{LK}} \qquad (7*)$$

The following equation does *only* apply to the host region, since (as shown in the discontinuous lines of Figure 1) domestic production (and its price) is the result of a CES amalgamation of national firms and MNEs' production into a unique composite good:

$$p_{iH}^{Y} = \left(\left(\theta_{iH}^{YF}\ (p_{iH}^{YF})^{(1-\sigma_{iH}^{FN})}\right)+\left(1-\theta_{iH}^{YF}\right)p_{iH}^{YN}\ {}^{(1-\sigma_{iH}^{FN})}\right)^{\left(1/(1+\sigma_{iH}^{FN})\right)} \qquad (8*)$$

where θ_{iH}^{YF} is the share of MNEs' production in gross production in sector i of the host region (H), and σ_{iH}^{FN} is the elasticity of substitution between national and foreign production.

For each i good and sector there are, once MNEs are introduced, two different "varieties", i.e., a foreign and a national one. Thus, in the country hosting MNEs, our model duplicates the sources of production of each good and aggregates both varieties (i.e., the national and the foreign one) into a unique composite good i (i.e., the "domestic" good). This domestic good is that available for either final or intermediate consumption.

Both MNEs and domestic firms produce under constant returns to scale. The differences in technology among MNEs and domestic firms are given by their different input mix of intermediates, labour, and capital. As expected, real data on the use of inputs tell us that MNEs are much more capital intensive than domestic firms, and that MNEs have greater reliance on imported intermediates compared to their national counterparts (see Figure 2 in Chapter 4). Furthermore, there is an additional source of differentiation regarding technology between MNEs and domestic firms, namely, the specific capital that each type of firm uses.

2.2. Remuneration of Capital as a Specific Factor

While labour is considered to be perfectly mobile across sectors, and internationally immobile, capital is considered to be sector-specific.

The introduction of capital as a specific factor is related to the conclusion of the literature (shown in Chapter 2) that MNEs possess a "very distinctive bundle of capabilities" (Barba Navaretti and Venables, 2004, p. 278), "proprietary assets" (e.g., Caves, 2007, chapters 1 and 2), and the idea that MNEs have some "ownership advantages" on which the OLI paradigm is based (Dunning, 1977b, 2000). These advantages give them a *different and superior technology* compared to national firms, which is embedded in our model in the assumption that capital is sector-specific. MNEs tend to have higher capital intensity, bigger size, and a higher imported content in their intermediates compared to national firms. Many of these are observable characteristics and are present in the data we use[2], but there is an intangible feature which is the specificity of MNEs' assets conveyed in the assumption of capital being sector- and firm-type-specific. This assumption, thus, introduces a distinction in the capital used by the foreign and domestic part of the same sector, so that, for example, the machines used by MNEs in the chemicals sector are different from the machines used by the national firms producing in the same sector of the host economy.

In the standard GTAP model, capital of the different sectors is aggregated into a national price of capital for each country. This is still present here. In this model though, as can be seen in Figure 2, discontinuous lines account for the fact that total capital in each sector is provided in the country hosting MNEs, not only by national firms but also by MNEs. These discontinuous lines again imply an addition of this model with respect to the standard GTAP version. The lower part of Figure 2 shows that a CET combination of MNEs' and national firms' capital gives total capital in each sector. In the upper part of the figure, the CET amalgamation of capital in each sector yields total

---

[2] Exact data on this are given in the next chapter, in which Figure 2 offers details on the different input uses in gross production of national firms versus MNEs.

capital in the economy. This particular order in the nests implies that it is easier to transfer capital between foreign and domestic firms producing in the same sector than to transfer capital among different sectors. This is an issue which has received some attention in the few CGE models that include MNEs (Petri, 1997; Hanslow et al., 1999; Lee and van der Mensbrugghe, 2001) and for which eventually the present specification seems to be most appropriate.

$$\Gamma_H = \Gamma(dfm_{KiH}); \; dfm_{KiH} = \Psi(dfm^N_{KiH}, dfm^F_{KiH})$$

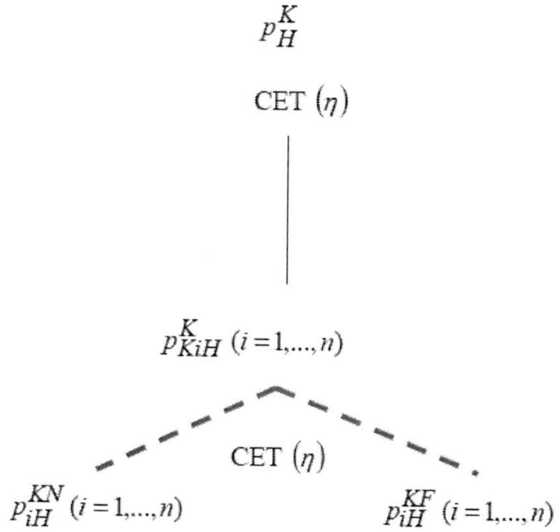

$$p^K_H$$

CET (η)

$$p^K_{KiH} \; (i=1,...,n)$$

CET (η)

$$p^{KN}_{iH} \; (i=1,...,n)$$ $$p^{KF}_{iH} \; (i=1,...,n)$$

Figure 2. Specific factor's aggregation in the host region.

It is clear from the assumption of specific capital that this factor exhibits differential prices according to the sector in which it is located, and according to whether it is owned by MNEs or by national firms. Note that due to the different technologies, the costs of MNEs versus those of domestic firms will differ and, consequently, in equilibrium, the price of the different varieties of the same good will also differ. These differences in prices across varieties of the same good imply that goods are not homogenous within the same sector. This violates the condition of homogenous goods necessary for perfect competition to hold, thus creating a climate of competition more appropriate for the presence of MNEs.

Mathematically, the CET revenue function aggregating the capital of national firms and that of MNEs in each sector, is represented by the following equation:

$$p_{jH}^{K} = \left(\left(\theta_{vfmjF} \left(p_{jH}^{KF} \right)^{(1+\eta)} \right) + \left(\left(1 - \theta_{vfmjF} \right) \left(p_{jH}^{KN} \right)^{(1+\eta)} \right) \right)^{\left(\frac{1}{(1+\eta)} \right)} \quad (9^*)$$

where θ_{vfmjF} is the value share of MNEs' capital in sector j's capital in the host economy; η is the elasticity of transformation of capital which, due to the specificity of capital, is very close to zero[3]; p_{jH}^{K} is the price of capital in the jth sector of the host economy, stemming from the price of capital of national firms and MNEs producing in that sector.

Note that this CET combination is not necessary for the capital of each sector in the rest of the world, which only has national firms producing. The return to capital at the national level has the following CET revenue function:

$$p_{r}^{K} = \left(\sum_{j} \theta_{jr}^{K} \left(p_{jr}^{K} \right)^{(1+\eta)} \right)^{\left(\frac{1}{(1+\eta)} \right)} \quad (10)$$

where θ_{jr}^{K} is the share of capital employed in sector j in region r; p_{r}^{K} is the composite price of capital, i.e., the upper price in Figure 2, which is also the return to capital for the whole economy in each region. This CET function originally stems from a maximisation problem from the GTAP model, which sought to send capital to the sectors in which its return was higher. Due to our specific capital assumption the maximisation problem no longer holds, but the CET form which aggregates sectoral prices of capital into the national price is preserved. The price of capital at the national level is used as income of the regional representative household, as will be seen below (Chapter 4). Nevertheless, in the simulations considering the impact of profit repatriation (see Chapter 5), part of the remuneration of foreign capital in the host region will be sent to ROW. Thus, some of the benefits generated in the host region do not remain there, i.e., they are subtracted from the income of the representative household and included in the income of the representative household in ROW.

---

[3] It is set at a value equal to 10^{-6}, instead of 0, because it eases the computation of the model.

2.3. Final Domestic Demand

So far, the production in each sector has been described. We look now at the three categories of final domestic demand of the model, i.e., investment, private consumption, and public consumption.

Regarding investment, $\bar{I}_{ir}$, the amount of output that each sector produces for investment goods remains fixed in real terms during the simulation. Since this is a static model, current investment does not augment the productive stock of capital available to firms. This is consistent with the interpretation of results from this model (and from the GTAP model) as a medium-term shock involving approximately three or four years.

We turn now to the other two categories of final domestic demand, which require a longer explanation.

Public Consumption
Public consumption follows the scheme shown in Figure 3.

$$G_H = G_H(ddgm_{iH}, digm_{iH})$$

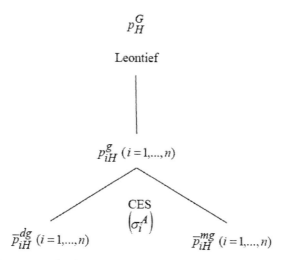

Figure 3. Public consumption in the host region.

This reflects that public consumption is a Leontief aggregation of n components, being these components, in turn, composite commodities. The latter composites are Armington CES aggregations (see section 2.4) of domestic and imported commodities.

The top Leontief form implies that the amount spent on each composite commodity i, remains unchanged during the simulation, whereas its internal composition will vary in terms of the domestic and imported share, according to the price of imports versus domestically produced goods.

Taking into account that $ddgm_{ir}$ is public demand for domestic goods and $digm_{ir}$ is public demand for imported goods, with $\bar{p}_{ir}^{dg}$ and $\bar{p}_{ir}^{mg}$ being their tax-inclusive prices, respectively, public consumption is obtained from the minimisation of the cost of a given level of aggregate public consumption:

$$\underset{ddgm_{ir},digm_{ir}}{min} \qquad \Sigma_i\left(\bar{p}_{ir}^{dg} ddgm_{ir} + \bar{p}_{ir}^{mg} digm_{ir} \right)$$

$$\text{s.t.} \qquad G_r = G_r\left(ddgm_{ir}, digm_{ir} \right)$$

The Armington-CES combinations of domestic and imported varieties have the following unit cost:

$$p_{ir}^g = \left[\left(\theta_{ir}^{dg}\left(\bar{p}_{ir}^{dg}\right)^{\left(1-\sigma_i^A\right)} \right) + \left(\left(1-\theta_{ir}^{dg}\right)\left(\bar{p}_{ir}^{mg}\right)^{\left(1-\sigma_i^A\right)} \right) \right]^{1/\left(1-\sigma_i^A\right)} \qquad (11)$$

where θ_{ir}^{dg} is the share of domestic good i in public consumption.

Each component, i, is aggregated to form public consumption using a Leontief technology. This Leontief amalgamation exhibits a unit cost function which is shown in the left-hand side of equation (12). The price of public expenditure appears at the right-hand side. Thus, the following equation shows the zero-profit condition of public consumption:

$$\sum_i \left(\theta_{ir}^g\, p_{ir}^g \right) = p_r^G \qquad (12)$$

where θ_{ir}^g is the share of good i in total public consumption, and p_{ir}^g is the tax- inclusive price of good i purchased for public consumption in region r.

Input demands are CES, so that for the demand of domestic public output this yields:

$$ddgm_{ir} = vdgm_{ir}\ G_r \left(\frac{p_{ir}^g}{\overline{p}_{ir}^{dg}} \right)^{\sigma_i^A} \tag{13}$$

where $vdgm_{ir}$ is the public demand for the ith domestic good in the benchmark and G_r is one plus the percentage change in public consumption. The CES input demand for the imported public output is:

$$digm_{ir} = vigm_{ir}\ G_r \left(\frac{p_{ir}^g}{\overline{p}_{ir}^{mg}} \right)^{\sigma_i^A} \tag{14}$$

where $vigm_{ir}$ is the public demand of the ith imported good in the benchmark.

Private Consumption

Private consumption is characterised by a Cobb-Douglas combination of composite goods of domestic and imported inputs, as shown in Figure 4.

Since public consumption and investment are fixed, private household consumption is the element that adjusts to satisfy the household's budget constraint in each region. In so doing utility maximization will lead to the minimization of the cost of aggregate private consumption, i.e.:

$$\min_{ddpm_{ir}, dipm_{ir}} \quad \Sigma_i \left(\overline{p}_{ir}^{dc} ddpm_{ir} \right) + \left(\overline{p}_{ir}^{mc} dipm_{ir} \right)$$

$$\text{s.t.} \quad C_r(ddpm_{ir}, dipm_{ir}) = C_r$$

where, similarly to the notation for public consumption, $ddpm_{ir}$ is the private demand for the ith domestic good, and $dipm_{ir}$ is the private demand for the ith imported good, being $\overline{p}_{ir}^{dc}$ and $\overline{p}_{ir}^{mc}$ their tax-inclusive prices, respectively.

$$C_H = C_H(ddpm_{iH}, dipm_{iH})$$

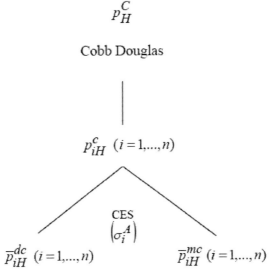

Figure 4. Private consumption in the host region.

The aggregation of domestic and imported varieties into a composite good exhibits the following Armington CES unit cost function:

$$p_{ir}^c = \left[\left(\theta_{ir}^{dc}\left(\bar{p}_{ir}^{dc}\right)^{1-\sigma_i^A}\right) + \left(\left(1-\theta_{ir}^{dc}\right)\left(\bar{p}_{ir}^{mc}\right)^{1-\sigma_i^A}\right)\right]^{1/\left(1-\sigma_i^A\right)} \quad (15)$$

where θ_{ir}^{dc} is the share of the domestic commodity i in private consumption.

The Cobb-Douglas aggregation at the top of Figure 4 yields a unit cost function which appears in the left-hand side of the following equation. By equating this to the price of consumption that appears in the right-hand side, we again obtain the zero-profit condition, this time of consumption of the private good:

$$\prod_i \left(p_{ir}^c\right)^{\theta_{ir}^p} = p_r^C \quad (16)$$

where θ_{ir}^p is the value share of good i in private output, and p_{ir}^c is the tax-inclusive price of good i purchased for private consumption in region r.

The corresponding demand for the ith domestic good purchased for private consumption is:

$$ddpm_{ir} = vdpm_{ir} \; C_r \left(\left. p_{ir}^c \middle/ \bar{p}_{ir}^{dc} \right. \right)^{\sigma_i^A} \left(\left. p^C \middle/ p_{ir}^c \right. \right) \tag{17}$$

where $vdpm_{ir}$ is the private demand for the ith domestic good in the benchmark and C_r is one plus the percentage change in national private consumption in region r. Finally, the private demand of the ith imported good is:

$$dipm_{ir} = vipm_{ir} \; C_r \left(\left. p_{ir}^c \middle/ \bar{p}_{ir}^{mc} \right. \right)^{\sigma_i^A} \left(\left. p^C \middle/ p_{ir}^c \right. \right) \tag{18}$$

where $vipm_{ir}$ is the private demand of the ith imported good in the benchmark.

2.4. Foreign Sector

The GTAP project is particularly devoted to the general equilibrium analysis of trade and resource shocks. As a consequence, the modelisation of the foreign sector offers several interesting features that are preserved in this model. One of these features is that it takes full account of destination/source policy instruments (tariffs or subsidies) and transport margins (associated with transport costs) *at the level of disaggregated regions and commodities*. Another interesting feature is that in GTAP, contrary to most models of global trade, imports are traced to specific uses. In other words, the model specifies whether imports are for private, public, or intermediate consumption. The latter characteristic will be apparent in one of the market-clearing equations below (see equation 27). At the moment, we will describe how imports and transport services are modeled.

Imports

In GTAP the choice among imports from different sources is based on Armington's idea of regionally differentiated products (Armington, 1969), so that each region produces its own distinctive variety of each commodity, which is imperfectly substitutable with respect to the variety produced by the other regions. This Armington assumption allows to reflect the empirical evidence of cross-hauling.

In a 2-region model the scheme of imports' demand is considerably simplified as imports of one region are just exports from the other region, with no other competing source of imports. As mentioned earlier, the model does not only take into account the volume of commodities traded but also transport and insurance services associated with trade flows.

The usual cost minimisation problem arises:

$$\begin{array}{c} min \\ dxmd_{isr}, dtwr_{jisr} \end{array} \qquad \overline{py}_{isr}^{m} dxmd_{isr} + \sum_j \overline{pt}_{jisr}^{m} dtwr_{jisr}$$

$$\text{s.t.} \qquad M_{ir}(dxmd_{isr}, dtwr_{jisr}) = M_{ir}$$

where $dxmd_{isr}$ stands for the amount of physical units of exports of the good i from region s to region r (or imports of good i in r coming from s). The flows originated by these exports/imports are associated with different transport services j (insurance, transport...), needed to move good i from region s to region r, $dtwr_{jisr}$. The movement of physical units is subject to export subsidies and import tariffs, with subsidies paid by the government in the exporting region, and tariffs collected by the government in the importing region, resulting in a final price $\overline{py}_{isr}^{m}$. The price of transport services $\overline{pt}_{jisr}^{m}$ only includes import tariffs.

The volume of commodities and transport margins is aggregated through a Leontief technology, which yields a Leontief unit cost function at the right-hand side of equation (20), which equated to the total price of imports, p_{ir}^{M}, leads to the zero-profit condition of this sector:

$$p_{ir}^{M} = \theta_{isr}^{ym} \cdot \overline{py}_{isr}^{m} + \sum_j \theta_{jisr}^{t} \overline{pt}_{jisr}^{m} \qquad (19)$$

where θ_{isr}^{ym} is the share of the amount of physical units in imports, and θ_{jisr}^{t} is the share of the amount of transport services in imports.

Input demands for the share of goods (excluding transport services) in imports are given by:

$$dxmd_{isr} = vxmd_{isr} \times M_{ir} \tag{20}$$

where $vxmd_{isr}$ is the physical volume of imports of good i in region r in the benchmark, and M_{ir} is one plus the percentage increase in imports of good i from region r.

In turn, input demands for transport services are:

$$dtwr_{jisr} = vtwr_{jisr} \times M_{ir} \tag{21}$$

where $dtwr_{jisr}$ is the transport service j associated with the trade flow of good i from region s to region r in the benchmark. Let us explain in more detail how transport services work.

Transport Services

In this model transport services constitute a sector on its own. This sector assembles transport services into a composite good used to move merchandise trade among regions. This is an "artificial" sector in the sense that is not "another sector" in any of the economies in the model. On the contrary, it is only part of the production of some sectors of the economy, mostly services, that is devoted to these transport services.

To obtain the price of one of these transport services, say insurance, this "artificial" sector takes the price and amount of insurance devoted to transport services in the two regions and combines them into an insurance composite of international transport services. More generally, composite international transport services are provided as a global activity, whose inputs are international transport services from each region. The production function assembling regional transport services has a Cobb-Douglas form, which shows that the price of the international transport service i, p_i^T, is an aggregation of its price in the two regions (p_{iH}^Y and p_{iRow}^Y).

The cost minimisation problem is:

$$\text{min} \qquad \sum_r p_{ir}^{Y}.dst_{ir}$$
$$dst_{ir}$$

$$\text{s.t} \qquad YT_i(dst_{ir}) = YT_i$$

where dst_{ir} is the amount of production of good i that is used as a transport service, and YT_j is one plus the percentage change in the world production of the jth international transport service.

The zero-profit condition has on its left-hand side a Cobb-Douglas technology unit cost function which is equal to the price of transport services (which appears in the right-hand side), as follows:

$$\prod_r \left(p_{ir}^{Y}\right)^{\theta_{ir}^{t}} = p_i^{T} \qquad\qquad (22)$$

where θ_{ir}^{t} represents the benchmark share of the amount of production of good i devoted to transport services in region r, in the amount of world production of good i devoted to transport services in the whole world.

The foreign sector is closed by assuming that the difference between the value of imports and exports of goods and services is fixed. This is the natural consequence of having investment and savings fixed in the model.

This explanation of transport services closes the part of equations in the model that describe the behaviour and the way of adjustment after a change in any of the parameters or variables in the model. As stated earlier, it is based on a neoclassical microeconomic optimising behaviour. The rest of the chapter describes some accounting relationships on which the general equilibrium nature of the model rests, providing to the model the conditions to reach equilibrium.

2.5. Income Balance Condition

To keep the focus on the production side of the model, there is a representative household in each region. All income earned from factor endowments (labour and capital) as well as all taxes levied in a region, accrue to the representative household of that region (except for the simulations in which we consider profit repatriation —Chapter 5—, in which part of the remuneration of foreign capital in the host economy goes to ROW).

Remember that the amount of physical units purchase for both public consumption and investment are fixed, so that only private household expenditure will adjust to satisfy the budget constraint. The following equation resembles the budget available for private consumption of the representative household, $raINC_r$. This is obtained by deducting expenses on public consumption and investment from the disposable regional income.

$$raINC_r = vb_r - \left(p_r^G \ \overline{vgm}_r\right) - \sum_i \left(p_{ir}^Y \ \overline{I}_{ir}\right) + \sum_f \left(p_r^f \ evom_{fr}\right) + \qquad + $$

$$revt_r^y + revt_r^L + revt_r^K + revt_r^{fd} + revt_r^{fm} + revt_r^{pd} + revt_r^{pm} +$$

$$+ \ revt_r^{gd} + revt_r^{gm} + revt_r^{xs} + revt_r^{ms} \qquad\qquad (23)$$

where vb_r is the negative of the current account balance, $evom_{fr}$ is the total endowment of factor f in region r, and all the terms beginning by $revt$ are the revenues of different types of taxes which are specified in the Appendix.

In the case in which we consider the effects of profit repatriation (Chapter 5), two new equations arise when modifying equation (23). These are equations (23*) and (23*bis) for ROW and the host region, respectively:

$$raINC_{ROW} = vb_{ROW} - \left(p_{ROW}^G \ \overline{vgm}_{ROW}\right) - \sum_i \left(p_{iROW}^Y \ \overline{I}_{ir}\right) + \sum_f \left(p_{ROW}^f \ evom_{fROW}\right) +$$

$$revt_{ROW}^y + revt_{ROW}^L + revt_{ROW}^K + revt_{ROW}^{fd} + revt_{ROW}^{fm} + revt_{ROW}^{pd} + revt_{ROW}^{pm}$$

$$+ \ revt_{ROW}^{gd} + revt_{ROW}^{gm} + revt_{ROW}^{xs} + revt_{ROW}^{ms}$$

$$+ \%\boldsymbol{Profit \ Rep}_j \left(\left(FDIf_{KjH} - 1\right) p_H^K \ vfm_{KjH}^F\right) \qquad (23*)$$

$$raINC_H = vb_H - \left(p_H^G \ \overline{vgm}_H\right) - \sum_i \left(p_{iH}^Y \ \overline{I}_{iH}\right) + \sum_f \left(p_r^f \ evom_{fH}\right) + \qquad +$$

$$revt_H^y + revt_H^L + revt_H^K + revt_H^{fd} + revt_H^{fm} + revt_H^{pd} + revt_H^{pm} +$$

$$+ \ revt_H^{gd} + revt_H^{gm} + revt_H^{xs} + revt_H^{ms}$$

$$- \%Profit\ Rep_j \left(\left(FDIf_{KjH} - 1 \right) p_H^K\ vfm_{KjH}^F \right) \qquad (23^*\ bis)$$

The last line in equations (23*) and in (23*bis) are the only terms added to the original equation (23) when we take into account the impact of profit repatriation. The parameters *%Profit Rep_j* and *FDIf_{Kjr}* are new and are not present in the GTAP model. To understand their role we have to explain how we are simulating the entry of MNEs. This is as follows. We simulate the arrival of new MNEs in a particular sector, j, of the host economy, H (some MNEs were previously present). Their arrival increases the capital stock of the sector j in which they act. In particular, they increase the amount of *foreign* capital in that sector j. $FDIf_{Kjr}$ takes the value of one plus the percentage increase in the foreign capital stock held by MNEs of sector j. When profit repatriation takes place, part of the remuneration of the extra capital added by the arrival of new MNEs is sent from the host economy to ROW. The parameter *%Profit Rep_j* indicates the percentage of extra capital in the foreign part of sector j, whose remuneration ($p_H^K\ vfm_{KjH}^F$) is repatriated.

The model in Chapter 4 uses equation (23), in Chapter 5 this equation is replaced by the expressions in equations (23*) and (23*bis). We continue now with the rest of equations in the model, which are common for the final specification of the model in both chapters 4 and 5.

2.6. Market-Clearing Equations

Private Consumption

$$raINC_r = C_r\ vpm_r\ p_r^C \qquad (24)$$

where C_r is one plus the percentage change in private consumption, vpm_r is the value of private consumption in the benchmark, and p_r^C is the price of private consumption.

Public Consumption

$$G_r = 1 \qquad (25)$$

Firms' Output

$$Y_{ir} \, vom_{ir} = \sum_j ddfm_{ijr} + ddpm_{ir} + ddgm_{ir} + dxmd_{irs} + dst_{ir} + \bar{I}_{ir} \quad (26)$$

where Y_{ir} is one plus the percentage change in sectoral output, and vom_{ir} is its value in the benchmark.

Imports

$$M_{ir} \, vim_{ir} = \sum_j difm_{ijr} + dipm_{ir} + digm_{ir} \qquad (27)$$

where vim_{ir} is the physical volume of imports in sector i of region r in the benchmark. Note that, as mentioned before, imports may refer to intermediates, public consumption, or private consumption.

Transport Services

$$YT_j \, vtw_j = \sum_i \sum_s \sum_r dtwr_{jisr} \qquad (28)$$

where, YT_j is one plus the percentage change in the world production of the jth international transport service, and vtw_j is the world production of the international transport service of good j in the benchmark.

Labour

$$evom_{Lr} = \sum_i dfm_{Lir} \qquad (29)$$

Capital

$$NEWevom_{Kr} = evom_{Kr} \, FT_{Kr} \qquad (30*)$$

where $NEWevom_{Kr}$ is the value of the capital stock in the economy r after the entrance of MNEs, and FT_{Kr} is one plus the percentage change in the capital stock.

$$vfm^o_{Kjr}\, FDIf_{Kjr}\left(p^{Ko}_{jr}\Big/ p^K_{jr}\right)^\eta = dfm^o_{Kjr} \qquad (31^*)$$

Remember that $FDIf_{Kjr}$ takes a value of one plus the percentage increase in the foreign capital stock held by MNEs, after the arrival of new MNEs in sector j. For national firms, and for the MNEs not receiving any additional capital, $FDIf_{Kjr}$ takes a value of one.

The increase in the capital stock of the foreign part of the sector to which MNEs go also increases the total volume of capital that the whole sector owns. This is reflected in the following equation whose parameter FDI_{Kjr} takes again a value of one plus the percentage increase in the total capital (national plus MNE) of that sector:

$$vfm_{Kjr}\, FDI_{Kjr}\left(p^K_{jr}\Big/ p^K_r\right)^\eta = dfm_{Kjr} \qquad (32^*)$$

Note that equations (31^*) and (32^*) are CET demand equations of the o-type firms in sector j, and total capital demand in sector j, respectively. When the number of MNEs increases these demands for capital also increase.

3. OVERVIEW OF THE MODEL

A final brief description of the model may be useful as a summary. The present model is an extension of a 2-region, 2-factor, 20-sector version of the GTAP model (Hertel, 1997), including MNEs. The GTAP model is a static general equilibrium model of the world economy, with which medium term impacts of different shocks can be evaluated. In its mathematical form, the model is a system of non-linear equations, derived from microeconomic optimisation theory using a dual approach together with national accounts identities.

In the model there is a *representative household* in each region, who embodies all types of agents in the economy. His income stems from the remuneration of all factors of production together with fiscal revenues from several taxes. In the simulations considering profit repatriation, however, part of the remuneration of foreign capital is subtracted from the income of the representative household from the host region to add it to the one in ROW. In any case, the representative household fully spends his income in investment, government consumption, and public consumption. To simplify, the real levels of investment and public consumption do not change after an entry of MNEs, but private consumption does.

Regarding firms' behaviour, two main departures from the GTAP standard model arise from the presence of MNEs. On the one hand, each good in the host economy will be produced not only by domestic firms but also by MNEs. On the other hand, capital, as a factor of production, can be now either foreign or domestic; in other words, the capital stock in the host country can be owned either by national firms or by MNEs. Capital is modeled as a specific factor in order to satisfy the extended conclusion in the literature that MNEs have some "specific assets" and "ownership advantages".

For each *i* good and sector there are, after introducing MNEs, two different "varieties" − a foreign and a national one −. Thus, in the country hosting MNEs, our model duplicates the sources of production of each good and combines both varieties into a unique composite good *i* − the "domestic" good −. This domestic good is the one available for final or intermediate consumption. MNEs and domestic firms produce under constant returns to scale, using as inputs both domestically-produced and imported intermediate goods, as well as two primary factors, labour and capital. However, the differences in technology between national firms and MNEs appear once the real data on intermediates, labour and capital are introduced in the model equations. As expected, one then realises how MNEs are much more capital intensive than national firms, or their greater reliance on imported intermediates as compared to their national counterparts. Furthermore, an additional source of differentiation regarding technology between MNEs and national firms stems from the assumption of specific capital. Capital will therefore exhibit different prices according not only to the type of good for which it is used, as in the standard GTAP model, but also according to whether it is used for production of the foreign or the national variety of that good.

The standard GTAP model (and this extension) offers a detailed description of international trade in the economies analysed. It takes into account not only the volume of commodities traded, but also transport and insurance services associated with trade flows. Furthermore, trade flows are subject to export subsidies and import tariffs which are specified at the level of commodities and region.

Some final comments are related to primary factor endowments. Labour is fully mobile across sectors and its endowment is exogenously fixed. Capital endowments, in contrast, will vary according to MNEs' entry. This is modeled as leading to changes in the capital stock held by foreign MNEs installed in the economy, i.e., as increasing the capital stock held by the "foreign" part of the production of goods. Note that MNEs' entrance causes a higher level of capital available for MNEs whose technology differs from national firms in the manner described above.

APPENDIX. COMPLETE LIST
OF VARIABLES AND PARAMETERS

Endogenous Variables

Production

$difm_{ijr}^{o}$ Demand for imported intermediates from sector i to be used by o-type firms in sector j in region r

$difm_{ijr}$ Total demand for the imported intermediate i in sector j in region r

$ddfm_{ijr}^{o}$ Demand for domestic purchases of intermediates from sector i to be used by o-type firms in sector j in region r

$ddfm_{ijr}$ Total demand for domestic purchases of intermediate i in sector j in region r

dfm_{fir}^{o} Demand for primary factor f by o-type firms in sector i in region r

dfm_{fir} Total demand for primary factor f in sector i in region r

$NEWevom_{Kr}$ Value of the capital stock after MNEs' entry in region r

FT_{Kr} One plus the percentage change in the capital stock in region r

$\bar{p}_{jr}^{fo}$ Tax-inclusive price of factor f used by o-type firms in sector j in region r

$\bar{p}_r^{L}$ Tax-inclusive wage in region r

$\bar{p}_{jr}^{Ko}$ Tax-inclusive price of capital in o-type firms in sector j in region r

$\bar{p}_{ijr}^{d}$ Tax-inclusive price of the domestically purchased intermediate i to be used in sector j in region r

$\bar{p}_{ijr}^{m}$ Tax-inclusive price of the imported intermediate i to be used in sector j in region r

p_{jr}^{Yo} Price of good j produced by o-type firms, excluding taxes or subsidies, in region r

p_{jr}^{K} Price of capital in sector j in region r

p_r^{K} Price of capital in region r

p_{jr}^{Y} Price of good j before taxes

Y_{jr}^{o} One plus the percentage change in gross output of o-type firms in sector j in region r

Y_{jr} One plus the percentage change in total gross output in sector j in region r

Public Consumption

$ddgm_{ir}$ Demand for domestic purchases of good i for public consumption in region r

$digm_{ir}$ Demand for imports of good i for public consumption in region r

G_r One plus the percentage change in national public consumption in region r

$\overline{p}_{ir}^{dg}$ Tax-inclusive price of public consumption of the ith domestic good in region r

$\overline{p}_{ir}^{mg}$ Tax-inclusive price of public consumption of the ith imported good in region r

p_{ir}^{g} Tax-inclusive price of good i purchased for public consumption in region r

p_{r}^{G} Price of public consumption in region r

Private Consumption

$ddpm_{ir}$ Demand for domestic purchases of good i for private consumption in region r

$dipm_{ir}$ Demand for imports of good i for private consumption in region r

$raINC_{r}$ Budget available for private consumption of the representative household in region r

C_{r} One plus the percentage change in national private consumption in region r

$\overline{p}_{ir}^{dc}$ Tax-inclusive price of private consumption of the ith domestic good in region r

$\overline{p}_{ir}^{mc}$ Tax-inclusive price of private consumption of the ith imported good in region r

p_{ir}^{c} Tax-inclusive price of good i purchased for private consumption in region r

p_{r}^{C} Price of private consumption in region r

Imports and Transport Services

$dxmd_{isr}$ Demand for physical units of imports of good i in region r coming from region s

$dtwr_{jisr}$ Demand for the transport service j needed for transport of good i from region s to region r

dst_{ir}	Production of good i used as a transport service in region r
M_{ir}	One plus the percentage increase in imports of good i in region r
p_{ir}^M	Price of imports of good i, including transport services, in region r
$\overline{py}_{isr}^m$	Price of the volume of physical imports, including tariffs and subsidies, of good i in the route from s to r
$\overline{pt}_{jisr}^m$	Price of the transport service j, including tariffs, of good i in the route from s to r
p_i^T	Price of the transportation service i
YT_j	One plus the percentage change in the world production of the jth international transport service

Taxes and Subsidies

$revt_r^y$	Total payments of subsidies on output in region r
$revt_r^f$	Total income from taxes on primary factors in region r
$revt_r^{fd}$	Total income from taxes on domestic intermediates in region r
$revt_r^{fm}$	Total income from taxes on imported intermediates in region r
$revt_r^{pd}$	Total income from taxes on private consumption of domestic goods in region r
$revt_r^{pm}$	Total income from taxes on private consumption of imported goods in region r
$revt_r^{gd}$	Total income from taxes on public consumption of domestic goods in region r
$revt_r^{gm}$	Total income from taxes on public consumption of imported goods in region r
$revt_r^{xs}$	Total payments of subsidies on exports in region r
$revt_r^{ms}$	Total income from tariffs on imports in region r

Exogenous Variables and Parameters

Production

$evom_{fr}$ — Total endowment of factor f in region r

θ^{O}_{fjr} — Share of the factor f in value added in o-type firms in sector j in region r

θ^{O}_{dijr} — Share of the domestic intermediate input i in its total use in o-type firms in sector j in region r

θ^{O}_{ijr} — Share of the intermediate input i (domestic plus imported) in gross production of the o-type firms in sector j

θ^{fo}_{jr} — Share of value added in gross production of the o-type firms in sector j in region r

θ^{YF}_{iH} — Share of MNEs' production in gross production in the host economy

θ_{vfmjF} — Share of MNEs' capital in total capital in sector j in the host economy

θ^{K}_{jr} — Share of capital employed in sector j in region r

$vdfm^{O}_{ijr}$ — Benchmark value of the domestic purchases of intermediates from sector i to be used by o-type firms in sector j in region r

$vdfm_{ijr}$ — Benchmark value of the total domestic purchases of intermediates from sector i in sector j in region r

vfm^{O}_{fir} — Benchmark value of the demand for the primary factor f by o-type firms in sector j in region r

vfm_{fir} — Benchmark value of the total demand for the primary factor f in sector j in region r

$vifm^{O}_{ijr}$ — Benchmark value of the imported intermediates from sector i to be used by o-type firms in sector j in region r

$vifm_{ijr}$ Benchmark value of the total demand for the imported intermediate i in sector j in region r

vom_{ir} Benchmark value of the sectoral gross production in region r

Demand

$\bar{I}_{ir}$ Fixed investment expenditure in sector i in region r

Public Consumption

θ_{ir}^{dg} Share of the domestic good i in public consumption in region r

θ_{ir}^{g} Share of the good i in total public consumption in region r

$vdgm_{ir}$ Benchmark value of the domestic purchases of good i for public consumption in region r

$vigm_{ir}$ Benchmark value of the imports of good i for public consumption in region r

$\overline{vgm}_{r}$ Benchmark value of total (imported plus domestic) national public consumption in region r

Private Consumption

θ_{ir}^{dc} Share of the domestic good i in private consumption in region r

θ_{ir}^{p} Share of the good i in total private consumption in region r

$vdpm_{ir}$ Benchmark value of the domestic purchases of good i for private consumption in region r

$vipm_{ir}$ Benchmark value of the imports of good i for private consumption in region r

vpm_{r} Benchmark value of total national private consumption in region r

Foreign Sector

vb_{r} Negative of the current account balance of region r in the benchmark

vim_{ir} Benchmark physical volume of imports in sector i in region r

Transport Services

θ_{isr}^{ym} Share of the amount of physical units of goods (excluding transport services) in imports of region r

θ_{jisr}^{t} Share of the amount of transport services in imports of region r

θ_{ir}^{t} Share of the part of production of good i devoted to transport services in region r in the part of world production of good i devoted to transport services

$vxmd_{isr}$ Benchmark amount of physical units of imports of the good i in region r coming from region s

$vtwr_{jisr}$ Benchmark amount of the transport service j needed for transport of good i from region s to region r

vst_{jr} Benchmark production of good j used as a transport service in region r

vtw_{j} Benchmark aggregate of international transport services in sector j in the world

Taxes

t_{ijr}^{fd} Tax rate of the domestic intermediates from sector i to be used in sector j in region r

t_{ijr}^{fm} Tax rate of the imported intermediates from sector i to be used in sector j in region r

t_{jr}^{f} Tax rate on the factor f used in sector j in region r

t_{jr}^{y} Output subsidy rate in sector j in region r

t_{ir}^{gd} Tax rate on the domestic public good i purchased domestically in region r

t_{ir}^{gm} Tax rate on the imported public good i in region r

t_{ir}^{pd} Tax rate on the domestic private good i purchased domestically in region r

t_{ir}^{pm} Tax rate on the imported private good i in region r

t_{isr}^{ms} Import tariff rate on the good i exported from s to r

t_{isr}^{xs} Export subsidy rate on the good i exported from s to r

Elasticities

σ_i^A Elasticity of substitution between imports and domestic production in sector i (Armington elasticity)

σ_i^{LK} Elasticity of substitution between labour and capital in sector i

σ_{iH}^{FN} Elasticity of substitution between domestic and foreign production in sector i in the host economy

η Elasticity of transformation of capital across sectors

Simulation Parameters

%Profit Rep$_j$ Percentage of extra capital in the foreign part of sector j, whose remuneration is repatriated

$FDIf_{Kjr}$ One plus the percentage increase in the stock of capital held by foreign MNEs in sector j in region r

FDI_{Kjr} One plus the percentage increase in the total stock of capital of sector j in region r

Chapter 4

SIMULATING THE ENTRY
OF MULTINATIONALS WITHOUT
PROFIT REPATRIATION

ABSTRACT

This chapter discusses the sources of the benchmark dataset used for the simulations performed in this book. It also explains how the simulation of the entry of MNEs works, in order to derive the effects of a higher involvement of MNEs in some particular sectors of a host economy. The analysis is applied to the Czech Republic, a country that has received substantial inflows of foreign direct investment in the last few years. The results of the model are in accordance with the predictions of the factor-specific model within the theory of international trade (Jones, 2002, 2000, 1971; Mussa, 1974; Neary, 1978). Given its general equilibrium nature, these results cover both aggregate and sectoral variables. We, thus, shed light on the impact of MNEs on GDP, wages, rental rate of capital, CPI, exports, imports and welfare. Regarding sectoral variables we offer the effects on production, prices, intermediate costs, value added, exports and imports (at a 20-sectors disaggregation level). The sensitivity analysis presented does not alter the causation chain of adjustments across the economy, nor does it affect the main outcomes, providing a successful test for the robustness of the model.

1. INTRODUCTION

Computable General Equilibrium (CGE) models have been described as "theory with numbers" (e.g., O'Rourke, 1995). The previous chapter develops "the theory" and this and the next one go on with "the numbers". We, thus, turn now to the empirical side of the model.

Any CGE model builds on an initial dataset which is the numerical solution of the model − the benchmark equilibrium −. After having calibrated the model, the benchmark simultaneously satisfies all the model equations, and a simulation can be run. This basically consists of a shock, which changes one or more parameters and/or variables of the model. This leads to a new solution called the counterfactual equilibrium. The comparison between the counterfactual and the benchmark equilibria provides the impact of the shock simulated. A description of the calibration procedure can be found in Dawkins et al. (2001).

In this chapter we discuss the sources of the benchmark dataset (section 2), explain how the simulation of the entry of MNEs works (section 3), and provide the results (section 4). Finally, we present a sensitivity analysis (section 5), and draw the main conclusions (section 6).

2. THE DATA

As explained in the previous chapter, our model is an extension of a 2-region, 2-factor, 20-sector version of GTAP. The two regions in this simulation are the Czech Republic and the Rest of the World (ROW), the two factors are labour and capital, and the twenty sectors appear in Table 1. Disaggregation to this level was made using the GEMPACK software package, and was the maximum sectoral disaggregation possible in order to use three different sources of data. The main source has been the GTAP6 Data Base (Dimaranan, 2007). Most of the production data for the Czech Republic, however, had to be split into a foreign and a national part. The information to assign which part is related to national firms and which one to MNEs has been obtained from two sources supplying data about MNEs' activities in the Czech Republic: the OECD (2007) database "The role of MNEs", and the Czech National Bank's (2004) "2001 Foreign direct investment".

Table 1. Definition of sectors and their relative weight in the Czech economy, 2001

	% on gross output	% on capital	% on private consumption	% on imports	% on exports	MNEs' % on gross output	MNEs' % on capital
01/05 Agriculture, hunting and fishing	3.02	4.49	3.08	2.20	1.09	0.57	0.57
10/14 Mining and quarrying	1.04	3.13	0.74	4.72	0.89	18.70	27.35
15/16 Food, beverages and tobacco	7.60	8.34	26.94	2.98	2.92	31.50	50.92
17/19 Textiles, wearing apparel, leather, footwear	3.06	2.01	7.12	5.33	5.71	26.50	23.92
20 Wood and wood products, except furniture	1.90	1.80	0.67	1.67	3.97	23.80	22.05
21/22 Paper; printing, publishing and recorded media	2.42	2.54	1.78	2.98	2.84	45.30	52.46
23 Petroleum	1.01	0.14	4.40	1.41	0.39	1.00	1.00
24/25 Chemicals, rubber and plastics	4.42	3.66	3.71	12.84	8.73	42.60	49.13
26 Non-metallic mineral products	2.60	3.38	0.17	2.50	4.55	49.00	58.58
27/28 Basic and fabricated metal products	7.62	5.34	0.25	9.95	10.74	24.00	28.91
34 Motor vehicles	6.48	2.98	3.93	7.55	14.06	90.70	89.45
35 Other transport equipment	1.06	0.40	0.74	1.10	1.46	23.00	18.53
30/33 Electronics	2.72	1.96	1.76	9.44	6.56	62.98	58.80
29 Machinery and equipment n.e.c.	8.60	3.82	7.50	20.40	19.46	29.30	24.06
36/37 Furniture, manufacturing n.e.c.	1.29	1.13	1.99	1.14	1.55	29.90	34.26
40/45 Electricity, gas and water supply; construction	11.03	9.91	6.13	1.56	2.61	11.90	12.61
50/55 Trade, repair; hotels and restaurants	4.13	5.25	2.93	1.15	0.62	30.80	36.20
60/64 Transport, storage and communication	6.38	8.46	4.59	2.60	4.66	10.80	9.50
65/74 Finance, insurance, real estate, business activities	11.88	20.60	11.09	6.59	4.67	22.60	10.67
75-79 NACE Other services	11.74	10.66	10.45	1.89	2.51	1.01	1.01
01/99 Total Czech economy	100	100	100	100	100	29.10	28.50

Notes: Author's own elaboration from Dimanaran (2007), OECD (2007) and Czech National Bank (2004). The definitions of the sectors follow the ISIC Rev 3 Classification.

Table 1 shows the relative importance of the 20 sectors within the economy of the Czech Republic and also gives some information on the sectoral weight of MNEs. All the data refer to the year 2001. The first and second columns show the percentage of each sector on the total gross output and total capital[13] of the Czech economy, i.e. the weights of national *and* foreign production and capital in each sector over their corresponding totals of the Czech economy. The third column gives the percentage that each sector represents on final private consumption. The fourth and fifth columns give the weight of each sector on imports and exports, respectively, in terms of international prices. Finally, the sixth and seventh columns show the shares of MNEs in gross production and capital, respectively, in each sector. It is remarkable the important weight of MNEs in *nearly all sectors* of the economy; for the economy as a whole, the weights of MNEs on gross production and capital amount to 29.1 and 28.5 per cent, respectively.

We will simulate the entry of multinational enterprises (MNEs) in five different sectors of the Czech economy. These sectors are: 1) Chemicals, rubber and plastics (Chemicals, henceforth), 2) Motor vehicles, 3) Electronics, 4) Trade, repair; hotels and restaurants (Trade, henceforth), and 5) Finance, insurance, real estate, business activities (Finance, henceforth). We offer extensive information regarding the impact of MNEs in these sectors. The choice of sectors has tried to combine their importance as FDI recipients, as well as their relative weight in the overall Czech economy. Also, we incorporate both manufacturing and services sectors, which is rather uncommon in the empirical literature; and, in the case of manufactures, the particular sectors chosen represent mostly dynamic activities, i.e., they are classified as medium- and high-technology sectors.

Even though the shock takes place initially in each of the five sectors above, in order to account for the impact of MNEs, the Czech economy and ROW have been disaggregated to the twenty-sector level mentioned earlier. This allows us to derive a full set of sectoral effects. Aggregate results will be also analysed. In so doing we will have a comprehensive picture of MNEs' effects thanks to the general equilibrium nature of the model.

Turning to another different type of data, those on elasticities also deserve some attention. The elasticity of transformation of capital across sectors is set

---

[13] Strictly speaking "capital" stands for what national accounts statistics denote "property income".

at 10^{-6} in order to fulfil the specific capital assumption[14]. The elasticity of substitution between national and foreign production within the Czech Republic is given the same value to that between domestic and imported goods (Armington elasticity supplied by GTAP). For the rest of elasticities the GTAP values have been taken. These are calculated by the GTAP team from econometric evidence; see Hertel (1997) and Dimaranan (2007, chapter 20) for details.

Finally, due to the Walrasian nature of the model, the monetary variables (values and prices) are set with respect to a numeraire. We have followed the practice of using the Consumer Price Index (CPI) as the numeraire[15]. CPI weights are the share of sectoral private consumption displayed in column 3 of Table 1.

3. SIMULATING THE ENTRY OF MNES WITHOUT PROFIT REPATRIATION

The entry of MNEs is simulated as a capital increase in the foreign share of each of the five sectors in turn, while capital in the rest of sectors remains fixed, due to its sector-specific nature. Notice that in the case of transition economies, such as the Czech Republic, the idea of MNEs leading to an inflow of capital, instead of a mere change in ownership, seems appropriate for three reasons. First, because the weight of *greenfield* investment among total flows of FDI is bigger than for developed countries. According to Schöllmann (2001, p. 384), "no transition country shows the high share of acquisitions in overall FDI that is familiar in more mature market economies". The second reason lies in the evidence of large amounts of obsolete capital stocks in the transition economies (Krkoska, 2001b; Bornstein, 2001; Lizal and Svegnar, 2002). Therefore, even the flows linked to acquisitions need to replace the

---

[14] As previously explained capital specificity accounts for the specific assets that MNEs have compared to national firms. Notice that the elasticity is set at a value equal to 10^{-6}, instead of 0, in order to facilitate the computation of the model.

[15] The GTAP6inGAMS selects by default a different variable as the numeraire. This variable is the budget available for private consumption in ROW ($raINC_{Row}$, see equation (23) in Chapter 3). The interpretation of the results with respect to this numeraire would be complex, though. Therefore, in our results, we present all values and monetary variables in terms of the CPI, i.e. using the CPI as the numeraire, instead of the default numeraire. The only exception is, however, the CPI itself, which continues to be expressed in terms of the default numeraire.

existing capital and are, consequently, linked to an increase in capital. Third, foreign investors, particularly in the Czech Republic, have been found to exhibit the highest propensities to invest in gross capital formation (Lizal and Svegnar, 2002).

The amount by which foreign capital is increased in our simulations following the entry of MNEs is 50 per cent. This increase may seem excessively high; nonetheless, it is not so disproportionate according to the growth of FDI inflows received in the Czech Republic since the transition phase began, as was commented in Chapter 1.

In terms of the model some equations need to be modified with respect to their original form in the GTAP standard version to introduce the shock of the entry of MNEs. The model (and our extensions), is explained at length in the previous chapter. Here, we just explain which parameters need to be modified or added in order to introduce the shock. Logically, the increase in capital endowments available for MNEs will result in: 1) changes in factor market equations; 2) an increase in total capital endowments of the host economy; 3) an impact on the rental rate of capital.

1) A larger amount of capital is available for MNEs in the sector where their entry takes place, which means that the demand for capital in that *foreign* part of the sector will increase. Thus, in equation (31*), which represents the demand for capital of the foreign-owned firms (MNEs), an increase is included through the parameter $FDIf_{Kjr}$, which is not present in the standard GTAP model:

$$vfm^o_{Kjr}\, FDIf_{Kjr} \left(\frac{p^{Ko}_{jr}}{p^{K}_{jr}} \right)^{\eta} = dfm^o_{Kjr} \qquad (31^*)$$

For the particular sector j receiving MNEs, $FDIf_{KjH}$ takes a value of 1.5, which increases by 50 percent its initial level in the benchmark, vfm^F_{KjH}. For domestic firms in ROW, and national firms and MNEs not receiving any additional capital in the host economy, $FDIf_{Kjr}$ takes a value of one.

The increase in the capital stock of the foreign part of the sector boosts the *total* volume of capital that the whole sector owns. In equation (32*), i.e., the equation for *total* capital demand in a sector, its initial value in the benchmark is vfm_{Kjr} will increase by a percentage (i.e., the new parameter FDI_{Kjr} takes a value of one plus a percentage change), that varies across simulations depending on the share of MNEs in the initial level of the demand for capital in that sector:

$$vfm_{Kjr} \cdot FDI_{Kjr} \left(\frac{p_{jr}^K}{p_r^K} \right)^{\eta} = dfm_{Kjr} \qquad (32*)$$

For national firms, and for the MNEs not receiving any additional capital in the host economy, as well as for firms in ROW, FDI_{Kjr} takes a value of one.

2) The initial total capital endowments in the host economy, $evom_{KH}$, will be exogenously increased, taking a new level $\psi evom_{KH}$ in equation (30*) (notice that $\psi evom_{KROW}$, i.e., capital endowments in ROW, remain at its benchmark level, though):

$$\psi evom_{Kr} = evom_{Kr} \cdot FT_{Kr} \qquad (30*)$$

3) The rental rate (price) of capital, both at the sectoral level and at the national level has to be modified. The equation of the price of capital at the sectoral level is (9*). In that equation the parameter θ_{vfmjF} – i.e., the value share of MNEs' capital in sector j's capital in the host economy – will have to be modified to account for a higher share of MNEs:

$$p_{jH}^K = \left(\left(\theta_{vfmjF} \left(p_{jH}^{KF} \right)^{(1+\eta)} \right) + \left(\left(1 - \theta_{vfmjF} \right) \left(p_{jH}^{KN} \right)^{(1+\eta)} \right) \right)^{\left(1/(1+\eta) \right)} \qquad (9*)$$

The equation for the national price of capital is (10). In that equation, the parameter θ_{jr}^K -i.e., the share of capital employed in sector j in region r- has to be modified for each sector j, to account for the adjustment in the shares over total capital across sectors in the economy:

$$p_r^K = \left(\sum_j \theta_{jr}^K \left(p_{jr}^K \right)^{(1+\eta)} \right)^{\left(1/(1+\eta) \right)} \qquad (10)$$

These changes will endogenously modify equation (23), i.e., the equation for
the representative household's income in the host economy, since he will now
receive the remuneration of higher capital endowments. On the other hand, the
exogenous changes we have just described will also endogenously affect the
goods market equations, since the sector receiving MNEs will have a higher
amount of capital to produce. This will affect its output and price levels,
which, in turn, will unleash a chain of adjustments in goods and factor markets
equations in the rest of sectors in the economy. How this process occurs is
explained in the next section.

4. SIMULATION RESULTS

4.1. Aggregate Results

The results from the above simulations on the main macroeconomic
variables appear in Table 2. Each column gives the percentage change in real
terms with respect to the benchmark in a particular aggregate variable, after
the entry of MNEs in any of the sectors appearing on the left-hand side of the
table. The variables considered are: the real wage and the real rental rate of
capital; the real GDP measured at factor costs; welfare, proxied by the change
in real private consumption, which in turn, due to its Cobb-Douglas form, is
the same as the variation in real income of the representative household[16]; the
CPI; and the real value of imports and exports (both measured at international
prices).

The wage of the economy − the same for all sectors, due to the assumption
of full mobility of labour − increases in all cases. Conversely, the aggregate
rental rate of capital − a weighted average of its price in all sectors − goes
down. The theory of international trade under the assumption of specific
capital (i.e., Jones, 1971, 2000, 2002; Mussa, 1974; Neary, 1978) predicts an
evolution of factor prices in accordance with these findings. The fall in the
capital rental rate makes sense in a context where more capital is added to an

---

[16] Hertel (1997, chapter 1) explains that percentage changes in welfare can be proxied in this
model by the variation in real private consumption, when investment and public
consumption are fixed in real terms, as is the case in our simulations. Additionally, the
evolution of real private consumption is modeled using a Cobb-Douglas function. Income
elasticity is unitary in this type of functions so that increases in private consumption have
the same percentage as variations in the households' income.

economy with a fixed stock of labour. Labour will tend to be more productive (resulting in a wage increase) and capital will be less productive (inducing a fall in its remuneration). Note also, that the amount of the fall in the rental rate of capital tends to be proportional to the percentage increase in the capital used in the economy that MNEs bring about (see Table 1), so aggregate capital remuneration tends to get worse the higher the increase in capital.

**Table 2. Simulation results: Effects on aggregate variables
(percent change from benchmark)**

	Wage	Rental rate of capital	GDP	Welfare	CPI	Imports	Exports
Chemicals	0.23	-0.55	0.30	0.61	0.08	1.30	1.36
Motor vehicles	0.05	-1.17	0.11	0.20	-0.10	0.59	0.61
Electronics	0.21	-0.34	0.23	0.40	0.09	0.93	0.97
Trade	0.09	-0.51	0.27	0.69	-0.01	0.18	0.19
Finance	0.20	-0.61	0.35	0.72	-0.14	0.50	0.52

The entry of MNEs leads to small improvements in GDP and welfare. What are the forces behind these two latter outcomes? For motor vehicles, GDP and welfare exhibit the lowest increase across sectors because of a higher fall in the rental of capital and a lower increase in the wage. This less favourable evolution of factor prices, compared to the rest of sectors, leaves little scope for GDP at factor costs to increase. Nor does it help to obtain a sufficient increase in income, so that a significant rise in private consumption (and thus in welfare) can be achieved. The impact is still positive but much more reduced than in the rest of sectors. Results on GDP and Welfare are not only driven by changes in factor prices, though, they are also driven by the magnitude of the increase in the aggregate capital stock involved in the shock. Electronics yields relatively high factor prices after the shock, compared to Chemicals or Finance. However, its impact on GDP and welfare is not higher than the cases of Chemicals or Finance because of the smaller increase in the capital stock that MNEs from Electronics means in the economy.

Another factor accounting for the evolution of welfare is the CPI. Only for Trade there is a slightly higher impact on welfare than that expected according to the evolution of factor prices and its GDP growth. In the rest of sectors GDP and welfare tend to move proportionally. The small wedge between GDP and welfare in Trade can be better seen with a comparison in the evolution of the entry of MNEs in Trade versus that in Chemicals. The impact on the aggregate stock of capital is very close for both sectors. This means that their size, in terms of the capital they use, is relatively similar. The higher increase in the real wage and the similar impact on the real rent of capital produced in Chemicals, compared to that in Trade, pulls the GDP higher after the entry of MNEs in Chemicals. However, the results are reversed for welfare. In terms of welfare, MNEs from Trade produce a slightly higher increase than those in Chemicals. This is related with the evolution of the CPI. Remember that our representative household devotes its income to private consumption, investment and public consumption (eq (23)). Investment and public consumption are fixed in real terms. Therefore, a higher (lower) CPI involves that the fixed amounts of physical units acquired for investment and public consumption become more expensive (cheaper). In other words, if prices increase (decrease), income will be more (less) reduced by the fixed amount of physical units acquired for investment and public output, leaving less (more) room for private consumption. Because prices (the CPI) increase by more after entry of MNEs in Chemicals, private consumption (and welfare) increases by less in Chemicals than in Trade.

The CPI[17] itself changes rather slightly across the simulations. It increases for the entry of MNEs in Chemicals and Electronics and decreases with their entry in Motor vehicles, Finance and Trade (the decrease is particularly small in this latter case). Its evolution is related to a complex interplay of the weight of goods stemming from the twenty sectors in final consumption, as well as their role as intermediates used in other sectors in the economy.

Finally, the last two columns in Table 2 give the impact of the entry of MNEs on real aggregate imports and exports. As explained in Chapter 3, one of the closure rules of the model is that the trade balance is fixed in real terms. Accordingly, exports and imports values adjust under this constraint, which matches the empirical evidence that the Czech Republic has exhibited trade deficits since the transition from communism took place (WIIW, several

---

[17] As mentioned in footnote 15, the CPI is the numeraire for the rest of variables in the model, although the CPI itself is expressed with respect to the default numeraire set by GTAP6inGAMS, i.e., with respect to $raINC_{row}$. This means that values in this column, strictly, cannot be interpreted as a standard CPI. But note that, for the particular simulation performed here (MNEs' entry) the impact on $raINC_{row}$ is negligible, since shocks in the Czech Republic are unlikely to affect ROW in an important extent. So, in this case, eventually, the evolution of the CPI in terms of $raINC_{row}$ should be a good proxy for the evolution of a standard CPI.

years). Imports and exports increase after the entry of MNEs in all sectors – an increase due to the higher level of economic activity that MNEs bring about –.

Let us analyse first the impact of MNEs on imports. The value of imports increases by more when MNEs come to Chemicals and Electronics, as shown in Table 2. The entry of MNEs in the services sectors, by contrast, produces lower increases in imports. What is behind this evolution? Intermediates account for the most important share in imports in the Czech Republic, as in most countries, but in the Czech case with an outstanding 82.8% of total aggregate imports. Private consumption and government consumption account for 15.5% and 1.6% of imports, respectively. As a consequence, the evolution of imports will tend to be more related to the path of production than to that of consumption. Indeed, one can check that the impact of MNEs on imports is not proportional to that in the column of private consumption (i.e., the welfare column). It is more related, though, to the share on imports in the sector receiving MNEs (see Table 1). Note that the main microeconomic impact takes place in the sector receiving MNEs, whose increase in production will be the highest among all sectors (as will be clearer below). If that sector has an important weight in imports, the impact on aggregate imports will be greater. Thus, the weight in imports of Chemicals (12.8%), Electronics (9.4%), Motor vehicles (7.5%), Finance (6.5%) and Trade (1.1%) explain their relative positions in aggregate imports.

On the other hand, the increase in exports is related to the important fall in the price of the good sold in the sector receiving MNEs (as will be seen below), which greatly enhances the competitiveness of that sector.

Let us briefly summarise the results for aggregate variables, shown in Table 2. We have simulated the entry of MMEs in five different sectors. While the aggregate rental rate of capital decreases in all cases, the aggregate wage always increases. Factor prices, together with the corresponding increase in capital, are behind the evolution of the GDP, measured at factor costs. This experiences small increases, in general, ranging from 0.11 per cent in Motor vehicles to 0.35 per cent in the case of Finance. We have proxied the evolution of welfare using the variation in real private consumption, which, in turn, due to its Cobb-Douglas form, is the same as the variation in real income of the representative household. As with GDP, the impact on welfare is small and variations across sectors are reduced. For a policy-maker interested in offering incentives to different types of MNEs, welfare considerations may slightly increase the value of MNEs coming to the Trade sector, though. Finally, the value of imports and exports always increases, preserving an exogenous trade deficit. However, MNEs in services lead to a smaller increase in trade activity as compared to MNEs in manufactures.

Are these the outcomes we should expect? We have already mentioned the consistency between the results obtained for factor prices and the theory of international trade under the assumption of specific capital. The GDP at factor costs follows the evolution of both factor prices and the aggregate stock of capital. The rest of aggregates, however, such as imports, exports and welfare, have not received much attention in the theory of specific capital. The outcomes for these latter variables may be related to the evolution of the CPI (in the case of welfare) and certainly rely heavily on the role of intermediates (in the case of imports and exports). Therefore, changes in these latter aggregate variables become an empirical issue, particularly in a 20-sector framework. In this sense, the computable nature of the model facilitates taking into account the simultaneous interactions of prices and the weight of intermediates in all sectors.

4.2. Sectoral Analysis

Tables 3, 4, 5 and 6 show, respectively, the effects on production, prices, exports and imports for the twenty sectors representing the Czech economy, following the entry of MNEs in each of the five sectors selected. Logically, the first and main impact of the shock takes place in the sector receiving MNEs. As a first step, we will look at the evolution of this particular sector.

The amount of capital that the sector receiving MNEs uses increases considerably as a result of the shock. Therefore its *production* will always rise (Table 3). Increases in production are of a considerable magnitude except for MNEs arriving to Finance. This has to do with the fact that MNEs' share on gross output and capital in Finance is the smallest among the five sectors considered (Table 1).

The *price* of the good sold by this sector will diminish (Table 4). The increase in capital strongly lowers its rental rate, driving costs of production and prices down in that sector (sectoral prices in this Walrasian model resemble costs, see equation (4*)).

Because of the fall in its price, the export competitiveness of the sector will improve, which results on a significant increase in its *exports* (Table 5).

Finally, note the fact that production in each sector relies to an important extent on intermediates stemming from the same sector (data on this latter fact are not shown here but are intuitive). As a consequence, *imports* of the sector receiving MNEs also experience an increase (Table 6), because a relevant amount of intermediates from that sector are imported in order to get its increase in production.

Table 3. Simulation results: effects on sectoral production (percent change from benchmark)

	Chemicals	Motor Vehicles	Electronics	Trade	Finance
Agriculture, hunting and fishing	-0.01	0.03	-0.04	0.06	0.06
Mining and quarrying	-0.01	0.00	-0.01	0.00	0.00
Food, beverages and tobacco	0.24	0.10	0.13	0.33	0.36
Textiles, wearing apparel, leather, footwear	-0.05	0.08	-0.31	0.13	0.26
Wood and wood products, except furniture	-0.24	0.07	-0.31	-0.01	0.11
Paper; printing and publishing	-0.12	0.07	-0.20	0.02	0.23
Petroleum	0.16	0.04	0.09	0.21	0.22
Chemicals, rubber and plastics	13.97	0.08	-0.21	-0.01	0.12
Non-metallic mineral products	-0.14	0.08	-0.18	0.00	0.12
Basic and fabricated metal products	-0.41	0.08	-0.42	-0.04	0.20
Motor vehicles	-0.11	16.89	-0.12	0.03	0.17
Other transport equipment	-0.16	0.29	-0.08	0.19	0.35
Electronics	-0.20	0.07	17.95	-0.01	0.21
Machinery and equipment n.e.c.	-0.18	1.80	-0.16	0.06	0.24
Furniture, manufacturing n.e.c.	-0.05	0.08	-0.21	0.14	0.24
Electricity, gas and water supply; construction	0.05	0.09	0.03	0.23	0.33
Trade, repair; hotels and restaurants	0.06	0.18	0.00	5.65	0.59
Transport, storage and communication	-0.12	0.11	-0.13	0.12	0.18
Finance, insurance, real estate, business activities	-0.02	0.05	-0.05	0.10	2.12
Other services	0.03	0.05	0.00	0.12	0.18

What about the rest of sectors? Generally, their responses exhibit very low percentage changes. Although, as the Czech economy has been split into these twenty sectors, small percentage variations may imply greater effects than what could be *a priori* expected.

Let us turn to *output* responses of the sectors not directly involved in the shock (Table 3). There are two different patterns, one for the entry of MNEs in Chemicals and Electronics, and another for their entry in the rest of sectors. For the former most sectors reduce production; for the latter most sectors increase it. These patterns are related to the evolution of demand. Figure 1 (see below) shows the different uses of sectoral production, together with their relative importance across sectors. Gross production can be devoted to five different uses: 1) Intermediates 2) Investment, 3) Exports, 4) Private consumption, and 5) Public consumption. This is clear in equation (26) in the model.

**Table 4. Simulation results: effects on sectoral prices
(percent change from benchmark)**

	Chemicals	Motor vehicles	Electronics	Trade	Finance
Agriculture, hunting and fishing	0.05	0.11	0.01	0.12	0.22
Mining and quarrying	-0.08	0.09	-0.09	0.02	0.14
Food, beverages and tobacco	0.13	0.10	0.09	0.17	0.23
Textiles, wearing apparel, leather, footwear	-0.03	0.09	-0.01	0.03	0.13
Wood and wood products, except furniture	-0.04	0.08	-0.04	0.02	0.13
Paper; printing and publishing	-0.03	0.09	-0.03	0.04	0.13
Petroleum	-0.05	0.09	-0.05	0.04	0.15
Chemicals, rubber and plastics	-2.33	0.08	-0.05	0.03	0.13
Non-metallic mineral products	-0.05	0.08	-0.05	0.02	0.12
Basic and fabricated metal products	-0.03	0.08	-0.04	0.02	0.12
Motor vehicles	-0.04	-3.44	-0.05	0.02	0.11
Other transport equipment	-0.04	0.06	-0.07	0.01	0.12
Electronics	-0.06	0.08	-1.92	0.02	0.12
Machinery and equipment n.e.c.	-0.05	-0.13	-0.06	0.02	0.12
Furniture, manufacturing n.e.c.	-0.02	0.09	-0.02	0.04	0.14
Electricity, gas and water supply; construction	0.06	0.09	0.02	0.09	0.16
Trade, repair; hotels and restaurants	0.13	0.06	0.09	-2.75	0.09
Transport, storage and communication	0.05	0.06	0.02	0.04	0.13
Finance, insurance, real estate, business activities	0.07	0.07	0.03	0.11	-1.48
Other services	0.12	0.07	0.10	0.07	0.07

The information in the Figure remarks the importance of the share devoted to intermediates. Analysing how this contributes to the level of sectoral production is possible but complex, due to the 20-sector nature of the model. We can see however, that the weight of exports and private consumption is also of considerable relevance. Indeed, by looking at the evolution of these two latter variables the response in sectoral output can be traced.

For the analysis of exports a comparison between domestic and foreign prices is in order. Their differential will give us the clue regarding the export competitiveness of the sectors from the Czech Republic. Table 4 provides the evolution of sectoral *prices*. As happened with output, prices exhibit two different patterns, related to the same two groups of sectors for which sectoral patterns of output exist. On the one hand, the entry of MNEs in Chemicals and Electronics leads to a fall in prices in most of the rest of sectors. On the other hand, nearly all sectoral prices increase when MNEs enter in Motor vehicles, Trade and Finance.

Table 5. Simulation results: effects on sectoral exports
(percent change from benchmark)

	Chemicals	Motor vehicles	Electronics	Trade	Finance
Agriculture, hunting and fishing	-0.57	-0.03	-0.46	-0.46	-0.37
Mining and quarrying	-0.04	0.00	-0.03	-0.03	-0.03
Food, beverages and tobacco	-1.01	-0.02	-0.83	-0.73	-0.45
Textiles, wearing apparel, leather, footwear	-0.35	0.04	-0.57	-0.14	0.06
Wood and wood products, except furniture	-0.28	0.05	-0.33	-0.07	0.05
Paper; printing and publishing	-0.28	0.02	-0.32	-0.14	0.07
Petroleum	-0.12	0.00	-0.13	-0.11	-0.05
Chemicals rubber and plastics	15.09	0.05	-0.25	-0.08	0.05
Non-metallic mineral products	-0.15	0.04	-0.20	-0.03	0.07
Basic and fabricated metal products	-0.34	0.06	-0.34	-0.04	0.15
Motor vehicles	-0.20	21.26	-0.21	-0.03	0.15
Other transport equipment	-0.30	0.24	-0.19	0.03	0.20
Electronics	-0.22	0.05	17.11	-0.05	0.16
Machinery and equipment n.e.c.	-0.24	1.70	-0.20	-0.01	0.18
Furniture, manufacturing n.e.c.	-0.44	0.04	-0.53	-0.21	-0.03
Electricity, gas and water supply; construction	-0.68	0.00	-0.53	-0.35	-0.10
Trade, repair; hotels and restaurants	-0.80	0.12	-0.68	11.22	0.18
Transport, storage and communication	-0.36	0.09	-0.32	-0.07	0.03
Finance, insurance, real estate, business activities	-0.58	0.08	-0.47	-0.35	6.37
Other services	-0.75	0.09	-0.73	-0.22	0.27

What is behind this evolution of sectoral prices? In the sectors not receiving MNEs output moves along with labour demand (capital is specific and remains fixed in each sector after the entry of MNEs, except for the sector to which MNEs arrive). After the entry of MNEs in Motor vehicles, Trade and Finance, the rest of sectors tend to increase production. This means that the rest of sectors are increasing their labour demands. In a context of rising wages factor costs increase. Simultaneously, an increase in intermediate costs also takes place since most sectors, in general, are increasing their prices which drives intermediates costs up. As a result of the increase in intermediates and factor costs, prices increase, in general, after the entry of MNEs in Motor vehicles, Trade and Finance. By contrast, for the entry of MNEs in Chemicals and Electronics, even though there is a general decrease in labour demand across sectors, wages are simultaneously rising, leaving an ambiguous result for factor prices.

**Table 6. Simulation results: effects on sectoral imports
(percent change from benchmark)**

	Chemicals	Motor vehicles	Electronics	Trade	Finance
Agriculture, hunting and fishing	0.31	0.05	0.22	0.31	0.26
Mining and quarrying	0.06	0.01	0.04	0.07	0.06
Food, beverages and tobacco	0.83	0.11	0.61	0.76	0.62
Textiles, wearing apparel, leather, footwear	0.30	0.07	0.13	0.35	0.34
Wood and wood products, except furniture	-0.06	0.04	-0.12	0.06	0.11
Paper; printing and publishing	0.07	0.06	-0.01	0.15	0.25
Petroleum	0.25	0.05	0.18	0.29	0.26
Chemicals, rubber and plastics	10.24	0.07	-0.07	0.08	0.16
Non-metallic mineral products	-0.06	0.08	-0.06	0.04	0.11
Basic and fabricated metal products	-0.30	0.02	-0.32	-0.05	0.10
Motor vehicles	0.06	3.87	0.07	0.12	0.14
Other transport equipment	0.05	0.17	0.05	0.23	0.29
Electronics	-0.07	0.08	10.55	0.07	0.21
Machinery and equipment n.e.c.	0.01	0.79	-0.01	0.13	0.19
Furniture, manufacturing n.e.c.	0.31	0.07	0.17	0.35	0.33
Electricity, gas and water supply; construction	0.38	0.06	0.26	0.39	0.34
Trade, repair; hotels and restaurants	0.46	0.11	0.32	1.43	0.49
Transport, storage and communication	0.15	0.04	0.11	0.17	0.15
Finance, insurance, real estate, business activities	0.29	0.10	0.20	0.32	2.67
Other services	0.47	0.02	0.41	0.29	0.09

The source for the decrease in prices, though, is the reduction in intermediate costs. After the entry of MNEs in Chemicals and Electronics general reductions in prices across sectors stem from lower intermediate costs faced by those sectors[18].

As is customary in CGE models, in Table 4, prices are expressed with respect to the numeraire, i.e., with respect to the CPI. This means that in order to see their evolution as a signal of the corresponding sector competitiveness

---

[18] See the evolution of factors' and intermediates' costs of production for national firms versus MNEs in Tables 8 to 12, below.

Sector	Intermediates	Investment	Exports	Private consumption	Public consumption
Agriculture, hunting and fishing	66.9	8.5	8.6	15.5	0.5
Mining and quarrying	76.4	2.7	19.2	1.8	
Food, beverages and tobacco	34.6	9.8	55.5	0.2	
Textiles, wearing apparel, leather, footwear	28.9		46.5	24.4	
Wood and wood products, except furniture	40.2	5.1	50.2	4.5	
Paper, printing and publishing	54.0	7.9	28.5	9.5	
Petroleum	74.9	0.0	9.5	15.5	
Chemicals, rubber and plastics	38.3	3.4	49.2	6.3	2.8
Non-metallic mineral products	44.2	13.3	41.7	0.9	
Basic and fabricated metal products	56.7	8.3	34.6	0.4	
Motor vehicles	35.1	2.5	55.8	6.7	
Other transport equipment	38.6	17.1	35.0	9.3	
Electronics	30.7	2.8	62.6	3.6	0.3
Machinery and equipment n.e.c.	31.7	3.7	57.9	6.7	0.1
Furniture, manufacturing n.e.c.	40.6	7.5	30.1	21.9	
Electricity, gas and water supply; construction	72.2	10.6	6.3	9.8	1.1
Trade, repair; hotels and restaurants	32.9	50.0	3.9	13.0	0.2
Transport, storage and communication	58.1	0.2	28.9	12.6	0.2
Finance, insurance, real estate, business activities	58.6	10.7	10.4	15.8	4.6
Other services	17.3	11.9	5.7	16.6	48.5

Notes: Author's own elaboration from Dimanaran (2007). The definitions of the sectors follow the ISIC Rev 3 Classification.
Figure 1. Output uses from sectors in the Czech Republic.

the information in that table should be analysed with care. Note that we want to compare the evolution of domestic prices versus the foreign ones. We know that the Czech Republic – a small economy – cannot affect world prices, but if domestic prices fall (i.e., the CPI falls) then foreign prices "become" more expensive, and vice versa. It is in the light of this latter assertion that the prices provided in Table 4 should be looked at, when we want to relate them with the volume of *exports* (Table 5).

As noted above Table 4 shows that after the entry of MNEs in Chemicals and Electronics most prices diminish, whereas for the rest of sector most prices increase. It is important to note, however, that the CPI increases after the entry of MNEs in Chemicals and Electronics. By contrast, it falls for Motor vehicles and Finance and remains nearly unchanged for Trade. So, in terms of export competitiveness, taking into account the outcome on the CPI, most of the original tendencies shown in the Table 4 are reversed. As a result, the entry of MNEs in Chemicals, Electronics and Trade results in a general decrease of sectoral exports – following a higher CPI – ; while for Motor vehicles and Finance, they result in a general increase in exports – due to the lower CPI – (Table 5).

The evolution of exports is the key to the evolution of sectoral production in most manufactures (the exceptions are Food and Petroleum). As can be seen in Figure 1, exports have a very important weight among the different uses of production for most manufacturing sectors. Thus, after the entry of MNEs entry in Chemicals and Electronics, and to a lesser extent in Trade, manufacturing sectors reduce production because of a fall in exports' demand. By contrast, gross output in manufacturing sectors increases as the evolution of exports does not depress production after the entry of MNEs in Motor vehicles and Finance.

Across the five simulations the sectors Food, Petroleum, Electricity, as well as all services sectors (with the exception of Transport) tend to follow a similar evolution. They are the only ones whose production is either not falling, or is increasing more or falling by less than in the rest of sectors. In other words, production tends to be higher in these sectors compared to the rest. This is because they are more responsive to the evolution of private consumption in the economy than to the evolution of exports. Private consumption just follows income, due to the Cobb-Douglas nature of the function for private consumption. It always increases in the five simulations, boosting production in these sectors for which it is more important.

Table 6 shows the sectoral evolution of *imports*. For the sectors not directly involved in the shock, imports again follow their respective production patterns. Thus most decreases in imports across sectors take place after the entry of MNEs in Chemicals and Electronics, which, remember, tend to depress production in most sectors. However, the CPI increases after the entry of MNEs in Chemicals and Electronics, making, in general, imports cheaper. Therefore decreases in imports only take place in a small number of sectors. On the contrary, after the entry of MNEs in Motor vehicles, Trade and Finance, most sectors increase imports. This is due, in general, to the increase in sectoral production taking place in most sectors.

To sum up, the entry of MNEs generates an important impact in the sector where they arrive. Its evolution is rather clear: production, exports and imports increase while the price falls. The impact for the rest of sectors in the economy tends to be small. Its sign, however, depends on the sector where MNEs enter. The entry of MNEs in Chemicals and Electronics tends, in general, to reduce production, following a general decrease in exports. On the contrary, the entry of MNEs in Motor vehicles and Finance, tends to boost production following a general increase in exports. For Trade most sectors increase production although there are exceptions related to the general increase in exports.

There is a small number of sectors, however, that across simulations exhibit higher levels of production. This is so because their production patters are linked to that of private consumption, which increases in all scenarios.

The level of imports across sectors moves along with the production pattern of the sector. So, to the general increase of production across sectors after the entry of MNEs in Motor vehicles, Finance and Trade, corresponds a general increase in imports. By contrast, to the general decrease of production across sectors after the entry of MNEs in Chemicals and Electronics, corresponds a decrease in imports. However, in some cases, in these two latter simulations, as Czech prices have increased and imports become cheaper, imports do increase.

Finally, after the entry of MNEs in Chemicals and Electronics prices tend to decrease, whereas they tend to increase for Motor vehicles, Trade and Finance.

This sectoral evolution offers a way to discriminate between the quite similar impact on GDP caused by the entry of MNEs in Chemicals, Finance, Electronics and Trade. If the policy maker is searching for a general increase in production across sectors, it may be preferable to offer incentives to attract MNEs to the two services sectors – that boost production and employment in other national and MNEs firms as well – than to these two manufactures sectors, which may entail a similar GDP impact, but whose positive effects will be highly concentrated in a few sectors, while depressing others.

Table 7 provides the evolution of production in both the national and MNEs' part of each of the twenty sectors. It basically gives more detail within the general tendencies highlighted so far. Most national firms and MNEs reduce (increase) production after the entry of MNEs in Chemicals and Electronics (Motor vehicles, Trade and Finance).

Figure 2 offers the different weights of intermediates (domestic and imported), labour and capital in total costs for national firms and MNEs in each sector. Responses in production do not seem to be related to the levels of labour intensity of the different national firms and MNEs within the same sector. Nor do they seem to affect differential responses across sectors. This outcome makes sense if we look at the importance of intermediates on total costs. The latter accounts, in general, for more than 60 per cent of total costs, and, in many cases it accounts for a higher share. As a consequence, value added (and, in turn, capital or labour intensity) accounts for a smaller share of costs and seems to be less important in determining responses in production.

The relevant share of intermediates in production again makes the analysis of sectors adjustment more complex, due to the 20-sector nature of the model. In order to obtain how intersectoral links affect results we need to rely on the general equilibrium nature of the model. In the light of the growing importance of fragmentation in today's world economy – alluded to in Chapter 1 – the capability of CGE models of taking into account sectoral links appears as an important advantage of this methodology.

Finally, Tables 8 to 12, show the evolution of factor costs, total intermediate costs and final prices of national firms versus MNEs for each of the five simulations (there is one table per simulation). There is a certain tendency for prices to increase by more (or decrease by less) in national firms than in MNEs. In other words, after the entry of MNE in any of the five sectors analysed, prices of national firms tend to be, in general, higher than those of MNEs. This is related to the more labour intensive technology of national firms versus MNEs. The former will tend to experience higher factor costs because of the wage increases that always arise after the entry of MNEs. And their higher factor costs will lead them to charge higher prices. However, there are some exceptions to this general tendency. These exceptions appear because of the important share of intermediates already alluded to. In some cases, the evolution of intermediate costs may counteract the pattern followed by factor costs. Note, also, that we still obtain the result that following the entry of MNEs in Chemicals and Electronics most national firms' and MNEs' prices decrease. By contrast, when MNEs come to Motor vehicles, Trade and Finance most national firms' and MNEs' prices increase.

Table 7. Simulation results: Effects on gross production of national firms and MNEs (percent change from benchmark)

	Chemicals		Motor vehicles		Electronics		Trade		Finance	
	MNEs	National firms	MNEs	National firms	MNEs	National firms	MNEs	National Firms	MNEs	National firms
Agriculture, hunting and fishing	-0.04	-0.01	0.01	0.03	-0.04	-0.04	-0.01	0.06	-0.01	0.06
Mining and quarrying	-0.01	-0.02	0.00	0.00	-0.01	-0.01	0.00	0.00	0.00	0.00
Food, beverages and tobacco	0.02	0.33	0.01	0.14	-0.07	0.23	0.10	0.44	0.12	0.47
Textiles, wearing apparel, leather, footwear	-0.12	-0.02	0.01	0.10	-0.27	-0.33	0.01	0.17	0.08	0.33
Wood and wood products, except furniture	-0.17	-0.27	0.02	0.08	-0.20	-0.35	-0.03	-0.01	0.02	0.14
Paper; printing and publishing	-0.16	-0.09	0.02	0.11	-0.28	-0.13	-0.01	0.05	0.20	0.26
Petroleum	-0.21	0.17	-0.03	0.04	-0.11	0.09	-0.05	0.21	-0.04	0.22
Chemicals, rubber and plastics	27.39	4.00	0.04	0.11	-0.27	-0.16	-0.04	0.01	0.08	0.15
Non-metallic mineral products	-0.20	-0.08	0.01	0.14	-0.31	-0.05	-0.05	0.05	0.07	0.16
Basic and fabricated metal products	-0.31	-0.44	-0.06	0.12	-0.37	-0.43	-0.11	-0.02	-0.01	0.27
Motor vehicles	-0.12	-0.07	20.52	0.20	-0.15	0.02	0.04	0.01	0.21	0.02
Other transport equipment	-0.14	-0.17	0.15	0.34	-0.10	-0.07	0.08	0.22	0.17	0.41
Electronics	-0.24	-0.13	0.05	0.10	25.78	4.62	-0.03	0.02	0.23	0.17
Machinery and equipment n.e.c.	-0.14	-0.20	0.74	2.24	-0.12	-0.18	0.00	0.08	0.08	0.31
Furniture, manufacturing n.e.c.	-0.09	-0.03	0.03	0.11	-0.20	-0.21	0.04	0.18	0.10	0.30
Electricity, gas and water supply; construction	-0.17	0.08	-0.05	0.10	-0.25	0.06	-0.03	0.27	-0.01	0.37
Trade, repair; hotels and restaurants	-0.07	0.12	0.03	0.25	-0.22	0.10	14.25	1.83	0.33	0.71
Transport, storage and communication	-0.11	-0.12	0.03	0.11	-0.07	-0.14	-0.02	0.14	0.00	0.20
Finance, insurance, real estate, business activities	0.09	-0.06	0.24	0.00	0.04	-0.08	0.22	0.07	9.55	-0.05
Other services	-0.02	0.03	0.16	0.04	0.11	0.00	0.07	0.12	0.09	0.18

Stacked bar chart. Horizontal axis: 0% to 100% (gridlines at 0%, 10%, 20%, 30%, 40%, 50%, 60%, 70%, 80%, 90%, 100%).

Category	% Labour	% Capital	% Domestic Intermediates	% Imported Intermediates
F: Agriculture, hunting and fishing	18.2	17.6	7.8	56.4
N: Agriculture, hunting and fishing	19.6	19.0	47.3	14.2
F: Mining and quarrying	8.1	76.4	8.8	6.6
N: Mining and quarrying	10.0	46.7	35.7	7.6
F: Food, beverages and tobacco	9.8	30.8	32.7	26.7
N: Food, beverages and tobacco	10.9	13.7	66.4	9.1
F: Wood and wood products, except furniture	15.9	10.4	7.8	65.9
N: Wood and wood products, except furniture	19.2	12.0	51.2	17.6
F: Paper; printing and publishing	12.9	15.5	29.5	42.1
N: Paper; printing and publishing	16.7	17.1	56.5	9.7
F: Paper; printing and publishing	11.9	21.1	42.1	24.9
N: Paper; printing and publishing	16.5	15.9	52.4	15.2
F: Petroleum	2.4		35.8	61.2
N: Petroleum	2.4		35.8	61.2
F: Chemicals, rubber and plastics	9.6	16.7	27.3	46.4
N: Chemicals, rubber and plastics	10.6	12.8	50.7	25.8
F: Non-metallic mineral products	12.9	27.2	38.0	22.0
N: Non-metallic mineral products	20.7	18.5	45.2	15.6
F: Basic and fabricated metal products	14.8	14.8	17.0	53.4
N: Basic and fabricated metal products	18.5	11.5	57.5	12.5

Legend: □ % Labour   ▨ % Capital   ▨ % Domestic Intermediates   □ % Imported Intermediates

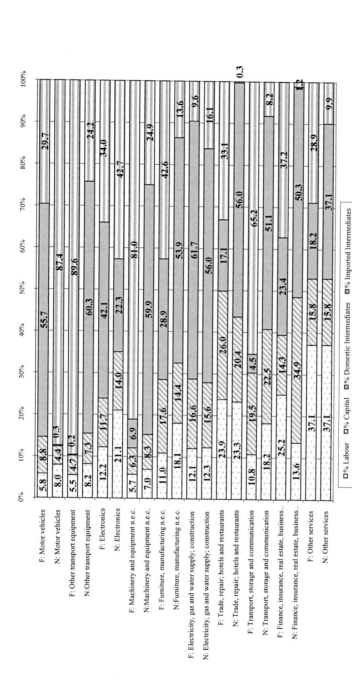

Notes: Author's own elaboration from Dimanaran (2007) and Czech National Bank (2004). The definitions of the sectors follow the ISIC Rev 3 Classification.

Figure 2. Percentage weight of inputs in MNEs (F) and National firms (N) per sector.

Table 8. Simulation results: Effects on factor and intermediate costs and prices of national firms and MNEs of the entry of MNEs in Chemicals (percent change from benchmark)

	MNEs			National firms		
	Factors' Costs	Intermediates' Costs	Price	Factors' costs	Intermediates' costs	Price
Agriculture, hunting and fishing	0.06	-0.08	-0.03	0.19	-0.04	0.05
Mining and quarrying	-0.09	-0.03	-0.08	-0.12	-0.01	-0.07
Food. beverages and tobacco	0.30	-0.08	0.07	0.61	0.01	0.16
Textiles, wearing apparel, leather, footwear	0.17	-0.10	-0.03	0.22	-0.15	-0.03
Wood and wood products, except furniture	0.07	-0.11	-0.06	0.02	-0.05	-0.03
Paper; printing and publishing	0.01	-0.09	-0.06	0.16	-0.09	-0.01
Petroleum	-0.23	-0.09	-0.09	0.71	-0.07	-0.05
Chemicals, rubber and plastics	-20.76	-0.26	-5.65	4.03	-0.71	0.40
Non-metallic mineral products	-0.11	-0.10	-0.11	0.18	-0.12	0.00
Basic and fabricated metal products	-0.02	-0.08	-0.06	0.01	-0.04	-0.02
Motor vehicles	0.08	-0.07	-0.04	0.20	-0.08	-0.05
Other transport equipment	0.14	-0.08	-0.06	0.12	-0.07	-0.04
Electronics	0.05	-0.10	-0.07	0.17	-0.15	-0.04
Machinery and equipment n.e.c.	0.11	-0.08	-0.06	0.05	-0.06	-0.05
Furniture, manufacturing n.e.c.	0.11	-0.13	-0.06	0.22	-0.11	0.00
Electricity, gas and water supply; construction	0.06	-0.09	-0.04	0.31	-0.01	0.08
Trade, repair; hotels and restaurants	0.19	-0.05	0.07	0.30	0.05	0.16
Transport, storage and communication	0.11	-0.07	-0.02	0.14	0.00	0.06
Finance, insurance, real estate, business activities	0.27	-0.07	0.06	0.12	0.04	0.08
Other services	0.23	-0.17	0.04	0.25	-0.02	0.12

Table 9. Simulation results: Effects on factor and intermediate costs and prices of national firms and MNEs of the entry of MNEs in Motor vehicles (percent change from benchmark)

	MNEs			National firms		
	Factors' Costs	Intermediates' costs	Price	Factors' costs	Intermediates' costs	Price
Agriculture, hunting and fishing	0.07	0.09	0.08	0.19	0.05	0.11
Mining and quarrying	0.10	0.08	0.10	0.12	0.06	0.09
Food, beverages and tobacco	0.07	0.07	0.07	0.21	0.08	0.11
Textiles, wearing apparel, leather, footwear	0.06	0.09	0.08	0.10	0.08	0.09
Wood and wood products, except furniture	0.07	0.07	0.07	0.11	0.08	0.09
Paper; printing and publishing	0.07	0.08	0.08	0.13	0.08	0.10
Petroleum	0.08	0.08	0.08	0.18	0.09	0.09
Chemicals, rubber and plastics	0.10	0.07	0.08	0.16	0.06	0.09
Non-metallic mineral products	0.07	0.07	0.07	0.15	0.06	0.10
Basic and fabricated metal products	0.00	0.09	0.06	0.11	0.08	0.09
Motor vehicles	-24.19	-0.74	-4.16	0.14	0.08	0.09
Other transport equipment	0.15	0.09	0.10	0.29	0.01	0.05
Electronics	0.09	0.08	0.08	0.10	0.08	0.09
Machinery and equipment n.e.c.	0.70	0.08	0.16	2.15	-0.68	-0.24
Furniture, manufacturing n.e.c.	0.08	0.08	0.08	0.12	0.08	0.09
Electricity, gas and water supply; construction	0.00	0.06	0.04	0.15	0.08	0.10
Trade, repair; hotels and restaurants	0.07	-0.01	0.03	0.18	-0.01	0.08
Transport, storage and communication	0.09	0.09	0.09	0.14	0.00	0.06
Finance, insurance, real estate, business activities	0.16	0.08	0.11	0.05	0.07	0.06
Other services	0.10	0.08	0.09	0.06	0.07	0.07

Table 10. Simulation results: Effects on factor and intermediate costs and prices of national firms and MNEs of the entry of MNEs in Electronics (percent change from benchmark)

	MNEs			National firms		
	Factors' Costs	Intermediates' costs	Price	Factors' costs	Intermediates' costs	Price
Agricultura, hunting and fishing	0.06	-0.08	-0.03	0.05	-0.01	0.01
Mining and quarrying	-0.11	-0.02	-0.09	-0.14	-0.02	-0.08
Food, beverages and tobacco	0.03	-0.04	-0.01	0.47	0.02	0.13
Textiles, wearing apparel, leather, footwear	0.07	-0.08	-0.04	0.05	-0.02	0.00
Wood and wood products, except furniture	0.02	-0.05	-0.03	-0.07	-0.02	-0.04
Paper; printing and publishing	-0.19	-0.04	-0.09	0.11	-0.03	0.02
Petroleum	-0.16	-0.05	-0.06	0.48	-0.07	-0.05
Chemicals, rubber and plastics	-0.15	-0.06	-0.09	0.06	-0.05	-0.02
Non-metallic mineral products	-0.32	-0.04	-0.15	0.18	-0.04	0.05
Basic and fabricated metal products	-0.08	-0.07	-0.07	0.00	-0.04	-0.03
Motor vehicles	0.03	-0.07	-0.05	0.22	-0.09	-0.05
Other transport equipment	0.14	-0.09	-0.07	0.16	-0.11	-0.07
Electronics	-12.79	-0.44	-3.40	2.60	-0.08	0.86
Machinery and equipment n.e.c.	0.10	-0.10	-0.07	0.04	-0.08	-0.06
Furniture, manufacturing n.e.c.	-0.05	-0.06	-0.06	0.08	-0.03	0.00
Electricity, gas and water supply; construction	-0.04	-0.13	-0.11	0.27	-0.05	0.04
Trade, repair; hotels and restaurants	0.07	-0.06	0.00	0.26	0.02	0.13
Transport, storage and communication	0.12	-0.08	-0.02	0.10	-0.03	0.03
Finance, insurance, real estate, business activities	0.23	-0.08	0.04	0.06	0.01	0.03
Other services	0.25	-0.05	0.11	0.21	-0.02	0.10

Table 11. Simulation results: Effects on factor and intermediate costs and prices of national firms and MNEs of the entry of MNEs in Trade (percent change from benchmark)

	MNEs			National firms		
	Factors' costs	Intermediates' costs	Price	Factors' costs	Intermediates' costs	Price
Agriculture, hunting and fishing	0.03	0.01	0.02	0.33	-0.02	0.12
Mining and quarrying	0.03	-0.10	0.01	0.04	0.00	0.02
Food, beverages and tobacco	0.37	-0.03	0.13	0.58	0.06	0.19
Textiles, wearing apparel, leather, footwear	0.10	-0.02	0.01	0.18	-0.02	0.04
Wood and wood products. except furniture	0.06	-0.04	-0.01	0.09	0.01	0.04
Paper; printing and publishing	0.08	0.01	0.03	0.13	0.01	0.05
Petroleum	-0.25	0.03	0.02	0.70	0.02	0.04
Chemicals. rubber and plastics	0.03	0.01	0.02	0.10	0.02	0.04
Non-metallic mineral products	0.01	-0.01	0.00	0.13	-0.02	0.04
Basic and fabricated metal products	0.01	-0.01	-0.01	0.08	0.01	0.03
Motor vehicles	0.14	0.00	0.02	0.10	0.01	0.02
Other transport equipment	0.15	0.01	0.03	0.25	-0.04	0.00
Electronics	0.07	0.00	0.02	0.10	-0.03	0.02
Machinery and equipment n.e.c.	0.09	0.00	0.01	0.17	-0.01	0.02
Furniture, manufacturing n.e.c.	0.14	-0.04	0.02	0.20	-0.02	0.05
Electricity, gas and water supply; construction	0.06	-0.11	-0.06	0.34	0.02	0.11
Trade, repair; hotels and restaurants	-17.97	-0.13	-9.02	1.03	-0.24	0.32
Transport, storage and communication	0.07	-0.04	-0.01	0.21	-0.07	0.04
Finance, insurance, real estate, business activities	0.19	-0.06	0.04	0.23	0.03	0.13
Other services	0.12	-0.10	0.01	0.13	0.00	0.07

Table 12. Simulation results: Effects on factor and intermediate costs and prices of national firms and MNEs of the entry of MNEs in Finance (percent change from benchmark)

	MNEs			National firms		
	Factors' costs	Intermediates' costs	Price	Factors' costs	Intermediates' costs	Price
Agriculture, hunting and fishing	0.15	0.13	0.14	0.46	0.07	0.22
Mining and quarrying	0.18	-0.04	0.14	0.25	0.01	0.14
Food. beverages and tobacco	0.53	0.02	0.22	0.72	0.08	0.24
Textiles, wearing apparel, leather, footwear	0.24	0.12	0.15	0.36	0.02	0.12
Wood and wood products. except furniture	0.21	0.05	0.09	0.31	0.06	0.14
Paper; printing and publishing	0.48	-0.01	0.15	0.40	-0.04	0.10
Petroleum	-0.14	0.00	0.00	0.82	0.13	0.15
Chemicals, rubber and plastics	0.31	0.08	0.14	0.34	0.06	0.13
Non-metallic mineral products	0.32	0.01	0.13	0.31	-0.01	0.11
Basic and fabricated metal products	0.19	0.07	0.10	0.33	0.03	0.12
Motor vehicles	0.44	0.05	0.10	0.20	0.14	0.15
Other transport equipment	0.31	0.14	0.16	0.48	0.03	0.10
Electronics	0.37	0.04	0.12	0.29	0.03	0.12
Machinery and equipment n.e.c.	0.26	0.11	0.13	0.49	0.04	0.11
Furniture, manufacturing n.e.c.	0.32	0.06	0.13	0.38	0.04	0.15
Electricity, gas and water supply; construction	0.19	-0.05	0.02	0.54	0.04	0.18
Trade, repair; hotels and restaurants	0.41	0.14	0.27	0.56	-0.41	0.01
Transport, storage and communication	0.19	0.14	0.15	0.35	-0.03	0.13
Finance, insurance, real estate, business activities	-13.68	0.13	-5.32	0.09	-0.67	-0.30
Other services	0.22	0.11	0.17	0.26	-0.15	0.07

5. SENSITIVITY ANALYSIS

We look now at how robust previous results are, when we change the values of the different elasticities in the model. For that purpose we present in this section the same simulation of the entry of MNEs into the five sectors above, but changing the values of three crucial elasticities: 1) the elasticity of substitution between imports and domestic production (i.e., the Armington elasticity); 2) the elasticity of substitution between national firms and MNEs' production; and 3) the elasticity of substitution between labour and capital. Obviously, the different combinations of elasticities across sectors are enormous, i.e., the costs of performing the so called Unconditional Systematic Sensitivity Analysis (UCSA) are high (Harrison et al., 1993). Therefore, we have opted for a simplifying strategy, namely, a Conditional Systematic Sensitivity Analysis (CSSA). This consists in choosing one of the three elasticities, double and halve its value in all of the twenty sectors (while holding the rest of elasticities at their initial benchmark level), and then compare the results for the aggregate and sectoral variables already analysed above.

Table 13 shows the results for the aggregate variables, in a structure analogous to that of Table 2, where the rows "double" and "half" denote, respectively, the results obtained when each of the elasticities analysed are multiplied or divided by two. The main conclusion arising from this table is that changes in elasticities preserve the general outcomes analysed earlier in this chapter. The differences are rather small for the elasticity of substitution between imports and domestic production (Table 13A) and for the elasticity of substitution between national firms and MNEs' production (Table 13B), and virtually non-existent for the elasticity of substitution between labour and capital (Table 13C).

For the two former cases, some comments may be in order. On the one hand, the wage in the economy increases as it did before. We can now add that the increase is higher the higher is the elasticity. On the other hand, the aggregate rental rate of capital decreases, as before, but the decrease is, in general, smaller the higher is the elasticity. Following a higher increase in the wage and a smaller fall in the rental of capital when the elasticity is higher, a greater increase in GDP is obtained. The same applies to the increase in private consumption and thus in welfare. Finally, when the elasticity of substitution between imports and domestic production is higher the volume of foreign trade is smaller, while the results are mixed for the elasticity of substitution between national firms and MNEs' production.

Table 13. Sensitivity analysis: effects on aggregate variables of changes in elasticities (percent change from benchmark)

A)   Elasticity of substitution between imports and domestic production

		Wage	Rental rate of capital	GDP	Welfare	CPI	Imports	Exports
Chemicals	Half	0.23	-0.57	0.28	0.59	0.08	1.37	1.42
	Double	0.25	-0.52	0.32	0.65	0.08	1.21	1.26
Motor vehicles	Half	0.03	-1.19	0.09	0.19	-0.11	0.73	0.76
	Double	0.08	-1.13	0.14	0.24	-0.09	0.36	0.37
Electronics	Half	0.20	-0.34	0.22	0.40	0.10	0.95	0.99
	Double	0.22	-0.34	0.23	0.42	0.08	0.88	0.92
Trade	Half	0.05	-0.52	0.25	0.66	-0.03	0.23	0.24
	Double	0.15	-0.50	0.31	0.72	0.01	0.14	0.15
Finance	Half	0.18	-0.63	0.33	0.69	-0.16	0.58	0.60
	Double	0.21	-0.57	0.38	0.75	-0.11	0.39	0.40

B)   Elasticity of substitution between national firms and MNEs' production

		Wage	Rental rate of capital	GDP	Welfare	CPI	Imports	Exports
Chemicals	Half	0.22	-0.56	0.28	0.59	0.08	1.29	1.34
	Double	0.26	-0.52	0.33	0.67	0.10	1.33	1.38
Motor vehicles	Half	0.05	-1.17	0.11	0.20	-0.10	0.59	0.61
	Double	0.06	-1.16	0.12	0.22	-0.10	0.59	0.62
Electronics	Half	0.20	-0.35	0.22	0.39	0.09	0.92	0.95
	Double	0.22	-0.33	0.23	0.42	0.10	0.94	0.98
Trade	Half	0.08	-0.52	0.26	0.66	-0.02	0.19	0.20
	Double	0.13	-0.49	0.30	0.74	0.00	0.17	0.17
Finance	Half	0.19	-0.62	0.34	0.70	-0.14	0.50	0.52
	Double	0.21	-0.57	0.37	0.75	-0.13	0.49	0.51

C) Elasticity of substitution between labour and capital

		Wage	Rental rate of capital	GDP	Welfare	CPI	Imports	Exports
Chemicals	Half	0.23	-0.55	0.30	0.61	0.08	1.30	1.36
	Double	0.23	-0.55	0.30	0.61	0.08	1.30	1.36
Motor vehicles	Half	0.05	-1.17	0.11	0.20	-0.10	0.59	0.61
	Double	0.05	-1.17	0.11	0.21	-0.10	0.59	0.61
Electronics	Half	0.21	-0.34	0.23	0.40	0.09	0.93	0.97
	Double	0.21	-0.34	0.23	0.40	0.09	0.93	0.97
Trade	Half	0.09	-0.51	0.27	0.69	-0.01	0.18	0.19
	Double	0.09	-0.51	0.27	0.69	-0.01	0.18	0.19
Finance	Half	0.20	-0.61	0.35	0.72	-0.14	0.50	0.52
	Double	0.20	-0.61	0.35	0.72	-0.14	0.50	0.52

The reason for a higher increase in the wage, with the higher value of these two elasticities, is due to the impact in the sectors receiving MNEs. The sector to which MNEs arrive increases production by more the higher the elasticity is. Therefore, it is demanding more labour to produce more, leaving less labour available for the rest of sectors, which pushes the wage up.

After showing the macroeconomic panorama, we go on to the analysis of the microeconomic results. Tables 14, 15 and 16 reproduce the effects on sectoral production, prices, exports and imports (in parts A, B, C, and D, respectively) of changes in each of the three elasticities.

For the elasticity of substitution between imports and domestic production (Table 14A), the main outcome is that, again, overall tendencies remain unchanged. The entry of MNEs in Chemicals and Electronics tends to reduce production in the rest of sectors, while concentrating it in the sector receiving MNEs. By contrast, the entry of MNEs in Finance and Motor vehicles does not result in a reduction of output in the rest of sectors. Only for Trade does the production level of some sectors, whose initial percentage changes were low, oscillate between small positive and small negative percentage changes (for the values half and double of the Armington elasticity, respectively). These results should be then familiar. What is remarkable here, however, is that for the five sectors receiving MNEs, the higher the elasticity assumed, the greater the concentration of production in the sector receiving MNEs. As already commented, there is a higher increase in labour demand in the sector receiving MNEs. More labour employed in the sector receiving MNEs leaves less labour available for the rest. As a consequence, the rest of sectors tend to experience lower increases in production for the higher value of the elasticity.

The higher the value of the Armington elasticity the smaller the fall in the price of the good sold by the sector receiving MNEs (Table 14B). This reduces the volume of exports from that sector (Table 14C). Its imports will also be smaller (Table 14D) because production in that sector, now relies more on domestic intermediates. When substitution between domestic and imported varieties is higher the domestic production is preferred, because its price has decreased considerably.

Table 14. Sensitivity analysis: Effects on sectoral variables of changes in the elasticity of substitution between imports and domestic production (percent change from benchmark)

A) Effects on sectoral output

	Chemicals		Motor vehicles		Electronics		Trade		Finance	
	Half	Double	Half	Double	Half	Double	Half	Double	Half	Double
Agriculture, hunting and fishing	0.00	-0.03	0.04	0.02	-0.03	-0.05	0.08	0.02	0.08	0.04
Mining and quarrying	-0.01	-0.01	0.00	0.00	-0.01	-0.01	0.00	-0.01	0.00	0.00
Food, beverages and tobacco	0.25	0.21	0.10	0.10	0.14	0.12	0.35	0.29	0.36	0.34
Textiles, wearing apparel, leather, footwear	-0.02	-0.12	0.11	0.03	-0.29	-0.34	0.20	0.00	0.32	0.18
Wood and wood products, except furniture	-0.24	-0.27	0.09	0.03	-0.32	-0.31	0.04	-0.10	0.15	0.04
Paper; printing and publishing	-0.11	-0.16	0.09	0.03	-0.19	-0.22	0.08	-0.06	0.27	0.17
Petroleum	0.20	0.14	0.04	0.04	0.11	0.06	0.22	0.17	0.21	0.20
Chemicals, rubber and plastics	13.43	15.01	0.10	0.05	-0.20	-0.22	0.03	-0.09	0.16	0.07
Non-metallic mineral products	-0.13	-0.17	0.10	0.05	-0.17	-0.19	0.05	-0.07	0.16	0.06
Basic and fabricated metal products	-0.39	-0.46	0.11	0.02	-0.41	-0.44	0.05	-0.18	0.26	0.10
Motor vehicles	-0.11	-0.13	16.47	17.68	-0.11	-0.12	0.07	-0.02	0.20	0.13
Other transport equipment	-0.14	-0.20	0.31	0.25	-0.07	-0.10	0.24	0.09	0.39	0.28
Electronics	-0.18	-0.25	0.10	0.02	17.36	18.99	0.06	-0.12	0.26	0.12
Machinery and equipment n.e.c.	-0.17	-0.21	1.78	1.83	-0.16	-0.17	0.11	-0.02	0.28	0.18
Furniture, manufacturing n.e.c.	-0.02	-0.10	0.10	0.05	-0.19	-0.23	0.20	0.03	0.28	0.17
Electricity, gas and water supply; construction	0.06	0.01	0.10	0.07	0.04	0.00	0.27	0.16	0.35	0.28
Trade, repair; hotels and restaurants	0.11	-0.02	0.19	0.17	0.05	-0.07	4.99	6.75	0.61	0.54
Transport, storage and communication	-0.11	-0.15	0.12	0.08	-0.12	-0.15	0.16	0.06	0.20	0.13
Finance, insurance, real estate, business activities	-0.01	-0.05	0.06	0.05	-0.04	-0.06	0.13	0.05	1.96	2.37
Other services	0.04	0.02	0.05	0.04	0.01	-0.02	0.13	0.09	0.18	0.16

Table 14. (Continued)

B) Effects on sectoral prices

	Chemicals		Motor vehicles		Electronics		Trade		Finance	
	Half	Double	Half	Double	Half	Double	Half	Double	Half	Double
Agriculture, hunting and fishing	0.07	0.02	0.11	0.10	0.03	0.00	0.14	0.08	0.25	0.18
Mining and quarrying	-0.08	-0.08	0.10	0.08	-0.09	-0.08	0.04	0.00	0.16	0.11
Food, beverages and tobacco	0.14	0.12	0.10	0.10	0.09	0.08	0.17	0.16	0.24	0.22
Textiles, wearing apparel, leather, footwear	-0.04	-0.03	0.09	0.08	-0.01	-0.01	0.04	0.03	0.14	0.11
Wood and wood products, except furniture	-0.04	-0.04	0.09	0.08	-0.04	-0.03	0.03	0.01	0.14	0.11
Paper; printing and publishing	-0.03	-0.03	0.09	0.08	-0.03	-0.03	0.05	0.03	0.14	0.11
Petroleum	-0.05	-0.05	0.10	0.08	-0.06	-0.05	0.06	0.02	0.17	0.12
Chemicals, rubber and plastics	-2.51	-2.03	0.09	0.08	-0.05	-0.05	0.04	0.01	0.15	0.11
Non-metallic mineral products	-0.05	-0.05	0.09	0.08	-0.06	-0.05	0.03	0.01	0.14	0.10
Basic and fabricated metal products	-0.03	-0.03	0.08	0.08	-0.04	-0.03	0.03	0.01	0.13	0.10
Motor vehicles	-0.05	-0.04	-3.50	-3.33	-0.06	-0.04	0.03	0.01	0.12	0.09
Other transport equipment	-0.05	-0.04	0.06	0.06	-0.07	-0.06	0.02	0.00	0.13	0.09
Electronics	-0.06	-0.05	0.09	0.08	-2.02	-1.74	0.03	0.01	0.13	0.10
Machinery and equipment n.e.c.	-0.05	-0.05	-0.13	-0.11	-0.07	-0.06	0.02	0.00	0.13	0.09
Furniture, manufacturing n.e.c.	-0.02	-0.02	0.09	0.08	-0.02	-0.01	0.05	0.03	0.15	0.12
Electricity, gas and water supply; construction	0.06	0.06	0.09	0.09	0.02	0.02	0.09	0.09	0.17	0.15
Trade, repair; hotels and restaurants	0.14	0.12	0.05	0.07	0.10	0.08	-2.94	-2.44	0.08	0.10
Transport, storage and communication	0.05	0.05	0.06	0.07	0.02	0.02	0.03	0.04	0.13	0.12
Finance, insurance, real estate, business activities	0.08	0.06	0.07	0.07	0.05	0.01	0.11	0.10	-1.56	-1.32
Other services	0.12	0.13	0.06	0.08	0.10	0.11	0.05	0.10	0.06	0.08

C) Effects on sectoral exports

	Chemicals		Motor vehicles		Electronics		Trade		Finance	
	Half	Double	Half	Double	Half	Double	Half	Double	Half	Double
Agriculture, hunting and fishing	-0.67	-0.46	-0.01	-0.06	-0.55	-0.34	-0.48	-0.40	-0.38	-0.33
Mining and quarrying	-0.06	-0.03	0.00	-0.01	-0.04	-0.02	-0.04	-0.03	-0.03	-0.02
Food. beverages and tobacco	-1.05	-0.96	0.04	-0.10	-0.90	-0.73	-0.66	-0.79	-0.37	-0.54
Textiles, wearing apparel, leather, footwear	-0.35	-0.38	0.09	-0.03	-0.61	-0.51	-0.04	-0.25	0.15	-0.06
Wood and wood products, except furniture	-0.29	-0.27	0.08	0.01	-0.35	-0.29	-0.01	-0.13	0.10	-0.01
Paper; printing and publishing	-0.31	-0.26	0.05	-0.01	-0.36	-0.26	-0.10	-0.18	0.14	0.00
Petroleum	-0.13	-0.12	0.01	-0.01	-0.15	-0.12	-0.09	-0.12	-0.03	-0.06
Chemicals, rubber and plastics	16.37	12.95	0.08	0.02	-0.27	-0.21	-0.04	-0.12	0.09	0.00
Non-metallic mineral products	-0.15	-0.14	0.06	0.01	-0.22	-0.17	0.01	-0.07	0.11	0.02
Basic and fabricated metal products	-0.36	-0.32	0.09	0.00	-0.37	-0.30	0.03	-0.13	0.22	0.06
Motor vehicles	-0.20	-0.21	21.67	20.52	-0.21	-0.19	0.01	-0.09	0.20	0.09
Other transport equipment	-0.31	-0.29	0.30	0.16	-0.20	-0.17	0.10	-0.06	0.27	0.10
Electronics	-0.22	-0.23	0.09	0.01	18.06	15.46	0.02	-0.13	0.23	0.07
Machinery and equipment n.e.c.	-0.25	-0.23	1.83	1.49	-0.21	-0.18	0.05	-0.08	0.24	0.10
Furniture, manufacturing n.e.c.	-0.45	-0.43	0.08	-0.02	-0.57	-0.46	-0.13	-0.30	0.05	-0.13
Electricity, gas and water supply; construction	-0.69	-0.66	0.04	-0.06	-0.56	-0.49	-0.27	-0.44	-0.02	-0.21
Trade, repair; hotels and restaurants	-0.85	-0.74	0.18	0.03	-0.73	-0.59	12.11	9.82	0.31	0.01
Transport, storage and communication	-0.37	-0.36	0.12	0.05	-0.33	-0.29	-0.01	-0.14	0.08	-0.04
Finance, insurance, real estate, business activities	-0.64	-0.52	0.11	0.04	-0.55	-0.35	-0.32	-0.39	6.80	5.60
Other services	-0.75	-0.78	0.16	-0.01	-0.74	-0.71	-0.08	-0.40	0.40	0.10

Table 14. (Continued)

D) Effects on sectoral imports

	Chemicals		Motor vehicles		Electronics		Trade		Finance	
	Half	Double	Half	Double	Half	Double	Half	Double	Half	Double
Agriculture, hunting and fishing	0.22	0.44	0.04	0.09	0.16	0.30	0.23	0.43	0.19	0.37
Mining and quarrying	0.06	0.06	0.01	0.02	0.04	0.04	0.06	0.07	0.06	0.07
Food, beverages and tobacco	0.61	1.25	0.08	0.20	0.44	0.88	0.57	1.14	0.48	0.92
Textiles, wearing apparel, leather, footwear	0.27	0.37	0.07	0.08	0.08	0.22	0.34	0.39	0.34	0.36
Wood and wood products, except furniture	-0.09	0.00	0.06	0.03	-0.16	-0.05	0.09	0.05	0.14	0.09
Paper; printing and publishing	0.04	0.12	0.07	0.05	-0.05	0.04	0.16	0.16	0.28	0.23
Petroleum	0.26	0.28	0.04	0.06	0.17	0.20	0.27	0.32	0.24	0.29
Chemicals, rubber and plastics	11.01	9.04	0.08	0.05	-0.09	-0.05	0.10	0.06	0.18	0.13
Non-metallic mineral products	-0.07	-0.04	0.11	0.05	-0.09	-0.02	0.08	0.01	0.15	0.06
Basic and fabricated metal products	-0.32	-0.28	0.05	-0.02	-0.34	-0.28	0.01	-0.11	0.16	0.03
Motor vehicles	0.04	0.08	5.14	1.51	0.06	0.08	0.14	0.11	0.16	0.11
Other transport equipment	0.02	0.10	0.21	0.12	0.03	0.08	0.26	0.20	0.34	0.24
Electronics	-0.07	-0.08	0.10	0.04	11.16	9.37	0.12	0.00	0.26	0.15
Machinery and equipment n.e.c.	-0.01	0.03	0.91	0.60	-0.02	0.01	0.15	0.10	0.22	0.16
Furniture, manufacturing n.e.c.	0.25	0.44	0.08	0.09	0.10	0.29	0.33	0.43	0.33	0.38
Electricity, gas and water supply; construction	0.25	0.63	0.05	0.11	0.16	0.42	0.32	0.57	0.31	0.45
Trade, repair; hotels and restaurants	0.32	0.70	0.12	0.12	0.22	0.49	3.11	-1.29	0.51	0.52
Transport, storage and communication	0.07	0.29	0.06	0.03	0.05	0.21	0.17	0.22	0.16	0.17
Finance, insurance, real estate, business activities	0.21	0.42	0.10	0.12	0.12	0.30	0.28	0.42	3.28	1.62
Other services	0.29	0.85	0.03	0.07	0.25	0.72	0.21	0.54	0.12	0.12

Table 15. Sensitivity analysis: Effects on sectoral variables of changes in the elasticity of substitution between national firms and MNE's production (percent change from benchmark)

A) Effects on sectoral output

	Chemicals		Motor vehicles		Electronics		Trade		Finance	
	Half	Double	Half	Double	Half	Double	Half	Double	Half	Double
Agriculture, hunting and fishing	-0.01	-0.02	0.03	0.03	-0.04	-0.04	0.06	0.05	0.06	0.06
Mining and quarrying	-0.01	-0.02	0.00	0.00	-0.01	-0.01	0.00	0.00	0.00	0.00
Food, beverages and tobacco	0.23	0.25	0.10	0.10	0.13	0.14	0.32	0.34	0.35	0.37
Textiles, wearing apparel, leather, footwear	-0.03	-0.09	0.08	0.07	-0.30	-0.33	0.15	0.08	0.27	0.24
Wood and wood products. Except furniture	-0.23	-0.29	0.07	0.06	-0.30	-0.33	0.01	-0.06	0.12	0.09
Paper; printing and publishing	-0.11	-0.16	0.07	0.06	-0.19	-0.21	0.04	-0.01	0.24	0.22
Petroleum	0.16	0.20	0.04	0.05	0.09	0.09	0.20	0.22	0.21	0.23
Chemicals, rubber and plastics	13.77	14.47	0.09	0.08	-0.20	-0.22	0.00	-0.05	0.13	0.11
Non-metallic mineral products	-0.13	-0.17	0.08	0.07	-0.17	-0.19	0.02	-0.04	0.13	0.10
Basic and fabricated metal products	-0.39	-0.48	0.08	0.06	-0.40	-0.44	-0.01	-0.11	0.21	0.17
Motor vehicles	-0.11	-0.14	16.82	17.01	-0.11	-0.12	0.04	0.01	0.18	0.16
Other transport equipment	-0.15	-0.19	0.29	0.28	-0.07	-0.09	0.20	0.15	0.35	0.33
Electronics	-0.18	-0.25	0.07	0.06	17.76	18.30	0.01	-0.07	0.22	0.18
Machinery and equipment n.e.c.	-0.17	-0.22	1.79	1.81	-0.15	-0.17	0.07	0.02	0.25	0.23
Furniture, manufacturing n.e.c.	-0.04	-0.08	0.09	0.08	-0.20	-0.22	0.15	0.10	0.24	0.22
Electricity, gas and water supply; construction	0.05	0.04	0.09	0.08	0.03	0.02	0.24	0.22	0.33	0.33
Trade, repair; hotels and restaurants	0.06	0.05	0.19	0.18	0.01	0.00	5.49	6.00	0.59	0.59
Transport, storage and communication	-0.11	-0.14	0.11	0.10	-0.12	-0.14	0.13	0.10	0.18	0.17
Finance, insurance, real estate, business activities	-0.02	-0.03	0.06	0.05	-0.04	-0.05	0.11	0.09	2.10	2.15
Other services	0.03	0.03	0.05	0.05	0.00	0.00	0.12	0.11	0.18	0.18

Table 15. (Continued)

B) Effects on sectoral prices

	Chemicals		Motor vehicles		Electronics		Trade		Finance	
	Half	Double	Half	Double	Half	Double	Half	Double	Half	Double
Agriculture, hunting and fishing	0.05	0.05	0.10	0.11	0.01	0.01	0.12	0.12	0.22	0.22
Mining and quarrying	-0.07	-0.09	0.09	0.09	-0.08	-0.09	0.02	0.01	0.15	0.13
Food, beverages and tobacco	0.13	0.15	0.10	0.10	0.08	0.09	0.16	0.18	0.23	0.24
Textiles, wearing apparel, leather, footwear	-0.03	-0.04	0.09	0.09	-0.01	-0.01	0.03	0.03	0.13	0.13
Wood and wood products, except furniture	-0.03	-0.04	0.08	0.08	-0.03	-0.04	0.03	0.02	0.13	0.13
Paper; printing and publishing	-0.03	-0.04	0.09	0.09	-0.03	-0.03	0.04	0.04	0.13	0.12
Petroleum	-0.04	-0.06	0.09	0.09	-0.05	-0.06	0.05	0.03	0.15	0.15
Chemicals, rubber and plastics	-2.30	-2.40	0.08	0.08	-0.05	-0.05	0.03	0.02	0.13	0.13
Non-metallic mineral products	-0.05	-0.06	0.08	0.08	-0.05	-0.05	0.02	0.01	0.13	0.12
Basic and fabricated metal products	-0.03	-0.04	0.08	0.08	-0.04	-0.04	0.02	0.02	0.12	0.11
Motor vehicles	-0.04	-0.05	-3.43	-3.47	-0.05	-0.05	0.02	0.01	0.11	0.11
Other transport equipment	-0.04	-0.05	0.06	0.06	-0.07	-0.07	0.01	0.00	0.12	0.11
Electronics	-0.05	-0.07	0.09	0.08	-1.90	-1.95	0.02	0.01	0.12	0.11
Machinery and equipment n.e.c.	-0.05	-0.06	-0.13	-0.13	-0.06	-0.07	0.02	0.01	0.12	0.11
Furniture, manufacturing n.e.c.	-0.02	-0.02	0.09	0.09	-0.01	-0.02	0.04	0.04	0.14	0.14
Electricity, gas and water supply; construction	0.06	0.07	0.09	0.09	0.02	0.02	0.09	0.09	0.16	0.16
Trade, repair; hotels and restaurants	0.13	0.14	0.06	0.06	0.09	0.09	-2.70	-2.86	0.09	0.10
Transport, storage and communication	0.05	0.05	0.06	0.06	0.02	0.02	0.04	0.04	0.13	0.13
Finance, insurance, real estate, business activities	0.07	0.08	0.07	0.07	0.03	0.04	0.10	0.12	-1.48	-1.48
Other services	0.11	0.13	0.07	0.07	0.10	0.11	0.06	0.09	0.06	0.07

C) Effects on sectoral exports

	Chemicals		Motor vehicles		Electronics		Trade		Finance	
	Half	Double	Half	Double	Half	Double	Half	Double	Half	Double
Agriculture, hunting and fishing	-0.55	-0.64	-0.03	-0.05	-0.44	-0.48	-0.43	-0.52	-0.35	-0.41
Mining and quarrying	-0.04	-0.05	0.00	-0.01	-0.03	-0.03	-0.03	-0.04	-0.02	-0.03
Food, beverages and tobacco	-0.96	-1.14	-0.01	-0.05	-0.81	-0.87	-0.67	-0.85	-0.42	-0.53
Textiles, wearing apparel, leather, footwear	-0.32	-0.43	0.05	0.02	-0.55	-0.60	-0.10	-0.22	0.08	0.01
Wood and wood products. Except furniture	-0.26	-0.33	0.06	0.04	-0.31	-0.34	-0.04	-0.12	0.06	0.03
Paper; printing and publishing	-0.27	-0.33	0.03	0.01	-0.31	-0.34	-0.12	-0.19	0.08	0.05
Petroleum	-0.12	-0.15	0.00	0.00	-0.13	-0.14	-0.10	-0.13	-0.04	-0.06
Chemicals, rubber and plastics	14.89	15.45	0.06	0.05	-0.24	-0.26	-0.07	-0.12	0.06	0.03
Non-metallic mineral products	-0.14	-0.18	0.04	0.04	-0.19	-0.21	-0.01	-0.06	0.08	0.06
Basic and fabricated metal products	-0.32	-0.39	0.06	0.04	-0.33	-0.36	-0.02	-0.10	0.16	0.12
Motor vehicles	-0.19	-0.24	21.19	21.41	-0.20	-0.22	-0.02	-0.07	0.16	0.13
Other transport equipment	-0.28	-0.35	0.25	0.23	-0.17	-0.20	0.05	-0.02	0.21	0.17
Electronics	-0.20	-0.27	0.06	0.04	16.98	17.46	-0.02	-0.10	0.17	0.14
Machinery and equipment n.e.c.	-0.22	-0.28	1.70	1.70	-0.19	-0.21	0.01	-0.05	0.19	0.16
Furniture, manufacturing n.e.c.	-0.41	-0.52	0.04	0.02	-0.50	-0.55	-0.17	-0.28	-0.01	-0.08
Electricity, gas and water supply; construction	-0.64	-0.76	0.01	-0.02	-0.51	-0.56	-0.31	-0.43	-0.08	-0.15
Trade, repair; hotels and restaurants	-0.76	-0.90	0.13	0.10	-0.65	-0.71	11.02	11.65	0.20	0.12
Transport, storage and communication	-0.34	-0.41	0.10	0.08	-0.30	-0.33	-0.04	-0.11	0.04	0.00
Finance, insurance, real estate, business activities	-0.55	-0.67	0.08	0.06	-0.44	-0.49	-0.32	-0.44	6.39	6.33
Other services	-0.71	-0.87	0.10	0.07	-0.70	-0.77	-0.16	-0.34	0.30	0.21

Table 15. (Continued)

D) Effects on sectoral imports

	Chemicals		Motor vehicles		Electronics		Trade		Finance	
	Half	Double	Half	Double	Half	Double	Half	Double	Half	Double
Agriculture, hunting and fishing	0.30	0.34	0.05	0.06	0.21	0.23	0.29	0.34	0.25	0.28
Mining and quarrying	0.06	0.06	0.01	0.01	0.04	0.04	0.06	0.07	0.06	0.06
Food, beverages and tobacco	0.79	0.92	0.10	0.13	0.59	0.64	0.72	0.85	0.59	0.68
Textiles, wearing apparel, leather, footwear	0.29	0.32	0.07	0.07	0.13	0.14	0.34	0.37	0.33	0.35
Wood and wood products, except furniture	-0.05	-0.08	0.05	0.04	-0.11	-0.12	0.07	0.04	0.11	0.10
Paper; printing and publishing	0.07	0.07	0.06	0.06	-0.01	-0.01	0.16	0.15	0.25	0.25
Petroleum	0.24	0.30	0.04	0.05	0.17	0.19	0.28	0.31	0.25	0.28
Chemicals, rubber and plastics	10.10	10.56	0.07	0.06	-0.07	-0.08	0.09	0.07	0.16	0.15
Non-metallic mineral products	-0.05	-0.08	0.09	0.08	-0.06	-0.06	0.05	0.01	0.12	0.10
Basic and fabricated metal products	-0.28	-0.34	0.03	0.01	-0.31	-0.33	-0.03	-0.09	0.11	0.08
Motor vehicles	0.06	0.05	3.85	3.92	0.06	0.07	0.12	0.11	0.14	0.14
Other transport equipment	0.05	0.04	0.17	0.17	0.05	0.05	0.23	0.22	0.29	0.29
Electronics	-0.06	-0.10	0.08	0.07	10.34	10.71	0.08	0.03	0.22	0.20
Machinery and equipment n.e.c.	0.01	0.00	0.79	0.79	-0.01	-0.01	0.13	0.12	0.19	0.19
Furniture, manufacturing n.e.c.	0.30	0.34	0.07	0.08	0.17	0.18	0.34	0.38	0.32	0.35
Electricity, gas and water supply; construction	0.36	0.42	0.06	0.07	0.25	0.27	0.37	0.43	0.33	0.37
Trade, repair; hotels and restaurants	0.44	0.50	0.11	0.12	0.31	0.33	1.38	1.55	0.47	0.52
Transport, storage and communication	0.14	0.16	0.04	0.04	0.10	0.11	0.16	0.18	0.14	0.16
Finance, insurance, real estate, business activities	0.28	0.31	0.10	0.11	0.20	0.20	0.32	0.35	2.66	2.67
Other services	0.45	0.53	0.01	0.03	0.40	0.43	0.26	0.34	0.07	0.12

Table 16. Sensitivity analysis: Effects on sectoral variables of changes in the elasticity of substitution between labour and capital (percent change from benchmark)

A) Effects on sectoral output

	Chemicals		Motor vehicles		Electronics		Trade		Finance	
	Half	Double	Half	Double	Half	Double	Half	Double	Half	Double
Agriculture, hunting and fishing	-0.01	-0.01	0.03	0.03	-0.04	-0.04	0.06	0.06	0.06	0.06
Mining and quarrying	-0.01	-0.01	0.00	0.00	-0.01	-0.01	0.00	0.00	0.00	0.00
Food, beverages and tobacco	0.24	0.24	0.10	0.10	0.13	0.13	0.33	0.33	0.36	0.36
Textiles wearing apparel, leather, footwear	-0.05	-0.05	0.08	0.08	-0.31	-0.31	0.13	0.13	0.26	0.26
Wood and wood products, except furniture	-0.24	-0.24	0.07	0.07	-0.31	-0.31	-0.01	-0.01	0.11	0.11
Paper; printing and publishing	-0.12	-0.12	0.07	0.07	-0.20	-0.20	0.02	0.02	0.23	0.23
Petroleum	0.16	0.16	0.04	0.04	0.09	0.09	0.21	0.21	0.21	0.22
Chemicals, rubber and plastics	13.97	13.97	0.08	0.08	-0.21	-0.21	-0.01	-0.01	0.12	0.12
Non-metallic mineral products	-0.14	-0.14	0.08	0.08	-0.18	-0.18	0.00	0.00	0.12	0.12
Basic and fabricated metal products	-0.41	-0.41	0.07	0.08	-0.42	-0.42	-0.04	-0.04	0.20	0.20
Motor vehicles	-0.11	-0.11	16.87	16.90	-0.12	-0.12	0.03	0.03	0.17	0.17
Other transport equipment	-0.16	-0.16	0.29	0.29	-0.08	-0.08	0.19	0.19	0.35	0.35
Electronics	-0.20	-0.20	0.07	0.07	17.95	17.95	-0.01	-0.01	0.21	0.21
Machinery and equipment n.e.c.	-0.18	-0.18	1.80	1.80	-0.16	-0.16	0.06	0.06	0.24	0.24
Furniture, manufacturing n.e.c.	-0.05	-0.05	0.08	0.08	-0.21	-0.21	0.14	0.14	0.24	0.24
Electricity, gas and water supply; construction	0.05	0.05	0.09	0.09	0.03	0.03	0.23	0.23	0.33	0.33
Trade, repair; hotels and restaurants	0.06	0.06	0.19	0.18	0.00	0.00	5.65	5.65	0.59	0.59
Transport, storage and communication	-0.12	-0.12	0.11	0.11	-0.13	-0.13	0.12	0.12	0.18	0.18
Finance, insurance, real estate.,business activities	-0.02	-0.02	0.06	0.05	-0.05	-0.05	0.10	0.10	2.12	2.12
Other services	0.03	0.03	0.05	0.05	0.00	0.00	0.12	0.12	0.18	0.18

Table 16. (Continued)

B) Effects on sectoral prices

	Chemicals		Motor vehicles		Electronics		Trade		Finance	
	Half	Double	Half	Double	Half	Double	Half	Double	Half	Double
Agricultura, hunting and fishing	0.05	0.05	0.11	0.10	0.01	0.01	0.12	0.12	0.22	0.22
Mining and quarrying	-0.07	-0.08	0.09	0.09	-0.09	-0.09	0.02	0.02	0.14	0.14
Food, beverages and tobacco	0.13	0.13	0.10	0.10	0.09	0.09	0.17	0.17	0.23	0.23
Textiles, wearing apparel, leather, footwear	-0.03	-0.03	0.09	0.09	-0.01	-0.01	0.03	0.03	0.13	0.13
Wood and wood products. Except furniture	-0.04	-0.04	0.08	0.08	-0.04	-0.04	0.02	0.02	0.13	0.13
Paper; printing and publishing	-0.03	-0.03	0.09	0.09	-0.03	-0.03	0.04	0.04	0.13	0.13
Petroleum	-0.05	-0.05	0.09	0.09	-0.05	-0.06	0.04	0.04	0.15	0.15
Chemicals, rubber and plastics	-2.33	-2.33	0.08	0.08	-0.05	-0.05	0.03	0.03	0.13	0.13
Non-metallic mineral products	-0.05	-0.05	0.08	0.08	-0.05	-0.05	0.02	0.02	0.12	0.12
Basic and fabricated metal products	-0.03	-0.03	0.08	0.08	-0.04	-0.04	0.02	0.02	0.12	0.12
Motor vehicles	-0.04	-0.04	-3.45	-3.44	-0.05	-0.05	0.02	0.02	0.11	0.11
Other transport equipment	-0.04	-0.04	0.06	0.06	-0.07	-0.07	0.01	0.01	0.12	0.12
Electronics	-0.06	-0.06	0.08	0.08	-1.92	-1.92	0.02	0.02	0.12	0.12
Machinery and equipment n.e.c.	-0.05	-0.05	-0.13	-0.13	-0.06	-0.06	0.02	0.02	0.12	0.12
Furniture, manufacturing n.e.c.	-0.02	-0.02	0.09	0.09	-0.02	-0.02	0.04	0.04	0.14	0.14
Electricity, gas and water supply; construction	0.06	0.06	0.09	0.09	0.02	0.02	0.09	0.09	0.16	0.16
Trade, repair; hotels and restaurants	0.13	0.13	0.06	0.06	0.09	0.09	-2.75	-2.75	0.09	0.09
Transport, storage and communication	0.05	0.05	0.06	0.06	0.02	0.02	0.04	0.04	0.13	0.13
Finance, insurance, real estate, business activities	0.07	0.07	0.07	0.07	0.03	0.03	0.11	0.11	-1.48	-1.48
Other services	0.12	0.12	0.07	0.07	0.10	0.10	0.07	0.07	0.07	0.07

C) Effects on sectoral exports

	Chemicals		Motor vehicles		Electronics		Trade		Finance	
	Half	Double	Half	Double	Half	Double	Half	Double	Half	Double
Agriculture, hunting and fishing	-0.57	-0.57	-0.03	-0.04	-0.46	-0.46	-0.46	-0.46	-0.37	-0.37
Mining and quarrying	-0.04	-0.04	0.00	0.00	-0.03	-0.03	-0.03	-0.03	-0.03	-0.03
Food, beverages and tobacco	-1.01	-1.01	-0.02	-0.03	-0.83	-0.83	-0.73	-0.73	-0.45	-0.45
Textiles, wearing apparel, leather, footwear	-0.35	-0.35	0.04	0.04	-0.57	-0.57	-0.14	-0.14	0.06	0.06
Wood and wood products. Except furniture	-0.28	-0.28	0.05	0.05	-0.33	-0.33	-0.07	-0.07	0.05	0.05
Paper; printing and publishing	-0.28	-0.28	0.02	0.02	-0.32	-0.32	-0.14	-0.14	0.07	0.07
Petroleum	-0.12	-0.12	0.00	0.00	-0.13	-0.13	-0.11	-0.11	-0.05	-0.05
Chemicals. Rubber and plastics	15.09	15.09	0.05	0.05	-0.25	-0.25	-0.08	-0.08	0.05	0.05
Non-metallic mineral products	-0.15	-0.15	0.04	0.04	-0.20	-0.20	-0.03	-0.03	0.07	0.07
Basic and fabricated metal products	-0.34	-0.34	0.05	0.06	-0.34	-0.34	-0.04	-0.04	0.15	0.15
Motor vehicles	-0.20	-0.20	21.24	21.27	-0.21	-0.21	-0.03	-0.03	0.15	0.15
Other transport equipment	-0.30	-0.30	0.24	0.24	-0.19	-0.19	0.03	0.03	0.20	0.20
Electronics	-0.22	-0.22	0.05	0.05	17.11	17.11	-0.05	-0.05	0.16	0.16
Machinery and equipment n.e.c.	-0.24	-0.24	1.70	1.70	-0.20	-0.20	-0.01	-0.01	0.18	0.18
Furniture, manufacturing n.e.c.	-0.44	-0.44	0.04	0.03	-0.53	-0.53	-0.21	-0.21	-0.03	-0.03
Electricity, gas and water supply; construction	-0.68	-0.68	0.00	0.00	-0.53	-0.53	-0.35	-0.35	-0.10	-0.10
Trade, repair; hotels and restaurants	-0.80	-0.80	0.12	0.12	-0.68	-0.68	11.22	11.22	0.18	0.18
Transport, storage and communication	-0.36	-0.36	0.09	0.09	-0.32	-0.32	-0.07	-0.07	0.03	0.03
Finance, insurance, real estate, business activities	-0.58	-0.58	0.08	0.08	-0.47	-0.47	-0.35	-0.35	6.37	6.37
Other services	-0.76	-0.75	0.09	0.09	-0.73	-0.73	-0.22	-0.22	0.27	0.27

Table 16. (Continued)

D) Effects on sectoral imports

	Chemicals		Motor vehicles		Electronics		Trade		Finance	
	Half	Double	Half	Double	Half	Double	Half	Double	Half	Double
Agriculture, hunting and fishing	0.31	0.31	0.05	0.05	0.22	0.22	0.31	0.31	0.26	0.26
Mining and quarrying	0.06	0.06	0.01	0.01	0.04	0.04	0.07	0.07	0.06	0.06
Food, beverages and tobacco	0.83	0.83	0.11	0.11	0.61	0.61	0.76	0.76	0.62	0.62
Textiles, wearing apparel, leather, footwear	0.30	0.30	0.07	0.07	0.13	0.13	0.35	0.35	0.34	0.34
Wood and wood products, except furniture	-0.06	-0.06	0.04	0.04	-0.12	-0.12	0.06	0.06	0.11	0.11
Paper; printing and publishing	0.07	0.07	0.06	0.06	-0.01	-0.01	0.15	0.15	0.25	0.25
Petroleum	0.25	0.25	0.04	0.05	0.18	0.18	0.29	0.29	0.26	0.26
Chemicals, rubber and plastics	10.24	10.24	0.07	0.07	-0.07	-0.07	0.08	0.08	0.16	0.16
Non-metallic mineral products	-0.06	-0.06	0.08	0.08	-0.06	-0.06	0.04	0.04	0.11	0.11
Basic and fabricated metal products	-0.30	-0.30	0.02	0.02	-0.32	-0.32	-0.05	-0.05	0.10	0.10
Motor vehicles	0.06	0.06	3.87	3.87	0.07	0.07	0.12	0.12	0.14	0.14
Other transport equipment	0.05	0.05	0.17	0.17	0.05	0.05	0.23	0.23	0.29	0.29
Electronics	-0.07	-0.07	0.08	0.08	10.55	10.56	0.07	0.07	0.21	0.21
Machinery and equipment n.e.c.	0.01	0.01	0.79	0.79	-0.01	-0.01	0.13	0.13	0.19	0.19
Furniture, manufacturing n.e.c.	0.31	0.31	0.07	0.07	0.17	0.17	0.35	0.35	0.33	0.33
Electricity, gas and water supply; construction	0.38	0.38	0.06	0.06	0.26	0.26	0.39	0.39	0.34	0.34
Trade, repair; hotels and restaurants	0.46	0.46	0.11	0.11	0.32	0.32	1.43	1.43	0.49	0.49
Transport, storage and communication	0.15	0.15	0.04	0.04	0.11	0.11	0.17	0.17	0.15	0.15
Finance, insurance, real estate, business activities	0.29	0.29	0.10	0.10	0.20	0.20	0.32	0.32	2.67	2.67
Other services	0.47	0.47	0.02	0.02	0.41	0.41	0.29	0.29	0.09	0.09

Production in the sector receiving MNEs also increases for a higher value of the elasticity of substitution between national firms and MNEs' production (Table 15A). The percentage changes between the two extreme values of this elasticity in sectoral production are much smaller, though, than for the previous one. The change in the price of the good sold by the sector directly involved in the shock is also smaller than for the Armington elasticity (Table 15B); as domestic and MNEs' varieties are easier to substitute for one another, variations in the final price amalgamating the prices of both varieties are softened. As a consequence, exports (Table 15C) from the sector tend to vary only slightly and so do imports (Table 15D).

Finally, Tables 16A-D give evidence of the absence of effects of a change in the elasticity of substitution between labour and capital at the sectoral level. The assumption of specific capital renders the analysis of substitution between labour and capital a nearly redundant exercise, although we have been careful to check this is true in our simulations.

All this empirical evidence should lead us to the conclusion that the results of the model, both at the sectoral and aggregate levels, are mainly unaffected when moving from a higher to a lower value of each of the elasticities analysed. In brief, changes in the elasticity of substitution between labour and capital and between national firms and MNEs' production leave our main findings unchanged, whereas changes in the Armington elasticity produce rather small adjustments that preserve previous conclusions.

6. CONCLUSIONS

The simulations performed in this chapter have tried to show the effects of a higher involvement of MNEs in some particular sectors of a host economy. More specifically, we have examined the impact of the entry of MNEs in five different sectors of the Czech economy, namely, Chemicals, Motor vehicles, Electronics, Trade, and Finance.

The results of the model are in accordance with the predictions of the factor-specific model within the theory of international trade (Jones, 2002, 2000, 1971; Mussa, 1974; Neary, 1978). Consistent with this theory, the aggregate wage rises, and the rental rate of capital decreases. Apart from their theoretical foundations these results for factor prices seem intuitive if we interpret them in the short-medium run which is the timing associated with our model. Given this timing, it makes sense that more MNEs in an economy may lead to a lower rental rate of capital, because they would lead to increased competition. Furthermore, sectoral results also show that the price of the good sold by the MNEs will fall. Remember that, as seen in Chapter 2, the impact of MNEs on concentration levels is a field where more empirical research is needed. In any case, an increase in competition seems reasonable, particularly in the short run.

The general equilibrium nature of the model allows us to derive the impact of the above mentioned changes in factor prices on GDP and welfare. Changes in these two latter aggregate variables are quantitatively small but positive. The entry of MNEs in Motor vehicles yields the least positive effects on GDP and welfare; MNEs from Chemicals, Electronics, Finance, and Trade lead to similar impacts on GDP and welfare.

The results suggest rather clear effects on the particular sector receiving FDI inflows. The entry of MNEs leads to an important increase in production as there is much more capital available for production. On the other hand, there is decrease in the price of the good sold by that sector. We have explained the reasons for this. The more capital there is in a sector, the lower its rental tends to be. This reduces costs and leads to a fall in the price of the goods of that sector. This will increase the export competitiveness of the sector. It also increases imports mainly due to the imported intermediates that the sector receiving MNEs uses to increase its level of production.

By contrast, for the rest of sectors different patterns can be identified depending on the sector where the entry of MNEs takes place. Their entry in the two services sectors boosts production in the rest of sectors of the economy. On the contrary, MNEs' arrivals to Chemicals and Electronics lead to a concentration of production in the sector receiving MNEs at the cost of reducing production in the rest of sectors. It should be noted, however, that in all of the five scenarios the impact of the entry of MNEs for the rest of sectors is quantitatively reduced.

The evolution of the demand side of the model seems quite relevant for sectoral responses. On the one hand, the effects of MNEs on export competitiveness are behind the response of most manufacturing sectors (with the exception of Food and Petroleum). On the other hand, the impact of MNEs on the income of the representative consumer leads the evolution of those sectors more responsive to private consumption. These are Food, Electricity and most services sectors (with the exception of Transport).

Another interesting result is the slight tendency for a different pattern of sectoral prices followed by national firms versus MNEs. National firms, in general, exhibit more labour intensive technologies than their MNEs counterparts acting in the same sector. As the entry of MNEs always bring about an increase in wages, national firms tend to experience a higher increase in factor costs, which, often, will lead to higher prices. Therefore, after the arrival of MNEs, prices of national firms tend to increase by more than prices of MNEs, within the same sector. These different levels of labour intensity do not seem to affect output responses of national firms versus MNEs, though. For production, the important weight of intermediates in costs seems to be blurring the possibility that national firms –the more labour-intensive firms– could suffer more from the increase in the aggregate wage. Such an effect does not arise in the model results. This points to the importance of taking into account intersectoral links in order to grasp the effects of the entry of MNEs. Given the relevance of intermediates and its growth, as pointed out in the introductory chapter, this seems to be a nice characteristic of this type of computable general equilibrium models.

On the other hand, the sensitivity analysis presented does not alter the causation chain of adjustments across the economy, nor does it affect the main outcomes. Indeed, having simulated MNEs arrivals with extreme values for different elasticities, does not vary neither the aggregate nor sectoral results in a meaningful manner. What is more, changes tend to be very small and, in some cases, non-existent.

Another final conclusion is related to methodological aspects. It is the inclusion of both an aggregate and sectoral perspective which leads to a better understanding of the main outcomes obtained. Having both sides enables the policy-maker to better analyse which sectors are the most relevant in order to achieve an increase in welfare, and what the costs are for the rest of sectors involved in the process.

Chapter 5

SIMULATING THE ENTRY OF MULTINATIONALS WITH PROFIT REPATRIATION

ABSTRACT

This chapter offers a quantitative approximation to the effects of profit repatriation compared to those of the initial FDI inflows, which have been analysed in the previous chapter. We find that the negative effects of profit repatriation are sizeable, and might even offset the positive impact of the entry of MNEs. Our simulations suggest that for the Czech Republic, profit repatriation above 50 per cent of MNEs' income leads to a decrease in the GDP, although the exact amount changes according to the sector where the entry of MNEs takes place. Empirical data available on the magnitude of profit repatriation indicate that this is likely to be higher than such 50 per cent threshold. Our analysis offers not only the same set of variables analysed for the impact of the entry of MNEs without profit repatriation (for the sake of comparison), but also the evolution of aggregate variables for different levels of profit repatriation. Finally, as happened in Chapter 4, the sensitivity analysis leads to conclude that the results are robust for different values of the elasticities.

1. INTRODUCTION

Chapter 4 has dealt with the impact of an increase in the capital stock and the corresponding higher national income that MNEs bring about. As one would expect, overall effects were positive, although unevenly distributed across sectors. In this chapter we look at a nearly unexplored effect of MNEs, namely, profit repatriation. As suggested by Caves (2007, chapter 9), and noted in Chapter 1, it is clear that the initial FDI flows necessary for a MNE to arise bring financial resources to the host country. But in some moment the affiliate begins to remit the profits earned towards the parent company (or other affiliate of the group) and these earnings may be large compared to the initial injection of FDI flows. The aim of the analysis in this chapter is to offer a quantitative approximation to the effects of profit repatriation compared to those of the initial FDI inflows, which have been analysed in the previous chapter.

To the best of our knowledge, among CGE studies only Gilham (2005) and Brown and Stern (2001) consider profit repatriation. The former, however, focuses exclusively on its impact in tourism activities, whereas the latter authors include a form of profit repatriation, which is fixed at the 10 per cent level. Analyses with alternative methodologies are also scarce. Indeed, Ietto-Gillies (2000) points to the small number of studies available on the effects of profit repatriation, despite the important magnitude of the phenomenon. Interestingly, the main conclusion from her analysis is the existence of different patterns across EU countries as net income recipients or debtors, obtaining considerable variation even within this group of developed economies. These patterns are mainly related to the different inward/outward FDI positions of the countries which, in turn, are in accordance to their stage in the investment development path of Dunning and Narula (1998), commented in Chapter 2. The author also emphasizes the problems with data on earnings[19], the existing lag between FDI inflows and their corresponding incomes, and the dynamics that this lag brings about. The intertemporal nature of the relationship between FDI and its returns involves not only cross-country distributional considerations but also dynamic or intergenerational ones).

On the other hand, some studies relate profit repatriation with some particular variables. Most of them have focused on their negative impact for the balance of payments; e.g., Fajnzylber and Martínez Tarragó (1976) for

---

[19] One of the reasons for the problems that appear with data on earnings is that they may be manipulated through transfer prices (Vaitsos, 1975) or channelled through other balance of payments components, such as royalties and fees for services (Vaitsos, 1974; Fajnzylber and Martínez Tarragó, 1976). These practices, in turn, are related to the fiscal treatment of the operations of the MNEs in host countries, and represent a way of avoiding taxation (Muñoz, Roldán and Serrano, 1978).

Mexico or Martínez González-Tablas (1979) for Spain. More recently, Barry and Bradley (1997) point to the importance of the magnitude of profit repatriation in the Irish economy over the period 1990-1995. During that period profit repatriation in the balance of payments "amounted to between 10 and 12 percent of overall GDP and to between 20 and 30 percent of GDP arising in manufacturing" (p. 1801); the effects of this important figures are not analysed though. Jansen (1995) offers an interesting model on the macroeconomic effects of FDI in Thailand, but regarding profit repatriation she just reports on the negative impact of capital repatriation on the current account. However, no attention is paid to the relative magnitude of this effect versus that of a negative trade balance which takes place simultaneously in the data she analyses, which is also contributing to the negative current account; therefore, we are left with no idea regarding the impact of profit repatriation. Ihrig (2000) provides a theoretical model of how restrictions on profit repatriation affect the amount of capital investment that MNEs undertake in the host economy and their technology transfers. The model is consistent with the behaviour of US MNEs in Brazil during the 1980s, but there is no further analysis on the impact for the host economy. Finally, Seabra and Flach (2005) test for Granger-causality between FDI and profit repatriation for the case of Brazil, over the period 1979-2003. They found unidirectional causality from FDI to profit outflows, while the effect was particularly stronger after five years (indicating that it takes time for the new capital to become fully profitable and generate profit outflows). Summarising, there are just a few studies available dealing with profit repatriation, the majority of them offering a descriptive analysis; however, the analysis of its links to FDI inflows, and the joint impact on the host economies –i.e., the focus of our study– still remains a mostly unexplored issue.

On the other hand, data from the latest World Investment Report (UNCTAD, 2006) suggest that, by and large, since the mid-1990s MNEs tend to repatriate more than 50 percent of the total income they generate; see Figure 1. This report differentiates between MNEs coming from developing countries and those from developed ones. Repatriation from the former seems to have begun later (probably because activities of MNEs from developing countries themselves have been low till recently). However, they have soon joined the patterns of repatriation exhibited by MNEs from developed countries. We will see that this general level of profit repatriation above 50 percent of the income generated is an important threshold for the impact on the GDP of the host economy. The results from this chapter show that –in the Czech case– when repatriation exceeds the 50 percent threshold its effects offset the positive impact of FDI inflows and begin to produce a fall in GDP. This suggests that the phenomenon of profit repatriation may be of great importance.

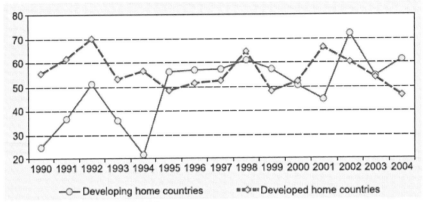

Source: UNCTAD (2006, p. 186).
Figure 1. Share of repatriated profits in total income on outward FDI flows (1990-2004).

Furthermore, in the last few years, the magnitude of profit repatriation seems to be increasing, which makes it worth to look at its impact. In particular, in the case of the Czech Republic, in 2003 profit repatriation, has exceeded the value of FDI inflows, i.e., loses from profit repatriation have exceeded the gains in financial resources derived from FDI inflows; see WIIW (several years). But we also know that data on profit repatriation may well underestimate the volume of incomes repatriated. The phenomenon is probably more important than what our data suggest. MNEs are more likely to make use of transfer prices than to giving information to fiscal authorities through the balance of payments. Unfortunately, there is not much information on transfer prices. In the absence of data on the "real" levels of profit repatriation, the potential for simulation of CGE models may offer an attractive way of exploring this issue of the impact of profit repatriation. Thus we will analyse different scenarios according to the level of profit repatriation.

The rest of the chapter is organised as follows. Section 2 explains how the simulation of profit repatriation has been implemented. Section 3 offers aggregate as well as sectoral results of the entry of MNEs with full profit repatriation. Section 4 looks at the impact on the main aggregate variables of different levels of profit repatriation. Section 5 presents a sensitivity analysis. Finally, section 6 provides some concluding remarks.

2. SIMULATING THE ENTRY OF MNES WITH FULL PROFIT REPATRIATION

The entry of MNEs leads to an increase in the capital endowment of the economy. In our simulations, this involves a capital increase in a particular sector, as we want to grasp the differential effects of MNEs according to the sector in which they operate. What we will consider in the new simulation is the effect of repatriation of the remuneration of the extra capital that the entry of MNEs adds. In other words, we continue assuming a 50 per cent increase in the capital stock of five particular sectors of the economy, as we did in the previous chapter, but now its remuneration will not be part of the income of the representative household of the host economy, but will increase the income of ROW. Note that we do not repatriate the remuneration of the already existing capital in any of the five sectors, but only the new addition of capital that the entry of MNEs we are simulating brings about. By comparing the results from Chapter 4 and Chapter 5 we have two extreme alternatives. In Chapter 4, all the remuneration of the extra capital remains in the host economy, whereas in Chapter 5 all the remuneration goes away, i.e., in the latter case we simulate *full* profit repatriation. As can be seen, strictly speaking, "profit repatriation" should be called "income repatriation", but we prefer to use that more common term (and will do it henceforth) once it is clear what we really denote.

We turn now to explain how the shock affects the equations of the model. The entry of MNEs will, as it did before, exogenously affect factor market equations (31*) and (32*), the total capital endowment (30*) and the price of this factor of production (9*) and (10) exactly as explained in the previous chapter, so we will not repeat that explanation here. Nevertheless, we should note that those changes in equations are also present in the model used for simulations along this chapter. The addition of profit repatriation just affects the representative households' income equations. We, therefore, concentrate on this aspect now.

Equation (23), which gives the value of the income available for private consumption in the standard GTAP model, will have, now, two different expressions, one for each of the two different regions. These appear in equations (23*) and (23*bis) for ROW and the host economy, respectively:

$$raINC_{ROW} = vb_{ROW} - \left(p_{ROW}^{G} \; \overline{vgm}_{ROW}\right) - \sum_{i}\left(p_{iROW}^{Y} \; \bar{I}_{ir}\right) \; +$$

$$\left(p^L_{ROW}\ evom_{LROW}\right) + \left(p^K_{ROW}\ \psi evom_{KROW}\right) +$$
$$+ revt^y_{ROW} + revt^L_{ROW} + revt^K_{ROW} + revt^{fd}_{ROW}$$
$$+ revt^{fm}_{ROW} + revt^{pd}_{ROW} + revt^{pm}_{ROW} +$$
$$+ revt^{gd}_{ROW} + revt^{gm}_{ROW} + revt^{xs}_{ROW} + revt^{ms}_{ROW}$$

$$+ \text{\%Profit Rep}_j\left(\left(FDIf_{KjH} - 1\right) p^K_H\ vfm^F_{KjH}\right) \qquad (23^*)$$

$$raINC_H = vb_H - \left(p^G_H\ \overline{vgm}_H\right) - \sum_i\left(p^Y_{iH}\ \bar{I}_{iH}\right) + \sum_f\left(p^f_r\ NEWevom_{fH}\right) +$$
$$+ \left(p^L_H\ evom_{LH}\right) + \left(p^K_H\ \psi evom_{KH}\right) +$$
$$+ revt^y_H + revt^L_H + revt^K_H + revt^{fd}_H + revt^{fm}_H + revt^{pd}_H + revt^{pm}_H +$$
$$+ revt^{gd}_H + revt^{gm}_H + revt^{xs}_H + revt^{ms}_H$$
$$- \text{\%Profit Rep}_j\left(\left(FDIf_{KjH} - 1\right) p^K_H\ vfm^F_{KjH}\right) \qquad (23^*\ bis)$$

The last lines in equations (23*) and (23*bis) are the only terms added to the original expression in equation (23), when we take into account the impact of profit repatriation. $FDIf_{Kjr}$ takes the value of one plus the percentage increase in the foreign capital stock held by MNEs of sector j; i.e., $FDIf_{KjH} = 1.5$ if j is the sector receiving MNEs, and $FDIf_{KjH} = 1$ otherwise. The parameter $\text{\%Profit Rep}_j$ indicates the percentage of extra capital in the foreign part of sector j, whose remuneration –i.e., $\left(FDIf_{KjH} - 1\right) p^K_H\ vfm^F_{KjH}$ – is sent from the host economy to ROW; i.e., $\text{\%Profit Rep}_j = 1$, except for the results in section 4, which consider different levels of profit repatriation ranging from 0 to 1.

The exogenous changes in the above equations will lead to a number of endogenous adjustments across the other equations of the model, namely, those for the factor and good markets, and the income of the representative agent. We go on now with how the adjustment takes place.

3. SIMULATION RESULTS

3.1. Aggregate Results

Table 1 shows the effects of the entry of MNEs when they repatriate all their income, together with those resulting from the mere entry of MNEs (i.e., those of Chapter 4), on the main aggregate variables. Each column gives the percentage change in real terms with respect to the benchmark in a particular aggregate variable. The variables considered are, as before: the real wage –the same in all sectors–; the real rental rate of capital –a weighted average of its price in all sectors–; the real GDP measured at factor costs; welfare, proxied by the change in real private consumption, which in turn, due to its Cobb-Douglas form, is the same as the variation in real income of the representative household[20]; the CPI[21]; and the real value of imports and exports (both measured at international prices).

As was the case in the previous chapter, the entry of MNEs brings about a decrease in the rental rate of capital together with an increase in the aggregate wage. Again, a higher volume of capital involves a lower marginal productivity of this production factor (i.e. its real rental rate diminishes) and a higher marginal productivity of labour (i.e., a higher real wage). As mentioned in Chapter 4, these results are consistent with the theory of international trade under the assumption of specific capital (i.e., Jones, 1971, 2000, 2002; Mussa, 1974; Neary, 1978).

Nevertheless, the additional effect that we now take into account, namely, profit repatriation, results in a reduction of the income available for the representative household. The circular flow of the economy implies that there is less income available for the remuneration of the domestic representative consumer, compared to Chapter 4 (see the column for welfare, showing that domestic income decreases in all scenarios). Consequently, in this simulation we obtain lower factor remunerations, i.e., the increase in the wage is smaller, and the decrease in the rental rate of capital is higher. This evolution of factor prices is an important force driving the results for GDP and welfare.

---

[20] See footnote 16 in Chapter 4.

[21] Regarding the inclusion of the CPI see footnotes 15 and 17 in Chapter 4.

Table 1. Simulation results: Effects on aggregate variables (percent change from benchmark)

	Wage		Rental rate of capital		GDP		Welfare		CPI		Imports		Exports	
	MNEs' entry	Profit Rep	MNEs' entry	Profit Rep	MNEs' entry	Profit Rep	MNEs' entry	Profit Rep	MNEs' entry	Profit Rep	MNEs' entry	Profit Rep	MNEs' entry	Profit Rep
Chemicals	0.23	0.17	-0.55	-0.64	0.30	-0.24	0.61	-0.39	0.08	-0.09	1.30	1.32	1.36	1.38
Motor vehicles	0.05	-0.06	-1.17	-1.30	0.11	-0.69	0.20	-1.28	-0.10	-0.35	0.59	0.62	0.61	0.65
Electronics	0.21	0.16	-0.34	-0.40	0.23	-0.12	0.40	-0.24	0.09	-0.02	0.93	0.95	0.97	0.98
Trade	0.09	0.02	-0.51	-0.61	0.27	-0.30	0.69	-0.38	-0.01	-0.20	0.18	0.20	0.19	0.21
Finance	0.20	0.10	-0.61	-0.71	0.35	-0.31	0.72	-0.52	-0.14	-0.35	0.50	0.52	0.52	0.54

Note: "MNE's entry" stands for the simulation without profit repatriation (see Chapter 4) and "Profit Rep" stands for the simulation with full profit repatriation.

As can be seen, GDP and welfare experience a small increase after the entry of MNEs when there is no profit repatriation, but fall unambiguously in all cases when there is full profit repatriation. The least favourable results are those for Motor vehicles, since in this case the amount of capital whose profit is repatriated is the highest among all sectors (see Table 1 of Chapter 4); in the opposite extreme, Electronics leads to the smallest fall in GDP, due to the smaller volume of capital involved in the shock.

The negative effect on welfare when there is full profit repatriation may seem surprising. For instance, in the well-known contribution of Mundell (1957), a positive (or null) welfare impact appears in a framework with profit repatriation. Mundell, however, assumes that both the incomes earned by domestic factors and commodities' prices are unchanged, and that all profits can be repatriated. In contrast, in our approach the general equilibrium model allows for changes in domestic factors' and commodities' prices, so national income can change not only due to changes in factor endowments. In the case of the mere entry of MNEs, the increase in the aggregate wage and the capital stock prevails over the fall in the rental rate of capital, leading to an increase in GDP and national income (the latter increasing welfare). Conversely, when there is full profit repatriation, the fall in the rental rate of capital, which now rewards only the stock of capital previous to the entry of more EMNs, prevails over the increase in the aggregate wage. In any event, recall that the previous results refer to the extreme case of *full* profit repatriation; we will find below the threshold levels of profit repatriation for which the effect on welfare becomes negative[22].

The general reduction in the CPI associated with profit repatriation would be due to the fall in aggregate demand following a reduction in income. In the absence of profit repatriation, we had seen different results for the CPI depending on the sector to which MNEs arrived.

Finally, the impact of profit repatriation on the value of exports and imports is small and the results are very similar to the case of no profit repatriation. Again, the key lies in the propensity to import of the sector to which MNEs arrive. The higher the share of this sector in aggregate imports of the Czech Republic (see Table 1 in Chapter 4), the higher the impact on total imports for that country. Exports of that sector also increase due to the fall in its price, thus driving aggregate exports up. Exports and imports values adjust

---

[22] Notice that Mundell (1957) briefly describes in p. 332 the case of changes in factors and commodities' prices, and confirms that world income would be reduced if capital was perfectly mobile among countries and profit repatriation occurred. This would make plausible a negative welfare effect on the host country.

under the constraint of a trade balance fixed in real terms, which matches the empirical evidence that the Czech Republic has exhibited trade deficits since the transition from communism took place (WIIW, several years). The impact on foreign trade for manufactures is higher than for the services sector.

Summing up, the introduction of profit repatriation leads to a very different panorama, as compared to the results in the previous chapter. The entry of MNEs may still benefit workers whose wages increase (except for the case of Motor vehicles). However, at the aggregate level the benefits of higher wages are offset by a larger fall in the remuneration of capital. This results in a decrease in GDP and welfare, whose magnitude slightly differs across sectors. Profit repatriation does not affect the volume of external trade.

3.2. Sectoral Analysis

Tables 2, 3, 4, and 5 show, respectively, the effects on production, prices, exports and imports for the twenty sectors representing the Czech economy, following the mere entry of MNEs (i.e., the results of Chapter 4), as well as when full profit repatriation is allowed in each of the five sectors selected. In both simulations, the first and main impact of the shock takes place in the particular sector receiving MNEs. Interestingly, the results for each of these five sectors are not significantly affected if profit repatriation is considered.

Recall that the amount of capital that the sector receiving MNEs uses increases considerably as a result of the shock. Therefore, its *production* will always rise (Table 2). The *price* of the good sold by this sector will diminish (Table 3) enhancing its competitiveness and, thus, increasing its *exports* (Table 4). Finally, *imports* also increase (Table 5), as more imported intermediates are used to increase the production in the sector directly involved in the shock.

For those sectors not directly involved in the shock *output* exhibits some general patterns across simulations (Table 2). Most manufacturing sectors tend to increase production after the entry of MNEs. By contrast, Food, Petroleum, and most services tend to decrease production. These patterns should be familiar. Output moves along with the demand side of the economy much in the same way as we explained in the previous chapter. There is a general tendency for exports to increase and for private consumption to decline, which underlies the sectoral patterns of production from Table 2. Let us see this in more detail.

As can be seen, in general, the shock causes an increase in domestic *prices* in all sectors across scenarios (Table 3). However, the CPI decreases in all simulations. The latter effect prevails, and, therefore, the shock causes a reduction in domestic prices *compared to foreign ones*. As a result, the export competitiveness of most sectors rises. There is a general increase in *exports* after the entry of MNEs (Table 4). This boosts production in most manufactures which are highly dependent on exports.

On the other hand, the evolution of private consumption just follows that of income. It will decline due to profit repatriation. As a consequence, those sectors whose production is more oriented to private consumption than to exports (see Figure 1 in Chapter 4) will experience a reduction in demand which will pull down their production levels.

The simulation of the entry of MNEs in Electronics deserves some comments. It may seem that it exhibits a different tendency to the one outlined above. It is true that most manufacturing sectors do not increase production after the entry of MNEs in this sector, as happened in the rest of simulations. However, note that even though production in manufactures still falls in this latter case, as it did in the simulation with zero profit repatriation, it falls by less now. Therefore, profit repatriation brings about an increase in production compared to the case of no profit repatriation. Note also that the decrease in production present in the simulation of profit repatriation of MNEs from Electronics is related to the general decrease in exports that takes place. Therefore, it is also following the demand pattern. Demand works differently for MNEs in Electronics, though, due to the smaller decrease in the CPI, which does not cause an increase in export competitiveness.

We should also note an exception to the otherwise demand driven production patterns we have identified. If the entry of MNEs takes place in the services sectors then production in the rest of services tends to increase. This occurs because intermediates linkages across services sectors are strong. As a consequence, the entry of MNEs in services pulls production up in the rest of services.

Finally, as we noted in the previous chapter, *imports* tend to follow the production pattern of their corresponding sector (Table 5). For those sectors decreasing production −those more responsive to private consumption− imports decrease. For most manufactures imports increase with production after the entry of MNEs in Motor vehicles, Trade, and Finance and decrease responding to a decrease in production in Electronics. Only in Chemicals are imports falling while production increases. But note that increases in production after the entry of MNEs in Chemicals are smaller than those taking place after the entry of MNEs in Motor vehicles, Trade, and Finance. If production increases by less in Chemicals its demand of imported intermediates may be smaller, or may even fall.

Table 2. Simulation results: Effects on sectoral production (percent change from benchmark)

	Chemicals		Motor Vehicles		Electronics		Trade		Finance	
	MNEs' entry	Profit Rep	MNEs' entry	Profit Rep	MNEs' entry	Profit Rep	MNEs' entry	Profit Rep	MNEs' entry	Profit Rep
Agriculture, hunting and fishing	-0.01	-0.02	0.03	0.02	-0.04	-0.05	0.06	0.05	0.06	0.05
Mining and quarrying	-0.01	0.00	0.00	0.02	-0.01	-0.01	0.00	0.01	0.00	0.02
Food, beverages and tobacco	0.24	-0.16	0.10	-0.49	0.13	-0.12	0.33	-0.09	0.36	-0.13
Textiles, wearing apparel, leather, footwear	-0.05	0.14	0.08	0.37	-0.31	-0.19	0.13	0.34	0.26	0.51
Wood and wood products, except furniture	-0.24	0.07	0.07	0.54	-0.31	-0.11	-0.01	0.32	0.11	0.50
Paper; printing and publishing	-0.12	0.06	0.07	0.35	-0.20	-0.08	0.02	0.22	0.23	0.47
Petroleum	0.16	-0.12	0.04	-0.33	0.09	-0.10	0.21	-0.11	0.22	-0.16
Chemicals, rubber and plastics	13.97	14.30	0.08	0.39	-0.21	-0.07	-0.01	0.21	0.12	0.38
Non-metallic mineral products	-0.14	0.09	0.08	0.43	-0.18	-0.03	0.00	0.25	0.12	0.41
Basic and fabricated metal products	-0.41	0.01	0.08	0.73	-0.42	-0.14	-0.04	0.42	0.20	0.74
Motor vehicles	-0.11	0.03	16.89	17.13	-0.12	-0.02	0.03	0.18	0.17	0.35
Other transport equipment	-0.16	0.01	0.29	0.55	-0.08	0.04	0.19	0.37	0.35	0.56
Electronics	-0.20	0.13	0.07	0.56	17.95	18.20	-0.01	0.34	0.21	0.62
Machinery and equipment n.e.c.	-0.18	0.02	1.80	2.12	-0.16	-0.02	0.06	0.28	0.24	0.50
Furniture, manufacturing n.e.c.	-0.05	0.04	0.08	0.22	-0.21	-0.15	0.14	0.23	0.24	0.35
Electricity, gas and water supply; construction	0.05	-0.12	0.09	-0.15	0.03	-0.08	0.23	0.06	0.33	0.13
Trade, repair; hotels and restaurants	0.06	-0.22	0.18	-0.22	0.00	-0.17	5.65	5.39	0.59	0.25
Transport, storage and communication	-0.12	-0.08	0.11	0.17	-0.13	-0.10	0.12	0.17	0.18	0.23
Finance, insurance, real estate, business activities	-0.02	-0.08	0.05	-0.02	-0.05	-0.08	0.10	0.04	2.12	2.05
Other services	0.03	-0.09	0.05	-0.13	0.00	-0.08	0.12	-0.01	0.18	0.03

Note: see Table 1.

Table 3. Simulation results: Effects on sectoral prices (percent change from benchmark)

	Chemicals		Motor Vehicles		Electronics		Trade		Finance	
	MNEs' entry	Profit Rep	MNEs' entry	Profit Rep	MNEs' entry	Profit Rep	MNEs' entry	Profit Rep	MNEs' entry	Profit Rep
Agriculture, hunting and fishing	0.05	0.01	0.11	0.05	0.01	-0.01	0.12	0.07	0.22	0.17
Mining and quarrying	-0.08	0.09	0.09	0.33	-0.09	0.02	0.02	0.19	0.14	0.34
Food, beverages and tobacco	0.13	-0.05	0.10	-0.17	0.09	-0.03	0.17	-0.02	0.23	0.01
Textiles, wearing apparel, leather, footwear	-0.03	0.04	0.09	0.19	-0.01	0.04	0.03	0.11	0.13	0.22
Wood and wood products, except furniture	-0.04	0.07	0.08	0.25	-0.04	0.03	0.02	0.14	0.13	0.26
Paper; printing and publishing	-0.03	0.06	0.09	0.22	-0.03	0.03	0.04	0.14	0.13	0.24
Petroleum	-0.05	0.06	0.09	0.25	-0.05	0.01	0.04	0.15	0.15	0.28
Chemicals, rubber and plastics	-2.33	-2.21	0.08	0.26	-0.05	0.03	0.03	0.16	0.13	0.28
Non-metallic mineral products	-0.05	0.08	0.08	0.28	-0.05	0.03	0.02	0.16	0.12	0.28
Basic and fabricated metal products	-0.03	0.09	0.08	0.25	-0.04	0.04	0.02	0.14	0.12	0.26
Motor vehicles	-0.04	0.08	-3.44	-3.26	-0.05	0.03	0.02	0.15	0.11	0.26
Other transport equipment	-0.04	0.08	0.06	0.24	-0.07	0.01	0.01	0.14	0.12	0.26
Electronics	-0.06	0.07	0.08	0.28	-1.92	-1.83	0.02	0.16	0.12	0.28
Machinery and equipment n.e.c.	-0.05	0.08	-0.13	0.07	-0.06	0.02	0.02	0.15	0.12	0.27
Furniture, manufacturing n.e.c.	-0.02	0.05	0.09	0.19	-0.02	0.03	0.04	0.11	0.14	0.22
Electricity, gas and water supply; construction	0.06	0.04	0.09	0.05	0.02	0.01	0.09	0.06	0.16	0.13
Trade, repair; hotels and restaurants	0.13	0.03	0.06	-0.08	0.09	0.03	-2.75	-2.84	0.09	-0.03
Transport, storage and communication	0.05	0.07	0.06	0.09	0.02	0.03	0.04	0.06	0.13	0.15
Finance, insurance, real estate, business activities	0.07	0.01	0.07	-0.03	0.03	-0.01	0.11	0.04	-1.48	-1.54
Other services	0.12	0.07	0.07	-0.01	0.10	0.07	0.07	0.01	0.07	0.00

Note: see Table 1.

Table 4. Simulation results: Effects on sectoral exports (percent change from benchmark)

	Chemicals		Motor vehicles		Electronics		Trade		Finance	
	MNEs' entry	Profit Rep	MNEs' entry	Profit Rep	MNEs' entry	Profit Rep	MNEs' entry	Profit Rep	MNEs' entry	Profit Rep
Agriculture, hunting and fishing	-0.57	0.36	-0.03	1.36	-0.46	0.14	-0.46	0.54	-0.37	0.78
Mining and quarrying	-0.04	0.02	0.00	0.09	-0.03	0.01	-0.03	0.04	-0.03	0.05
Food, beverages and tobacco	-1.01	0.65	-0.02	2.49	-0.83	0.24	-0.73	1.05	-0.45	1.61
Textiles, wearing apparel, leather, footwear	-0.35	0.35	0.04	1.10	-0.57	-0.11	-0.14	0.62	0.06	0.93
Wood and wood products, except furniture	-0.28	0.09	0.05	0.62	-0.33	-0.08	-0.07	0.34	0.05	0.52
Paper; printing and publishing	-0.28	0.14	0.02	0.66	-0.32	-0.04	-0.14	0.31	0.07	0.60
Petroleum	-0.12	0.12	0.00	0.35	-0.13	0.03	-0.11	0.16	-0.05	0.27
Chemicals rubber and plastics	15.09	15.38	0.05	0.49	-0.25	-0.06	-0.08	0.23	0.05	0.41
Non-metallic mineral products	-0.15	0.05	0.04	0.34	-0.20	-0.07	-0.03	0.19	0.07	0.32
Basic and fabricated metal products	-0.34	0.01	0.06	0.59	-0.34	-0.11	-0.04	0.34	0.15	0.59
Motor vehicles	-0.20	0.05	21.26	21.71	-0.21	-0.04	-0.03	0.24	0.15	0.47
Other transport equipment	-0.30	0.11	0.24	0.86	-0.19	0.08	0.03	0.47	0.20	0.70
Electronics	-0.22	0.13	0.05	0.59	17.11	17.37	-0.05	0.33	0.16	0.60
Machinery and equipment n.e.c.	-0.24	0.07	1.70	2.17	-0.20	0.00	-0.01	0.32	0.18	0.56
Furniture; manufacturing n.e.c.	-0.44	0.29	0.04	1.14	-0.53	-0.05	-0.21	0.58	-0.03	0.88
Electricity, gas and water supply; construction	-0.68	0.24	0.00	1.38	-0.53	0.07	-0.35	0.64	-0.10	1.04
Trade, repair; hotels and restaurants	-0.80	0.20	0.12	1.64	-0.68	-0.02	11.22	12.40	0.18	1.43
Transport, storage and communication	-0.36	0.06	0.09	0.73	-0.32	-0.04	-0.07	0.39	0.03	0.56
Finance, insurance, real estate, business activities	-0.58	0.31	0.08	1.44	-0.47	0.12	-0.35	0.60	6.37	7.47
Other services	-0.75	0.09	0.09	1.37	-0.73	-0.18	-0.22	0.69	0.27	1.33

Note: see Table 1.

To sum up, as in the simulations performed in Chapter 4, the entry of MNEs leads to an important impact in the sector where they arrive. Its evolution continues to be rather clear: production, exports and imports increase while the price falls. The impact for the rest of sectors in the economy tends to be small. Some clear patterns arise following the demand side of the model. Manufacturing sectors increase their output levels, compared to those obtained in the previous simulation. These sectors experience a favourable price evolution, due to the entry of MNEs, which boosts their exports. On the contrary, the sectors linked to private consumption tend to lose due to profit repatriation. The level of imports across sectors tends to move along with the production pattern of the corresponding sector.

Table 6 offers data on output responses of national and MNEs in each sector. As in the previous chapter, these do not seem to be consistent with different labour intensities across sectors or within the same sector. Recall the important weight of intermediates in total costs of production (Figure 2 in Chapter 4).

Tables 7 to 11 offer the evolution of prices for national firms and MNEs, together with their corresponding factor and intermediate costs. There is a certain tendency for factor costs to increase by more in national firms due to their more labour intensive technologies. However, there are exceptions to this. It is even less clear than in the previous chapter that the final price charged by national firms is higher. The reason for this latter result is that as the CPI is falling in all scenarios, MNEs which rely more on imported intermediates than national firms, experience higher increases in intermediate costs (this is particularly clear for Motor vehicles and Finance, simulations in which the fall in the CPI is stronger). The higher increase in intermediate costs pulls the prices of MNEs up. As a consequence, for the entry of MNEs in Motor vehicles and Finance, prices of MNEs tend to be higher than the ones in national firms. For the rest of scenarios the levels of the prices of national firms versus those of MNEs do not exhibit a clear tendency.

Table 5. Simulation results: Effects on sectoral imports (percent change from benchmark)

	Chemicals		Motor vehicles		Electronics		Trade		Finance	
	MNEs' entry	Profit Rep	MNEs' entry	Profit Rep	MNEs' entry	Profit Rep	MNEs' entry	Profit Rep	MNEs' entry	Profit Rep
Agriculture, hunting and fishing	0.31	-0.23	0.05	-0.74	0.22	-0.13	0.31	-0.27	0.26	-0.40
Mining and quarrying	0.06	-0.05	0.01	-0.15	0.04	-0.03	0.07	-0.05	0.06	-0.07
Food, beverages and tobacco	0.83	-0.56	0.11	-1.94	0.61	-0.29	0.76	-0.72	0.62	-1.08
Textiles, wearing apparel, leather, footwear	0.30	-0.20	0.07	-0.67	0.13	-0.19	0.35	-0.19	0.34	-0.27
Wood and wood products, except furniture	-0.06	-0.03	0.04	0.09	-0.12	-0.10	0.06	0.10	0.11	0.15
Paper; printing and publishing	0.07	-0.07	0.06	-0.15	-0.01	-0.10	0.15	0.00	0.25	0.08
Petroleum	0.25	-0.21	0.05	-0.56	0.18	-0.12	0.29	-0.22	0.26	-0.34
Chemicals, rubber and plastics	10.24	10.26	0.07	0.03	-0.07	-0.09	0.08	0.05	0.16	0.13
Non-metallic mineral products	-0.06	0.09	0.08	0.30	-0.06	0.04	0.04	0.19	0.11	0.29
Basic and fabricated metal products	-0.30	-0.04	0.02	0.42	-0.32	-0.15	-0.05	0.23	0.10	0.43
Motor vehicles	0.06	-0.01	3.87	3.79	0.07	0.02	0.12	0.05	0.14	0.05
Other transport equipment	0.05	-0.09	0.17	-0.03	0.05	-0.04	0.23	0.08	0.29	0.12
Electronics	-0.07	0.06	0.08	0.28	10.55	10.66	0.07	0.21	0.21	0.38
Machinery and equipment n.e.c.	0.01	-0.07	0.79	0.69	-0.01	-0.06	0.13	0.05	0.19	0.10
Furniture, manufacturing n.e.c.	0.31	-0.22	0.07	-0.71	0.17	-0.17	0.35	-0.21	0.33	-0.32
Electricity, gas and water supply; construction	0.38	-0.30	0.06	-0.93	0.26	-0.18	0.39	-0.33	0.34	-0.49
Trade, repair; hotels and restaurants	0.46	-0.35	0.11	-1.08	0.32	-0.20	1.43	0.60	0.49	-0.49
Transport, storage and communication	0.15	-0.11	0.04	-0.35	0.11	-0.06	0.17	-0.11	0.15	-0.17
Finance, insurance, real estate, business activities	0.29	-0.20	0.10	-0.61	0.20	-0.12	0.32	-0.19	2.67	2.06
Other services	0.47	-0.15	0.02	-0.91	0.41	0.01	0.29	-0.38	0.09	-0.68

Note: see Table 1.

Table 6. Simulation results: Effects on gross production of national firms and MNEs (percent change from benchmark)

	Chemicals		Motor vehicles		Electronics		Trade		Finance	
	MNEs	National firms	MNEs	National firms	MNEs	National firms	MNEs	National firms	MNEs	National firms
Agriculture, hunting and fishing	0.00	-0.02	0.06	0.02	-0.01	-0.05	0.02	0.05	0.03	0.05
Mining and quarrying	0.00	0.00	0.01	0.02	0.00	-0.01	0.00	0.01	0.01	0.02
Food, beverages and tobacco	-0.12	-0.18	-0.21	-0.61	-0.16	-0.10	-0.06	-0.11	-0.06	-0.16
Textiles, wearing apparel, leather, footwear	0.01	0.18	0.22	0.43	-0.18	-0.19	0.16	0.40	0.25	0.60
Wood and wood products, except furniture	-0.01	0.09	0.27	0.62	-0.10	-0.11	0.14	0.38	0.22	0.59
Paper; printing and publishing	-0.01	0.12	0.25	0.43	-0.18	0.01	0.15	0.28	0.39	0.53
Petroleum	0.01	-0.12	0.52	-0.34	0.00	-0.10	0.08	-0.12	0.09	-0.16
Chemicals, rubber and plastics	27.10	4.79	0.30	0.46	-0.15	-0.01	0.14	0.25	0.30	0.44
Non-metallic mineral products	0.00	0.18	0.32	0.54	-0.18	0.12	0.17	0.33	0.33	0.48
Basic and fabricated metal products	-0.14	0.06	0.21	0.89	-0.26	-0.10	0.08	0.53	0.21	0.90
Motor vehicles	0.01	0.12	20.76	0.47	-0.06	0.15	0.18	0.20	0.37	0.24
Other transport equipment	-0.02	0.02	0.34	0.63	-0.02	0.06	0.21	0.43	0.32	0.64
Electronics	0.11	0.16	0.58	0.53	26.06	4.81	0.35	0.33	0.67	0.53
Machinery and equipment n.e.c.	0.02	0.03	0.99	2.59	-0.01	-0.03	0.17	0.33	0.28	0.60
Furniture, manufacturing n.e.c.	-0.03	0.07	0.14	0.26	-0.16	-0.14	0.12	0.28	0.19	0.42
Electricity, gas and water supply; construction	-0.22	-0.10	-0.11	-0.16	-0.27	-0.05	-0.07	0.07	-0.05	0.15
Trade, repair; hotels and restaurants	-0.34	-0.16	-0.34	-0.17	-0.39	-0.08	13.81	1.64	0.02	0.36
Transport, storage and communication	0.02	-0.09	0.23	0.17	0.01	-0.11	0.12	0.18	0.16	0.24
Finance, insurance, real estate, business activities	-0.01	-0.10	0.13	-0.07	-0.01	-0.10	0.12	0.02	9.34	-0.08
Other services	0.19	-0.09	0.46	-0.13	0.25	-0.08	0.28	-0.01	0.34	0.03

Table 7. Simulation results: Effects on factor and intermediate costs and prices of national firms and MNEs of the entry of MNEs in Chemicals (percent change from benchmark)

	MNEs			National firms		
	Factors' costs	Intermediates' Costs	Price	Factors' costs	Intermediates' costs	Price
Agriculture, hunting and fishing	0.15	0.07	0.10	0.07	-0.04	0.01
Mining and quarrying	0.10	0.03	0.09	0.14	0.01	0.09
Food, beverages and tobacco	-0.18	-0.01	-0.08	-0.04	-0.03	-0.03
Textiles, wearing apparel, leather, footwear	0.17	0.04	0.08	0.26	-0.08	0.02
Wood and wood products, except furniture	0.16	0.00	0.04	0.24	0.00	0.08
Paper; printing and publishing	0.15	0.00	0.05	0.26	-0.02	0.07
Petroleum	0.33	0.03	0.04	-0.18	0.07	0.06
Chemicals, rubber and plastics	-21.08	-0.14	-5.65	4.70	-0.61	0.64
Non-metallic mineral products	0.16	-0.01	0.06	0.29	-0.03	0.10
Basic and fabricated metal products	0.06	0.05	0.05	0.20	0.05	0.10
Motor vehicles	0.17	0.06	0.07	0.22	0.09	0.10
Other transport equipment	0.16	0.09	0.09	0.18	0.05	0.07
Electronics	0.25	0.02	0.07	0.25	-0.03	0.07
Machinery and equipment n.e.c.	0.18	0.07	0.09	0.19	0.05	0.08
Furniture, manufacturing n.e.c.	0.13	-0.01	0.03	0.21	-0.02	0.05
Electricity, gas and water supply; construction	-0.05	-0.01	-0.02	0.07	0.04	0.04
Trade, repair; hotels and restaurants	-0.05	0.06	0.00	0.08	0.02	0.05
Transport, storage and communication	0.19	0.09	0.12	0.09	0.04	0.06
Finance, insurance, real estate, business activities	0.16	0.04	0.09	-0.04	0.01	-0.02
Other services	0.23	-0.06	0.09	0.14	-0.01	0.06

Table 8. Simulation results: Effects on factor and intermediate costs and prices of national firms and MNEs of the entry of MNEs in Motor vehicles (percent change from benchmark)

	MNEs			National firms		
	Factors' costs	Intermediates' Costs	Price	Factors' costs	Intermediates' Costs	Price
Agriculture, hunting and fishing	0.19	0.30	0.26	0.01	0.07	0.05
Mining and quarrying	0.39	0.16	0.36	0.51	0.09	0.33
Food, beverages and tobacco	-0.65	0.17	-0.16	-0.75	0.01	-0.17
Textiles, wearing apparel, leather, footwear	0.06	0.31	0.25	0.15	0.18	0.17
Wood and wood products, except furniture	0.20	0.23	0.22	0.45	0.15	0.25
Paper; printing and publishing	0.29	0.21	0.24	0.27	0.18	0.21
Petroleum	0.75	0.25	0.27	-1.03	0.29	0.25
Chemicals, rubber and plastics	0.35	0.25	0.28	0.38	0.22	0.25
Non-metallic mineral products	0.48	0.21	0.32	0.32	0.18	0.24
Basic and fabricated metal products	0.11	0.28	0.23	0.38	0.21	0.26
Motor vehicles	-24.07	-0.56	-3.99	0.15	0.33	0.31
Other transport equipment	0.17	0.34	0.33	0.38	0.18	0.21
Electronics	0.38	0.27	0.29	0.22	0.26	0.25
Machinery and equipment n.e.c.	0.81	0.32	0.38	2.37	-0.50	-0.06
Furniture, manufacturing n.e.c.	0.12	0.26	0.22	0.10	0.20	0.17
Electricity, gas and water supply; construction	-0.16	0.17	0.08	-0.21	0.15	0.05
Trade, repair; hotels and restaurants	-0.28	0.15	-0.06	-0.14	-0.05	-0.09
Transport, storage and communication	0.21	0.32	0.29	0.07	0.07	0.07
Finance, insurance, real estate, business activities	0.00	0.24	0.15	-0.19	0.02	-0.08
Other services	0.10	0.25	0.17	-0.10	0.08	-0.02

**Table 9. Simulation results: Effects on factor and intermediate costs
and prices of national firms and MNEs of the entry of MNEs
in Electronics (percent change from benchmark)**

	MNEs			National firms		
	Factors' Costs	Intermediates' Costs	Price	Factors' costs	Intermediates' Costs	Price
Agriculture, hunting and fishing	0.11	0.02	0.05	-0.03	0.00	-0.01
Mining and quarrying	0.02	0.02	0.02	0.04	0.00	0.02
Food, beverages and tobacco	-0.29	0.01	-0.11	0.05	-0.01	0.01
Textiles, wearing apparel, leather, footwear	0.07	0.02	0.03	0.07	0.02	0.04
Wood and wood products, except furniture	0.07	0.02	0.03	0.07	0.01	0.03
Paper; printing and publishing	-0.10	0.02	-0.02	0.17	0.02	0.07
Petroleum	0.22	0.02	0.03	-0.12	0.02	0.01
Chemicals, rubber and plastics	-0.05	0.02	0.00	0.15	0.02	0.05
Non-metallic mineral products	-0.14	0.02	-0.05	0.25	0.02	0.11
Basic and fabricated metal products	-0.04	0.02	0.00	0.12	0.02	0.05
Motor vehicles	0.09	0.01	0.02	0.23	0.02	0.05
Other transport equipment	0.15	0.02	0.03	0.20	-0.04	0.00
Electronics	-12.67	-0.36	-3.31	2.65	0.00	0.93
Machinery and equipment n.e.c.	0.15	0.00	0.02	0.14	0.00	0.02
Furniture, manufacturing n.e.c.	-0.04	0.02	0.00	0.08	0.02	0.04
Electricity, gas and water supply; construction	-0.11	-0.09	-0.09	0.11	-0.02	0.02
Trade, repair; hotels and restaurants	-0.09	0.01	-0.04	0.12	0.00	0.05
Transport, storage and communication	0.18	0.02	0.07	0.07	0.00	0.03
Finance, insurance, real estate, business activities	0.16	-0.01	0.06	-0.05	-0.02	-0.03
Other services	0.25	0.02	0.14	0.14	-0.01	0.07

Table 10. Simulation results: Effects on factor and intermediate costs and prices of national firms and MNEs of the entry of MNEs in Trade (percent change from benchmark)

	MNEs			National firms		
	Factors' Costs	Intermediates' costs	Price	Factors' costs	Intermediates' costs	Price
Agriculture, hunting and fishing	0.12	0.16	0.15	0.21	-0.01	0.07
Mining and quarrying	0.24	-0.04	0.19	0.32	0.02	0.19
Food, beverages and tobacco	-0.14	0.04	-0.03	-0.11	0.01	-0.02
Textiles, wearing apparel, leather, footwear	0.10	0.14	0.13	0.21	0.05	0.10
Wood and wood products, except furniture	0.15	0.08	0.10	0.32	0.07	0.15
Paper; printing and publishing	0.23	0.10	0.15	0.23	0.08	0.13
Petroleum	0.41	0.15	0.16	-0.32	0.17	0.15
Chemicals, rubber and plastics	0.21	0.14	0.16	0.26	0.12	0.16
Non-metallic mineral products	0.30	0.10	0.18	0.25	0.07	0.14
Basic and fabricated metal products	0.08	0.13	0.11	0.28	0.10	0.15
Motor vehicles	0.23	0.13	0.14	0.11	0.19	0.18
Other transport equipment	0.16	0.19	0.19	0.32	0.08	0.12
Electronics	0.28	0.13	0.17	0.19	0.10	0.13
Machinery and equipment n.e.c.	0.17	0.16	0.17	0.33	0.12	0.15
Furniture, manufacturing n.e.c.	0.17	0.09	0.11	0.19	0.07	0.11
Electricity, gas and water supply; construction	-0.06	-0.03	-0.04	0.09	0.07	0.07
Trade, repair; hotels and restaurants	-18.29	-0.01	-9.13	0.86	-0.27	0.23
Transport, storage and communication	0.15	0.13	0.14	0.16	-0.03	0.05
Finance, insurance, real estate, business activities	0.07	0.06	0.06	0.06	0.00	0.03
Other services	0.11	0.02	0.07	0.01	0.01	0.01

Table 11. Simulation results: Effects on factor and intermediate costs and prices of national firms and MNEs of the entry of MNEs in Finance (percent change from benchmark)

	MNEs			National firms		
	Factors' costs	Intermediates' costs	Price	Factors' costs	Intermediates' costs	Price
Agriculture, hunting and fishing	0.25	0.31	0.28	0.31	0.08	0.17
Mining and quarrying	0.42	0.02	0.36	0.57	0.03	0.34
Food, beverages and tobacco	-0.07	0.10	0.03	-0.08	0.03	0.00
Textiles, wearing apparel, leather, footwear	0.23	0.31	0.29	0.40	0.10	0.19
Wood and wood products, except furniture	0.31	0.18	0.22	0.58	0.12	0.28
Paper; printing and publishing	0.65	0.10	0.28	0.50	0.05	0.19
Petroleum	0.64	0.14	0.16	-0.37	0.30	0.28
Chemicals, rubber and plastics	0.51	0.23	0.30	0.52	0.18	0.26
Non-metallic mineral products	0.65	0.13	0.34	0.45	0.09	0.23
Basic and fabricated metal products	0.27	0.23	0.24	0.54	0.14	0.26
Motor vehicles	0.54	0.19	0.24	0.21	0.35	0.33
Other transport equipment	0.32	0.35	0.34	0.56	0.17	0.23
Electronics	0.61	0.19	0.29	0.38	0.18	0.25
Machinery and equipment n.e.c.	0.35	0.30	0.31	0.67	0.19	0.26
Furniture, manufacturing n.e.c.	0.34	0.21	0.25	0.37	0.14	0.21
Electricity, gas and water supply; construction	0.05	0.04	0.04	0.24	0.10	0.14
Trade, repair; hotels and restaurants	0.11	0.27	0.19	0.29	-0.44	-0.12
Transport, storage and communication	0.29	0.33	0.32	0.29	0.02	0.13
Finance, insurance, real estate, business activities	-13.84	0.27	-5.30	-0.06	-0.70	-0.39
Other services	0.22	0.24	0.23	0.11	-0.14	0.00

4. EFFECTS OF DIFFERENT LEVELS OF PROFIT REPATRIATION

In this section we look at how different levels of profit repatriation affect the main aggregate variables. More precisely, we present four Figures showing the percentage changes with respect to the benchmark of the wage, the rental rate of capital, GDP and welfare. Repatriation levels rank from no repatriation at all (i.e., results from Chapter 4) to full profit repatriation (i.e., previous results in this chapter). We, thus, cover the intermediate values between the two extreme results analysed.

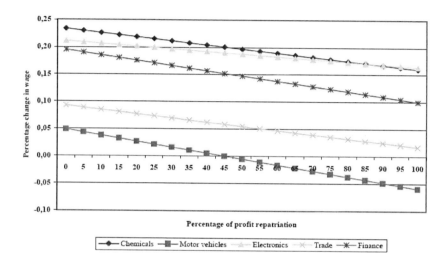

Figure 2. Effects on the wage of different levels of profit repatriation.

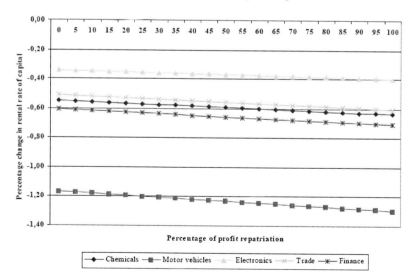

Figure 3. Effects on the rental rate of capital of different levels of profit repatriation.

Figure 2 shows the evolution of the wage. The higher the amount of profits repatriated the smaller the increases in the wage that the entry of MNEs brings about. This tends to happen at a similar rate for most sectors. It is remarkable, however, that for Motor vehicles beyond profit repatriation of approximately 45 per cent of capital remuneration, the wage begins to decrease with respect to its benchmark value. In the opposite extreme for Electronics profit repatriation is less harmful for the wage. The rate of decrease in percentage increases with respect to the benchmark is slower than for the rest of sectors. This is related to the smaller amount of capital involved in profit repatriation in this sector which accounts for a small part of capital from the Czech Republic.

Figure 3 shows the evolution of the rental rate of capital. The level of profit repatriation exerts a rather small influence on the percentage change of this variable. The amount of the fall in the rental rate of capital is related to the amount of capital involved in the shock. Thus, we obtain that for Electronics the fall is small whereas it is higher for Motor vehicles.

Figure 4 shows the evolution of the GDP. In general, when more than half of capital remuneration is repatriated GDP growth turns negative. No wonder that negative GDP growth appears earlier (after 15 per cent repatriation) in Motor vehicles. On the contrary, the entry of MNEs in Electronics yields negative GDP growth after higher levels of profits repatriation (65-70 per cent), and the percentage falls are smaller.

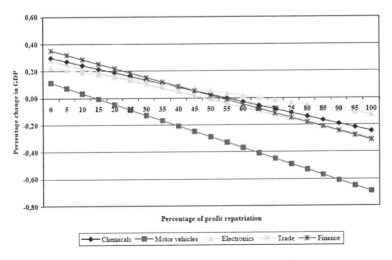

Figure 4. Effects on GDP of different levels of profit repatriation.

Finally, Figure 5 provides the evolution of welfare. In general it goes down, always compared to benchmark levels, for a slightly higher level of profit repatriation than that necessary for the increase in GDP to turn negative (around 60 per cent). Motor vehicles follows its usual less favourable tendency. Reductions in welfare after the entry of MNEs in this sector appear for smaller levels of profit repatriation (around 15 per cent). The entry of MNEs in Electronics with zero profit repatriation had led to slower increases in welfare but profit repatriation is less harmful for welfare in this sector (as happened with GDP).

All in all, the higher the level of profit repatriation, the lower the remunerations of factors of production tend to be, and consequently, the lower the levels of GDP and welfare, which are likely to decrease with respect to their benchmark level. The larger the amount of capital involved in the shock the more intense these tendencies are, and vice versa.

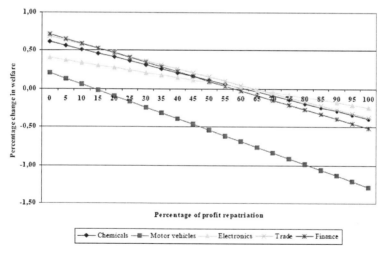

Figure 5. Effects on welfare of different levels of profit repatriation.

5. SENSITIVITY ANALYSIS

We check now the robustness of the results. We will follow the same procedure of Chapter 4, i.e., we double and halve the initial values of three crucial elasticities and rerun the simulations of this chapter. These elasticities are: 1) the elasticity of substitution between imports and domestic production

(Armington elasticity); 2) the elasticity of substitution between national and foreign firms' production; and 3) the elasticity of substitution between labour and capital.

Table 12 shows the effects on aggregate variables. Differences between the two extreme values of elasticities are small for the elasticity of substitution between imports and domestic production (Table 12A), tiny for the elasticity of substitution between national firms versus MNEs' production (Table 12B) and non-existent for the elasticity of substitution between labour and capital (Table 12C).

Regarding the Armington elasticity, the higher its value, the higher factor remunerations tend to be and with them GDP and welfare. The lower the elasticity, the higher the volume of foreign trade is. These logical results are the same as those obtained in Chapter 4. For the elasticity of substitution between national firms versus MNEs' production, as with the Armington elasticity, the higher its value the higher factor prices, GDP and welfare are. Although, percentage changes for this latter elasticity are really small. Nevertheless, in contrast with the Armington elasticity, the value of foreign trade is not determined by a higher or smaller value of the elasticity of substitution between national firms versus MNEs' production.

As noticed in Chapter 4, the reason for a higher wage, with the higher value of these two elasticities, is due to the impact on the sectors receiving MNEs. The sector to which MNEs arrive increases production by more the higher the elasticity is (although the percentage increase is very small for the elasticity of substitution between national firms and MNEs' production). Therefore, it is demanding more labour to produce more, leaving less labour available for the rest of sectors, which pushes the wage up.

With respect to the sectoral results, let us begin with changes in the Armington elasticity in the sector receiving MNEs. The higher the value of this elasticity, the larger *output* is (Table 13A), which means that more labour is being employed in that sector, compared to the amount of labour employed with the lower value of the elasticity. In contrast, the *price* of the good sold experiences a very similar reduction for the two extreme values of the elasticity (Table 13B). *Exports* decrease for the higher value of the elasticity because production will be more devoted to the domestic market instead of being exported (Table 13C). This tendency to rely more on domestic goods can also be seen in the evolution of imports. For the higher value of the elasticity, *imports* are also reduced because domestic varieties (which are cheaper compared to the benchmark) are more demanded when substitution between imports and domestic production is easier (Table 13D).

On the other hand, *output* tends to decrease, in general, in the sectors not directly involved in the shock for the high value of the elasticity compared to the low one (Table 13A). This is related to the evolution of exports, to be seen below, which exerts a lower demand pull on sectoral production. It is also related to the smaller amount of labour available for production because of the increase in output in the sector receiving MNEs. *Prices* are very similar for the two extreme values of the elasticities (Table 13B), but the reduction in the CPI is smaller with the higher elasticity so *exports* increase by less in that case (Table 13C). Due to the lower level of production the amount of *imports* is also lower for the highest elasticity (Table 13D).

Table 12. Sensitivity analysis: Effects on aggregate variables of changes in elasticities (percent change from benchmark)

A) Elasticity of substitution between imports and domestic production

		Wage	Rental rate of capital	GDP	Welfare	CPI	Imports	Exports
Chemicals	Half	0.14	-0.67	-0.27	-0.44	-0.11	1.47	1.53
	Double	0.20	-0.59	-0.20	-0.32	-0.06	1.12	1.16
Motor vehicles	Half	-0.09	-1.34	-0.73	-1.33	-0.40	0.88	0.92
	Double	-0.01	-1.23	-0.63	-1.21	-0.29	0.22	0.23
Electronics	Half	0.15	-0.41	-0.13	-0.26	-0.03	1.02	1.06
	Double	0.19	-0.39	-0.10	-0.21	-0.01	0.83	0.87
Trade	Half	-0.03	-0.63	-0.34	-0.43	-0.24	0.33	0.34
	Double	0.09	-0.58	-0.25	-0.32	-0.14	0.04	0.04
Finance	Half	0.07	-0.74	-0.35	-0.57	-0.39	0.70	0.72
	Double	0.09	-0.59	-0.25	-0.43	-0.26	0.25	0.26

B) Elasticity of substitution between nacional firms and MNEs' production

		Wage	Rental rate of capital	GDP	Welfare	CPI	Imports	Exports
Chemicals	Half	0.15	-0.65	-0.26	-0.09	-0.42	1.31	1.36
	Double	0.19	-0.61	-0.22	-0.08	-0.34	1.35	1.41
Motor vehicles	Half	-0.06	-1.30	-0.69	-0.35	-1.29	0.62	0.65
	Double	-0.05	-1.29	-0.68	-0.35	-1.27	0.62	0.65
Electronics	Half	0.16	-0.40	-0.13	-0.02	-0.25	0.94	0.98
	Double	0.17	-0.39	-0.11	-0.02	-0.23	0.96	0.99
Trade	Half	0.00	-0.62	-0.31	-0.20	-0.41	0.21	0.22
	Double	0.05	-0.59	-0.27	-0.18	-0.32	0.18	0.19
Finance	Half	0.10	-0.73	-0.32	-0.35	-0.54	0.52	0.54
	Double	0.11	-0.68	-0.29	-0.34	-0.48	0.51	0.53

C) Elasticity of substitution between labour and capital

		Wage	Rental rate of capital	GDP	Welfare	CPI	Imports	Exports
Chemicals	Half	0.17	-0.64	-0.24	-0.39	-0.09	1.32	1.38
	Double	0.17	-0.64	-0.24	-0.39	-0.09	1.32	1.38
Motor vehicles	Half	-0.06	-1.30	-0.69	-1.29	-0.35	0.62	0.65
	Double	-0.06	-1.30	-0.69	-1.28	-0.35	0.62	0.65
Electronics	Half	0.16	-0.40	-0.12	-0.24	-0.02	0.95	0.98
	Double	0.16	-0.40	-0.12	-0.24	-0.02	0.95	0.98
Trade	Half	0.02	-0.61	-0.30	-0.38	-0.20	0.20	0.21
	Double	0.02	-0.61	-0.30	-0.38	-0.20	0.20	0.21
Finance	Half	0.10	-0.71	-0.31	-0.52	-0.35	0.52	0.54
	Double	0.10	-0.71	-0.31	-0.52	-0.35	0.52	0.54

Note that Food and Petroleum experience a less intense reduction in production with the higher value of the Armington elasticity because there is more income available for private consumption.

For the other two elasticities, changes are either tiny regarding sectoral results (in the case of the elasticity of substitution between national firms versus MNEs' production in Table 14) or non-existent (for the elasticity of substitution between labour and capital in Table 15). This is consistent with the macroeconomic panorama shown above.

For a higher value of the elasticity of substitution between national firms and MNEs' production the level of *output* in the sector receiving MNEs is slightly higher (Table 14A). The *price* of the good sold by this sector tends to fall by more for a higher value of this elasticity with respect to the benchmark (although the difference for the two extreme values is tiny, see Table 14B). The smaller price with the higher elasticity (together with a CPI which remains nearly unchanged) increases the volume of *exports* very slightly (Table 14C). Finally, the volume of *imports* is also slightly higher with the higher elasticity following a higher production level in the sector receiving MNEs (Table 14D).

Table 13. Sensitivity analysis: Effects on sectoral variables of changes in the elasticity of substitution between imports and domestic production (percent change from benchmark)

A) Effects on sectoral output

	Chemicals		Motor vehicles		Electronics		Trade		Finance	
	Half	Double	Half	Double	Half	Double	Half	Double	Half	Double
Agriculture, hunting and fishing	-0.02	-0.03	0.00	0.03	-0.05	-0.05	0.05	0.03	0.05	0.05
Mining and quarrying	0.00	0.00	0.03	0.02	0.00	-0.01	0.02	0.01	0.02	0.01
Food, beverages and tobacco	-0.18	-0.14	-0.54	-0.42	-0.13	-0.11	-0.11	-0.08	-0.16	-0.08
Textiles, wearing apparel, leather, footwear	0.20	0.05	0.42	0.29	-0.16	-0.24	0.43	0.19	0.58	0.40
Wood and wood products. except furniture	0.13	-0.02	0.63	0.41	-0.08	-0.15	0.43	0.17	0.60	0.37
Paper; printing and publishing	0.10	0.00	0.38	0.28	-0.06	-0.11	0.29	0.12	0.52	0.37
Petroleum	-0.15	-0.09	-0.38	-0.26	-0.11	-0.09	-0.15	-0.08	-0.22	-0.08
Chemicals, rubber and plastics	13.69	15.30	0.44	0.32	-0.05	-0.10	0.27	0.10	0.43	0.29
Non-metallic mineral products	0.14	0.03	0.49	0.34	0.00	-0.06	0.33	0.14	0.48	0.31
Basic and fabricated metal products	0.09	-0.10	0.83	0.58	-0.10	-0.20	0.55	0.22	0.85	0.57
Motor vehicles	0.06	-0.02	16.75	17.88	-0.01	-0.05	0.24	0.10	0.40	0.27
Other transport equipment	0.05	-0.05	0.60	0.48	0.06	0.00	0.45	0.25	0.62	0.45
Electronics	0.20	0.03	0.65	0.43	17.63	19.21	0.45	0.17	0.72	0.47
Machinery and equipment n.e.c.	0.07	-0.04	2.13	2.11	0.00	-0.06	0.35	0.17	0.57	0.40
Furniture, manufacturing n.e.c.	0.08	-0.02	0.25	0.17	-0.13	-0.18	0.30	0.12	0.40	0.28
Electricity, gas and water supply; construction	-0.11	-0.13	-0.16	-0.15	-0.07	-0.10	0.08	0.01	0.14	0.11
Trade, repair; hotels and restaurants	-0.22	-0.23	-0.29	-0.13	-0.16	-0.20	4.68	6.55	0.21	0.29
Transport, storage and communication	-0.05	-0.12	0.20	0.13	-0.09	-0.13	0.22	0.09	0.27	0.18
Finance, insurance, real estate, business activities	-0.08	-0.08	-0.04	0.00	-0.08	-0.08	0.06	0.01	1.87	2.20
Other services	-0.08	-0.10	-0.13	-0.13	-0.07	-0.09	0.00	-0.03	0.03	0.04

Table 13. (Continued)

B) Effects on sectoral prices

	Chemicals		Motor Vehicles		Electronics		Trade		Finance	
	Half	Double	Half	Double	Half	Double	Half	Double	Half	Double
Agriculture, hunting and fishing	0.01	0.01	0.05	0.05	-0.01	-0.01	0.07	0.07	0.17	0.17
Mining and quarrying	0.09	0.09	0.33	0.33	0.02	0.02	0.19	0.19	0.34	0.34
Food, beverages and tobacco	-0.05	-0.05	-0.17	-0.17	-0.03	-0.03	-0.02	-0.03	0.01	0.01
Textiles, wearing apparel, leather, footwear	0.04	0.04	0.19	0.19	0.04	0.04	0.11	0.11	0.22	0.22
Wood and wood products. except furniture	0.07	0.07	0.25	0.25	0.03	0.03	0.14	0.14	0.26	0.26
Paper; printing and publishing	0.06	0.06	0.22	0.22	0.03	0.03	0.14	0.14	0.24	0.24
Petroleum	0.06	0.06	0.26	0.26	0.01	0.01	0.15	0.15	0.28	0.28
Chemicals, rubber and plastics	-2.21	-2.21	0.26	0.26	0.03	0.03	0.16	0.16	0.28	0.28
Non-metallic mineral products	0.08	0.08	0.28	0.28	0.03	0.03	0.16	0.16	0.28	0.28
Basic and fabricated metal products	0.09	0.09	0.25	0.25	0.04	0.04	0.14	0.14	0.26	0.26
Motor vehicles	0.08	0.08	-3.27	-3.26	0.03	0.03	0.15	0.15	0.26	0.26
Other transport equipment	0.08	0.08	0.24	0.24	0.01	0.01	0.14	0.14	0.26	0.26
Electronics	0.07	0.07	0.28	0.28	-1.83	-1.83	0.16	0.16	0.28	0.28
Machinery and equipment n.e.c.	0.08	0.08	0.07	0.07	0.02	0.02	0.15	0.15	0.27	0.27
Furniture, manufacturing n.e.c.	0.05	0.05	0.19	0.19	0.03	0.03	0.11	0.11	0.22	0.22
Electricity, gas and water supply; construction	0.04	0.04	0.05	0.05	0.01	0.01	0.06	0.06	0.13	0.13
Trade, repair; hotels and restaurants	0.03	0.03	-0.08	-0.08	0.03	0.03	-2.84	-2.84	-0.03	-0.03
Transport, storage and communication	0.07	0.07	0.09	0.09	0.03	0.03	0.06	0.06	0.15	0.15
Finance, insurance, real estate, business activities	0.01	0.01	-0.03	-0.03	-0.01	-0.01	0.04	0.04	-1.54	-1.54
Other services	0.07	0.07	-0.01	-0.01	0.07	0.07	0.01	0.01	0.00	0.00

Table 13. (Continued)

C) Effects on sectoral exports

	Chemicals		Motorvehicles		Electronics		Trade		Finance	
	Half	Double	Half	Double	Half	Double	Half	Double	Half	Double
Agriculture, hunting and fishing	0.52	0.19	1.75	0.92	0.21	0.08	0.77	0.30	1.06	0.45
Mining and quarrying	0.04	0.01	0.13	0.06	0.02	0.00	0.06	0.02	0.08	0.03
Food, beverages and tobacco	0.84	0.41	2.86	1.96	0.31	0.15	1.34	0.67	1.94	1.11
Textiles, wearing apparel, leather, footwear	0.49	0.17	1.32	0.80	-0.08	-0.16	0.83	0.33	1.16	0.62
Wood and wood products. except furniture	0.17	0.01	0.75	0.44	-0.06	-0.11	0.47	0.17	0.66	0.34
Paper; printing and publishing	0.22	0.05	0.83	0.45	-0.02	-0.06	0.45	0.15	0.78	0.37
Petroleum	0.16	0.08	0.40	0.27	0.04	0.01	0.21	0.10	0.32	0.18
Chemicals, rubber and plastics	16.77	13.15	0.61	0.34	-0.04	-0.07	0.33	0.10	0.53	0.26
Non-metallic mineral products	0.10	0.00	0.43	0.23	-0.06	-0.08	0.27	0.08	0.42	0.21
Basic and fabricated metal products	0.08	-0.07	0.74	0.39	-0.09	-0.14	0.49	0.15	0.75	0.38
Motor vehicles	0.10	0.00	22.18	20.87	-0.02	-0.06	0.32	0.13	0.56	0.33
Other transport equipment	0.18	0.02	1.02	0.64	0.12	0.03	0.61	0.27	0.86	0.47
Electronics	0.22	0.03	0.72	0.40	18.38	15.61	0.47	0.15	0.75	0.40
Machinery and equipment n.e.c.	0.13	0.00	2.38	1.85	0.03	-0.03	0.43	0.18	0.69	0.38
Furniture, manufacturing n.e.c.	0.42	0.14	1.37	0.84	-0.01	-0.09	0.79	0.32	1.10	0.58
Electricity, gas and water supply; construction	0.35	0.10	1.58	1.09	0.11	0.00	0.83	0.39	1.24	0.73
Trade, repair; hotels and restaurants	0.33	0.05	1.94	1.23	0.02	-0.08	13.48	10.75	1.74	0.96
Transport, storage and communication	0.12	-0.01	0.85	0.57	-0.02	-0.07	0.51	0.23	0.68	0.39
Finance, insurance, real estate, business activities	0.39	0.20	1.65	1.12	0.11	0.11	0.76	0.38	7.98	5.83
Other services	0.22	-0.09	1.60	1.05	-0.12	-0.26	0.94	0.34	1.59	0.96

Table 13. (Continued)

D) Effects on sectoral imports

	Chemicals		Motorvehicles		Electronics		Trade		Finance	
	Half	Double	Half	Double	Half	Double	Half	Double	Half	Double
Agriculture, hunting and fishing	-0.20	-0.23	-0.58	-0.90	-0.11	-0.13	-0.21	-0.28	-0.31	-0.42
Mining and quarrying	-0.05	-0.04	-0.15	-0.14	-0.03	-0.03	-0.05	-0.04	-0.08	-0.06
Food, beverages and tobacco	-0.49	-0.59	-1.53	-2.49	-0.26	-0.29	-0.58	-0.81	-0.85	-1.26
Textiles, wearing apparel. leather. footwear	-0.17	-0.21	-0.58	-0.78	-0.20	-0.16	-0.12	-0.23	-0.19	-0.33
Wood and wood products, except furniture	0.01	-0.07	0.23	-0.06	-0.09	-0.09	0.20	-0.01	0.27	0.02
Paper; printing and publishing	-0.03	-0.10	-0.04	-0.27	-0.10	-0.10	0.08	-0.07	0.19	-0.03
Petroleum	-0.22	-0.18	-0.53	-0.58	-0.13	-0.11	-0.24	-0.20	-0.35	-0.29
Chemicals, rubber and plastics	11.04	9.01	0.09	-0.05	-0.08	-0.09	0.11	-0.01	0.19	0.06
Non-metallic mineral products	0.14	0.05	0.41	0.18	0.05	0.04	0.29	0.09	0.40	0.17
Basic and fabricated metal products	0.02	-0.10	0.55	0.25	-0.13	-0.17	0.36	0.08	0.57	0.26
Motor vehicles	0.00	-0.03	5.09	1.39	0.03	0.02	0.09	0.00	0.11	-0.01
Other transport equipment	-0.06	-0.11	0.10	-0.20	-0.02	-0.06	0.18	-0.03	0.24	-0.01
Electronics	0.12	-0.01	0.37	0.15	11.30	9.56	0.31	0.08	0.48	0.25
Machinery and equipment n.e.c.	-0.05	-0.08	0.85	0.44	-0.05	-0.06	0.10	-0.02	0.17	0.02
Furniture, manufacturing n.e.c.	-0.19	-0.23	-0.56	-0.89	-0.18	-0.13	-0.13	-0.27	-0.20	-0.41
Electricity, gas and water supply; construction	-0.28	-0.28	-0.72	-1.23	-0.18	-0.16	-0.24	-0.40	-0.33	-0.63
Trade, repair; hotels and restaurants	-0.34	-0.30	-0.85	-1.35	-0.21	-0.15	2.43	-2.31	-0.30	-0.67
Transport, storage and communication	-0.10	-0.09	-0.20	-0.54	-0.06	-0.03	-0.02	-0.19	-0.06	-0.29
Finance, insurance, real estate, business activities	-0.19	-0.19	-0.48	-0.79	-0.13	-0.10	-0.15	-0.23	2.74	0.69
Other services	-0.17	-0.03	-0.65	-1.23	-0.04	0.17	-0.27	-0.39	-0.43	-0.93

Table 14. Sensitivity analysis: Effects on sectoral variables of changes in the elasticity of substitution between national firms and MNE's production (percent change from benchmark)

A) Effects on sectoral output

	Chemicals		Motor vehicles		Electronics		Trade		Finance	
	Half	Double	Half	Double	Half	Double	Half	Double	Half	Double
Agriculture, hunting and fishing	-0.02	-0.03	0.02	0.02	-0.05	-0.05	0.05	0.04	0.05	0.05
Mining and quarrying	0.00	0.00	0.02	0.02	0.00	-0.01	0.01	0.01	0.02	0.02
Food, beverages and tobacco	-0.17	-0.15	-0.49	-0.48	-0.12	-0.12	-0.10	-0.08	-0.13	-0.12
Textiles, wearing apparel, leather, footwear	0.16	0.11	0.38	0.36	-0.18	-0.20	0.36	0.29	0.52	0.49
Wood and wood products. except furniture	0.09	0.03	0.54	0.53	-0.10	-0.12	0.35	0.27	0.51	0.48
Paper; printing and publishing	0.07	0.03	0.35	0.34	-0.07	-0.09	0.24	0.18	0.47	0.45
Petroleum	-0.13	-0.11	-0.33	-0.33	-0.10	-0.09	-0.12	-0.10	-0.17	-0.15
Chemicals, rubber and plastics	14.08	14.71	0.39	0.38	-0.07	-0.08	0.22	0.17	0.38	0.36
Non-metallic mineral products	0.10	0.07	0.43	0.42	-0.02	-0.04	0.27	0.21	0.42	0.39
Basic and fabricated metal products	0.04	-0.04	0.73	0.71	-0.12	-0.16	0.45	0.35	0.75	0.70
Motor vehicles	0.04	0.01	17.07	17.26	-0.02	-0.03	0.20	0.16	0.35	0.33
Other transport equipment	0.03	-0.02	0.56	0.55	0.04	0.03	0.39	0.34	0.57	0.55
Electronics	0.15	0.09	0.57	0.55	18.01	18.54	0.37	0.28	0.63	0.59
Machinery and equipment n.e.c.	0.04	0.00	2.12	2.13	-0.02	-0.03	0.30	0.25	0.51	0.49
Furniture. manufacturing n.e.c.	0.05	0.02	0.23	0.21	-0.14	-0.16	0.25	0.20	0.36	0.34
Electricity, gas and water supply; construction	-0.12	-0.12	-0.15	-0.16	-0.08	-0.08	0.06	0.05	0.13	0.13
Trade, repair; hotels and restaurants	-0.21	-0.22	-0.22	-0.22	-0.17	-0.17	5.22	5.75	0.25	0.26
Transport, storage and communication	-0.07	-0.10	0.18	0.17	-0.10	-0.11	0.18	0.15	0.24	0.22
Finance, insurance, real estate, business activities	-0.08	-0.09	-0.02	-0.02	-0.08	-0.09	0.05	0.03	2.04	2.07
Other services	-0.08	-0.09	-0.13	-0.13	-0.08	-0.08	0.00	-0.01	0.03	0.03

Table 14. (Continued)

B) Effects on sectoral prices

	Chemicals		Motor vehicles		Electronics		Trade		Finance	
	Half	Double	Half	Double	Half	Double	Half	Double	Half	Double
Agriculture, hunting and fishing	0.01	0.01	0.05	0.05	-0.01	-0.01	0.07	0.08	0.17	0.17
Mining and quarrying	0.09	0.07	0.34	0.33	0.02	0.01	0.20	0.18	0.34	0.33
Food, beverages and tobacco	-0.05	-0.04	-0.17	-0.17	-0.03	-0.03	-0.03	-0.01	0.01	0.02
Textiles, wearing apparel, leather, footwear	0.04	0.04	0.19	0.19	0.04	0.04	0.11	0.11	0.22	0.21
Wood and wood products, except furniture	0.08	0.07	0.25	0.24	0.03	0.03	0.14	0.14	0.26	0.26
Paper; printing and publishing	0.06	0.06	0.22	0.22	0.03	0.03	0.14	0.13	0.24	0.23
Petroleum	0.06	0.05	0.26	0.25	0.01	0.01	0.16	0.15	0.28	0.27
Chemicals, rubber and plastics	-2.17	-2.27	0.27	0.26	0.03	0.03	0.16	0.15	0.28	0.27
Non-metallic mineral products	0.08	0.07	0.28	0.28	0.03	0.03	0.16	0.15	0.29	0.28
Basic and fabricated metal products	0.09	0.08	0.25	0.25	0.04	0.03	0.15	0.14	0.26	0.25
Motor vehicles	0.08	0.07	-3.25	-3.29	0.03	0.02	0.15	0.14	0.26	0.25
Other transport equipment	0.08	0.07	0.24	0.24	0.01	0.01	0.14	0.13	0.26	0.26
Electronics	0.08	0.07	0.28	0.28	-1.81	-1.87	0.16	0.15	0.28	0.27
Machinery and equipment n.e.c.	0.08	0.07	0.07	0.06	0.02	0.02	0.16	0.15	0.28	0.27
Furniture, manufacturing n.e.c.	0.05	0.04	0.19	0.18	0.03	0.03	0.11	0.11	0.22	0.22
Electricity, gas and water supply; construction	0.03	0.04	0.05	0.05	0.01	0.01	0.06	0.07	0.13	0.13
Trade, repair; hotels and restaurants	0.03	0.04	-0.08	-0.08	0.02	0.03	-2.79	-2.95	-0.03	-0.02
Transport, storage and communication	0.07	0.07	0.09	0.09	0.03	0.04	0.06	0.06	0.15	0.15
Finance, insurance, real estate, business activities	0.00	0.01	-0.03	-0.03	-0.01	-0.01	0.03	0.05	-1.55	-1.54
Other services	0.06	0.08	-0.02	-0.01	0.06	0.07	0.00	0.03	0.00	0.00

Table 14. (Continued)

C) Effects on sectoral exports

	Chemicals		Motorvehicles		Electronics		Trade		Finance	
	Half	Double	Half	Double	Half	Double	Half	Double	Half	Double
Agriculture, hunting and fishing	0.39	0.30	1.37	1.35	0.16	0.12	0.57	0.47	0.80	0.74
Mining and quarrying	0.03	0.02	0.09	0.09	0.01	0.01	0.04	0.03	0.06	0.05
Food, beverages and tobacco	0.71	0.54	2.50	2.46	0.26	0.21	1.11	0.92	1.64	1.53
Textiles, wearing apparel, leather, footwear	0.38	0.29	1.11	1.08	-0.10	-0.14	0.66	0.53	0.95	0.89
Wood and wood products. except furniture	0.11	0.06	0.62	0.61	-0.07	-0.10	0.36	0.29	0.53	0.50
Paper; printing and publishing	0.16	0.10	0.67	0.65	-0.03	-0.06	0.34	0.26	0.61	0.58
Petroleum	0.13	0.10	0.35	0.34	0.03	0.02	0.17	0.14	0.27	0.25
Chemicals, rubber and plastics	15.17	15.78	0.50	0.49	-0.05	-0.07	0.25	0.19	0.42	0.39
Non-metallic mineral products	0.06	0.03	0.35	0.34	-0.06	-0.08	0.20	0.16	0.33	0.31
Basic and fabricated metal products	0.03	-0.03	0.59	0.58	-0.10	-0.13	0.36	0.28	0.60	0.56
Motor vehicles	0.07	0.03	21.63	21.86	-0.03	-0.05	0.26	0.21	0.48	0.45
Other transport equipment	0.13	0.07	0.87	0.85	0.09	0.07	0.49	0.42	0.72	0.68
Electronics	0.15	0.09	0.59	0.57	17.18	17.72	0.36	0.28	0.61	0.58
Machinery and equipment n.e.c.	0.09	0.04	2.17	2.18	0.01	-0.01	0.34	0.28	0.57	0.54
Furniture, manufacturing n.e.c.	0.33	0.23	1.15	1.12	-0.03	-0.07	0.62	0.50	0.90	0.84
Electricity, gas and water supply; construction	0.28	0.17	1.39	1.36	0.08	0.04	0.68	0.55	1.06	0.99
Trade, repair; hotels and restaurants	0.25	0.12	1.65	1.62	-0.01	-0.05	12.20	12.83	1.45	1.38
Transport, storage and communication	0.08	0.02	0.74	0.72	-0.03	-0.05	0.41	0.34	0.57	0.53
Finance, insurance, real estate, business activities	0.35	0.24	1.44	1.42	0.13	0.09	0.65	0.52	7.51	7.41
Other services	0.14	0.00	1.39	1.35	-0.16	-0.21	0.75	0.57	1.36	1.28

Table 14. (Continued)

D) Effects on sectoral imports

	Chemicals		Motorvehicles		Electronics		Trade		Finance	
	Half	Double	Half	Double	Half	Double	Half	Double	Half	Double
Agriculture, hunting and fishing	-0.24	-0.20	-0.75	-0.74	-0.13	-0.12	-0.28	-0.24	-0.41	-0.38
Mining and quarrying	-0.05	-0.04	-0.15	-0.15	-0.03	-0.03	-0.05	-0.04	-0.07	-0.07
Food, beverages and tobacco	-0.60	-0.48	-1.95	-1.92	-0.30	-0.26	-0.76	-0.63	-1.11	-1.03
Textiles, wearing apparel, leather, footwear	-0.21	-0.18	-0.67	-0.66	-0.20	-0.19	-0.19	-0.17	-0.28	-0.26
Wood and wood products, except furniture	-0.02	-0.04	0.10	0.09	-0.09	-0.10	0.10	0.08	0.16	0.15
Paper; printing and publishing	-0.07	-0.07	-0.14	-0.15	-0.10	-0.10	0.01	0.00	0.08	0.08
Petroleum	-0.22	-0.18	-0.56	-0.55	-0.13	-0.11	-0.24	-0.20	-0.35	-0.32
Chemicals. rubber and plastics	10.10	10.55	0.03	0.03	-0.09	-0.09	0.06	0.04	0.13	0.12
Non-metallic mineral products	0.10	0.07	0.31	0.30	0.04	0.03	0.21	0.17	0.30	0.28
Basic and fabricated metal products	-0.02	-0.07	0.42	0.41	-0.14	-0.16	0.26	0.19	0.44	0.41
Motor vehicles	-0.01	-0.02	3.76	3.84	0.02	0.03	0.05	0.04	0.05	0.05
Other transport equipment	-0.09	-0.09	-0.03	-0.03	-0.04	-0.04	0.08	0.08	0.12	0.12
Electronics	0.07	0.04	0.28	0.27	10.58	10.81	0.22	0.17	0.39	0.36
Machinery and equipment n.e.c.	-0.06	-0.07	0.68	0.69	-0.06	-0.06	0.05	0.04	0.10	0.10
Furniture, manufacturing n.e.c.	-0.23	-0.20	-0.71	-0.70	-0.17	-0.16	-0.22	-0.19	-0.33	-0.30
Electricity, gas and water supply; construction	-0.32	-0.26	-0.94	-0.93	-0.19	-0.17	-0.35	-0.29	-0.50	-0.46
Trade, repair; hotels and restaurants	-0.37	-0.31	-1.08	-1.07	-0.20	-0.19	0.55	0.72	-0.51	-0.46
Transport, storage and communication	-0.12	-0.10	-0.35	-0.34	-0.06	-0.06	-0.12	-0.10	-0.18	-0.17
Finance, insurance, real estate, business activities	-0.21	-0.18	-0.61	-0.60	-0.12	-0.11	-0.20	-0.17	2.07	2.05
Other services	-0.18	-0.11	-0.91	-0.90	0.00	0.03	-0.41	-0.32	-0.69	-0.65

Table 15. Sensitivity analysis: Effects on sectoral variables of changes in the elasticity of substitution between labour and capital (percent change from benchmark)

A) Effects on sectoral output

	Chemicals		Motor vehicles		Electronics		Trade		Finance	
	Half	Double	Half	Double	Half	Double	Half	Double	Half	Double
Agriculture. hunting and fishing	-0.02	-0.02	0.02	0.02	-0.05	-0.05	0.05	0.04	0.05	0.05
Mining and quarrying	0.00	0.00	0.02	0.02	-0.01	-0.01	0.01	0.01	0.02	0.02
Food. beverages and tobacco	-0.16	-0.16	-0.49	-0.49	-0.12	-0.12	-0.09	-0.09	-0.13	-0.13
Textiles. wearing apparel. leather. footwear	0.14	0.14	0.37	0.37	-0.19	-0.19	0.34	0.34	0.51	0.51
Wood and wood products. except furniture	0.07	0.07	0.54	0.54	-0.11	-0.11	0.32	0.32	0.50	0.50
Paper; printing and publishing	0.06	0.06	0.35	0.35	-0.08	-0.08	0.22	0.22	0.47	0.47
Petroleum	-0.12	-0.12	-0.33	-0.33	-0.10	-0.10	-0.11	-0.11	-0.16	-0.16
Chemicals. rubber and plastics	14.30	14.30	0.39	0.39	-0.07	-0.07	0.21	0.21	0.38	0.38
Non-metallic mineral products	0.09	0.09	0.43	0.43	-0.03	-0.03	0.25	0.25	0.41	0.41
Basic and fabricated metal products	0.01	0.01	0.72	0.73	-0.14	-0.14	0.42	0.42	0.74	0.74
Motor vehicles	0.03	0.03	17.12	17.14	-0.02	-0.02	0.18	0.18	0.35	0.35
Other transport equipment	0.01	0.01	0.56	0.55	0.04	0.04	0.37	0.37	0.56	0.56
Electronics	0.13	0.13	0.56	0.56	18.20	18.20	0.34	0.34	0.62	0.62
Machinery and equipment n.e.c.	0.02	0.02	2.12	2.12	-0.02	-0.02	0.28	0.28	0.50	0.50
Furniture. Manufacturing n.e.c.	0.04	0.04	0.22	0.22	-0.15	-0.15	0.23	0.23	0.35	0.35
Electricity. gas and water supply; construction	-0.12	-0.12	-0.15	-0.16	-0.08	-0.08	0.06	0.06	0.13	0.13
Trade. repair; hotels and restaurants	-0.22	-0.22	-0.22	-0.22	-0.17	-0.17	5.39	5.39	0.25	0.25
Transport. storage and communication	-0.08	-0.08	0.18	0.17	-0.10	-0.10	0.17	0.17	0.23	0.23
Finance. insurance. real estate. business activities	-0.08	-0.08	-0.02	-0.02	-0.08	-0.08	0.04	0.04	2.05	2.05
Other services	-0.09	-0.09	-0.13	-0.13	-0.08	-0.08	-0.01	-0.01	0.03	0.03

Table 15. (Continued)

B) Effects on sectoral prices

	Chemicals		Motor Vehicles		Electronics		Trade		Finance	
	Half	Double	Half	Double	Half	Double	Half	Double	Half	Double
Agriculture, hunting and fishing	0.01	0.01	0.05	0.05	-0.01	-0.01	0.07	0.07	0.17	0.17
Mining and quarrying	0.09	0.09	0.33	0.33	0.02	0.02	0.19	0.19	0.34	0.34
Food, beverages and tobacco	-0.05	-0.05	-0.17	-0.17	-0.03	-0.03	-0.02	-0.03	0.01	0.01
Textiles, wearing apparel, leather, footwear	0.04	0.04	0.19	0.19	0.04	0.04	0.11	0.11	0.22	0.22
Wood and wood products, except furniture	0.07	0.07	0.25	0.25	0.03	0.03	0.14	0.14	0.26	0.26
Paper; printing and publishing	0.06	0.06	0.22	0.22	0.03	0.03	0.14	0.14	0.24	0.24
Petroleum	0.06	0.06	0.26	0.26	0.01	0.01	0.15	0.15	0.28	0.28
Chemicals, rubber and plastics	-2.21	-2.21	0.26	0.26	0.03	0.03	0.16	0.16	0.28	0.28
Non-metallic mineral products	0.08	0.08	0.28	0.28	0.03	0.03	0.16	0.16	0.28	0.28
Basic and fabricated metal products	0.09	0.09	0.25	0.25	0.04	0.04	0.14	0.14	0.26	0.26
Motor vehicles	0.08	0.08	-3.27	-3.26	0.03	0.03	0.15	0.15	0.26	0.26
Other transport equipment	0.08	0.08	0.24	0.24	0.01	0.01	0.14	0.14	0.26	0.26
Electronics	0.07	0.07	0.28	0.28	-1.83	-1.83	0.16	0.16	0.28	0.28
Machinery and equipment n.e.c.	0.08	0.08	0.07	0.07	0.02	0.02	0.15	0.15	0.27	0.27
Furniture, manufacturing n.e.c.	0.05	0.05	0.19	0.19	0.03	0.03	0.11	0.11	0.22	0.22
Electricity, gas and water supply; construction	0.04	0.04	0.05	0.05	0.01	0.01	0.06	0.06	0.13	0.13
Trade, repair; hotels and restaurants	0.03	0.03	-0.08	-0.08	0.03	0.03	-2.84	-2.84	-0.03	-0.03
Transport, storage and communication	0.07	0.07	0.09	0.09	0.03	0.03	0.06	0.06	0.15	0.15
Finance, insurance, real estate, business activities	0.01	0.01	-0.03	-0.03	-0.01	-0.01	0.04	0.04	-1.54	-1.54
Other services	0.07	0.07	-0.01	-0.01	0.07	0.07	0.01	0.01	0.00	0.00

Table 15. (Continued)

C) Effects on sectoral exports

	Chemicals		Motorvehicles		Electronics		Trade		Finance	
	Half	Double	Half	Double	Half	Double	Half	Double	Half	Double
Agriculture, hunting and fishing	0.36	0.36	1.36	1.36	0.14	0.14	0.54	0.54	0.78	0.78
Mining and quarrying	0.02	0.02	0.09	0.09	0.01	0.01	0.04	0.04	0.05	0.06
Food, beverages and tobacco	0.65	0.65	2.49	2.48	0.24	0.24	1.05	1.05	1.61	1.61
Textiles, wearing apparel, leather, footwear	0.35	0.35	1.10	1.10	-0.11	-0.11	0.62	0.62	0.93	0.93
Wood and wood products, except furniture	0.09	0.09	0.62	0.62	-0.08	-0.08	0.34	0.34	0.52	0.52
Paper; printing and publishing	0.14	0.14	0.66	0.66	-0.04	-0.04	0.31	0.31	0.60	0.60
Petroleum	0.12	0.12	0.35	0.35	0.03	0.03	0.16	0.16	0.27	0.27
Chemicals, rubber and plastics	15.38	15.38	0.49	0.49	-0.06	-0.06	0.23	0.23	0.41	0.41
Non-metallic mineral products	0.05	0.05	0.34	0.34	-0.07	-0.07	0.19	0.19	0.32	0.32
Basic and fabricated metal products	0.01	0.01	0.59	0.59	-0.11	-0.11	0.34	0.34	0.59	0.59
Motor vehicles	0.05	0.05	21.68	21.72	-0.04	-0.04	0.24	0.24	0.47	0.47
Other transport equipment	0.11	0.11	0.86	0.86	0.08	0.08	0.47	0.47	0.70	0.70
Electronics	0.13	0.13	0.59	0.59	17.37	17.37	0.33	0.33	0.60	0.60
Machinery and equipment n.e.c.	0.07	0.07	2.17	2.17	0.00	0.00	0.32	0.32	0.56	0.56
Furniture, manufacturing n.e.c.	0.29	0.29	1.14	1.14	-0.05	-0.05	0.58	0.58	0.88	0.88
Electricity, gas and water supply; construction	0.24	0.24	1.38	1.38	0.07	0.07	0.64	0.64	1.04	1.04
Trade, repair; hotels and restaurants	0.20	0.20	1.64	1.64	-0.02	-0.02	12.40	12.40	1.43	1.43
Transport, storage and communication	0.06	0.06	0.73	0.73	-0.04	-0.04	0.39	0.39	0.56	0.56
Finance, insurance, real estate, business activities	0.31	0.31	1.44	1.43	0.12	0.12	0.60	0.60	7.47	7.47
Other services	0.09	0.09	1.38	1.37	-0.18	-0.18	0.69	0.69	1.33	1.33

Table 15. (Continued)

D) Effects on sectoral imports

	Chemicals		Motorvehicles		Electronics		Trade		Finance	
	Half	Double	Half	Double	Half	Double	Half	Double	Half	Double
Agricultura, hunting and fishing	-0.23	-0.23	-0.74	-0.74	-0.13	-0.13	-0.27	-0.27	-0.40	-0.40
Mining and quarrying	-0.05	-0.05	-0.15	-0.15	-0.03	-0.03	-0.05	-0.05	-0.07	-0.07
Food, beverages and tobacco	-0.56	-0.56	-1.94	-1.94	-0.29	-0.29	-0.72	-0.72	-1.08	-1.08
Textiles, wearing apparel, leather, footwear	-0.20	-0.20	-0.67	-0.67	-0.19	-0.19	-0.19	-0.19	-0.27	-0.27
Wood and wood products, except furniture	-0.03	-0.03	0.10	0.09	-0.10	-0.10	0.10	0.10	0.15	0.15
Paper; printing and publishing	-0.07	-0.07	-0.15	-0.15	-0.10	-0.10	0.00	0.00	0.08	0.08
Petroleum	-0.21	-0.21	-0.56	-0.56	-0.12	-0.12	-0.22	-0.22	-0.34	-0.34
Chemicals, rubber and plastics	10.26	10.26	0.03	0.03	-0.09	-0.09	0.05	0.05	0.13	0.13
Non-metallic mineral products	0.09	0.09	0.30	0.30	0.04	0.04	0.19	0.19	0.29	0.29
Basic and fabricated metal products	-0.04	-0.04	0.42	0.42	-0.15	-0.15	0.23	0.23	0.43	0.43
Motor vehicles	-0.01	-0.01	3.79	3.79	0.02	0.02	0.05	0.05	0.05	0.05
Other transport equipment	-0.09	-0.09	-0.03	-0.03	-0.04	-0.04	0.08	0.08	0.12	0.12
Electronics	0.06	0.06	0.28	0.28	10.66	10.66	0.21	0.21	0.38	0.38
Machinery and equipment n.e.c.	-0.07	-0.07	0.69	0.69	-0.06	-0.06	0.05	0.05	0.10	0.10
Furniture, manufacturing n.e.c.	-0.22	-0.22	-0.71	-0.71	-0.17	-0.17	-0.21	-0.21	-0.32	-0.32
Electricity, gas and water supply; construction	-0.30	-0.30	-0.93	-0.93	-0.18	-0.18	-0.33	-0.33	-0.49	-0.49
Trade, repair; hotels and restaurants	-0.35	-0.35	-1.08	-1.07	-0.20	-0.20	0.60	0.60	-0.49	-0.49
Transport, storage and communication	-0.11	-0.11	-0.35	-0.35	-0.06	-0.06	-0.11	-0.11	-0.17	-0.17
Finance, insurance, real estate, business activities	-0.20	-0.20	-0.61	-0.61	-0.12	-0.12	-0.19	-0.19	2.06	2.06
Other services	-0.15	-0.15	-0.91	-0.91	0.01	0.01	-0.38	-0.38	-0.68	-0.68

Responses in the sectors not directly involved in the shock to changes in the value of the elasticity of substitution between national firms and MNEs' production are as follows. Regarding *output* levels, they are lower the higher level of the elasticity because production is more concentrated in the sector receiving MNEs (Table 14A). As already mentioned, the differences in output levels between the two extreme values are small though. *Prices* remain nearly unchanged for the two extreme values (Table 14B). Exports are slightly lower (Table 14C) and imports slightly larger (Table 14D) the higher the value of the elasticity. Both tendencies are related to the higher CPI (i.e., smaller fall in the CPI) which arises with the higher value of the elasticity of substitution between national firms versus MNEs' production.

All in all, sensitivity analysis leads to conclude that the previous results as well as the causation chains explained above are basically robust for different values of the elasticities.

6. CONCLUSIONS

The positive effects of an increase in FDI on GDP and welfare, due to the entry of MNEs, can be offset if the extent of profit repatriation is large. Our simulations suggest that, in general, profit repatriation above 50 per cent of MNEs' income leads to a decrease in the GDP of the host economy, although the exact amount changes according to the sector where the entry of MNEs takes place. Empirical data available on the magnitude of profit repatriation indicate that this is likely to be higher than such 50 percent threshold. Furthermore, we can guess that the level of profit repatriation may be higher than reported by MNEs for balance of payments statistics, as they may be trying to avoid taxation. Thus, profit repatriation, a nearly under-researched area, may have a considerable impact on the different effects that the entry of MNEs brings about.

Apart from the evolution of aggregate variables for different levels of profit repatriation, we have showed detailed results for profit repatriation of 100 per cent, i.e. when the remuneration of all the extra capital that new MNEs bring with them is fully repatriated. These are the results for which we give some conclusions henceforth.

Motor vehicles stands out as a sector showing the highest fall in GDP and welfare (-0.7 per cent and -1.28 per cent, respectively). These outcomes are consistent with those obtained in Chapter 4, in which the positive impact of

MNEs across scenarios is smallest for this sector. However, the entry of MNEs in Electronics yielded a slightly smaller positive impact on GDP than the rest of sectors in the case of no profit repatriation (i.e., in Chapter 4). By contrast, it exhibits now, with full profit repatriation, the less unfavourable outcomes for GDP and welfare (i.e., the smallest falls across simulations, -0.12 per cent and -0.24 per cent, respectively). These results seem to be related to the amount of capital involved in the shock. The larger the amount of capital repatriated the higher the fall in aggregate variables is. The remunerations of labour and capital are also behind the fall in GDP and welfare. Factor remunerations fall when profit repatriation takes place, compared to the scenario of no profit repatriation.

The impact of profit repatriation on foreign trade at the aggregate level is negligible. Results are very close to those obtained for the case of no profit repatriation. This is related to the evolution of the sector receiving MNEs, which is also very similar to that in the previous chapter. Production, exports and imports increase while the price falls. The increase in production leads to a higher level of imported intermediates in that sector which boosts aggregate imports. The reduction in the price of the good the sector sells increases its exports, driving aggregate exports up.

Across simulations, the evolution of the sectors not receiving MNEs moves along with the demand side of the model. The evolution of demand, in turn, boils down to the impact of MNEs in two variables, namely, the evolution of the CPI (which determines exports) and that of aggregate income (which determines private consumption). We had identified this demand-driven sectoral production in the previous chapter and it is reassuring to see it also holds in these latter simulations. Further, sensitivity analysis again shows that results are robust to changes in elasticities, giving support to the causation chain in adjustments in the model we have identified. However, the impact of MNEs on demand follows a different trend now.

The simulation of the entry of MNEs with full profit repatriation leads to a fall in the CPI, which enhances the export competitiveness of the majority of sectors of the economy. This will boost production of most manufactures which are highly dependent on exports. Thus, most manufacturing sectors exhibit higher levels of production in this scenario than in the case of no profit repatriation (Chapter 4). By contrast, those sectors more dependent on the evolution of private consumption have higher levels of production in the scenario with no profit repatriation, in which all income remains in the host economy.

As happened in the simulation with no profit repatriation, output responses of national firms versus MNEs do not seem to respond to the different levels of labour intensity across sectors. Their respective price levels do not seem either to be responding to different labour intensities. There was a certain tendency for prices of national firms to be higher in the simulations in the previous chapter. We attributed that to their higher labour intensities (compared to their MNEs' counterparts within the same sector). We noted that there were exceptions to this tendency, as well. This tendency is even less clear now. MNEs also experience a tendency to increase prices in this simulation. The reason for this is that MNEs, which rely heavily on imported intermediates, now face higher intermediate costs due to the fall in the CPI that makes imports relatively more expensive. For those scenarios in which the fall in the CPI is bigger (after the entry of MNEs in Motor vehicles and Finance), MNEs charge higher prices than domestic firms, following the higher increase in their intermediates costs.

Thus, intermediates linkages across sectors are important for the determination of prices and for the determination of output. In both cases, they seem to be more important than relative labour intensities. This gives support to thge use of CGE methodologies which deal carefully with intermediate links across sectors.

The results from this and the former chapter should not be strictly taken at their face value. Nevertheless, they surely suggest that profit repatriation has an important negative effect. They, further, suggest that there are different effects of the entry of MNEs according to the sector in which it takes place and, also, different patterns of adjustments to the shock across sectors. The use of a computable general equilibrium (CGE) models facilitates obtaining more accurate sectoral effects at an important level of disaggregation. These outcomes may be useful for the policy-maker to identify which type of MNEs are less harmful for a host country, in this case, for the Czech Republic. This differentiation in sectoral responses is, however, absent in many analyses of the impact of MNEs on host economies.

Finally, it is important to note, however, that the results obtained are applicable for a short and medium run period, which is the timing associated to our model. Furthermore, in the real world, the positive impact of MNEs on the capital stock of the host economy takes place previously than their impact through profit repatriation. This implies that the host economy may benefit from the presence of MNEs for some time. Nevertheless, the sooner profits are repatriated, the sooner their negative impact appears.

Chapter 6

CONCLUSIONS

It is time to evaluate the conclusions of this study, as well as a number of possible extensions. The structure of this final chapter then responds to two simple questions: what has been done? and, what is left?

1. WHAT HAS BEEN DONE?

The contributions of this book could be summarised in the main following points:

1) The Use of a General Equilibrium Methodology to Analyse the Impact of MNEs

The most important objective of this book has been to include foreign-owned companies (i.e., multinational enterprises, MNEs) in a computable general equilibrium (CGE) model. This has been a challenge because CGE models are already complex without MNEs. Indeed, as mentioned in Chapter 2, till very recently, this methodology has not considered the presence of MNEs, and only a handful of studies have been successful in doing it. The comments of Shoven and Whalley (1984, p. 1047) may be relevant in this respect: "One of the most common problems encountered by (CGE) modelers is the necessity to be simultaneously a "jack of all trades." Modelers must know general-equilibrium theory so that their models have a sound theoretical basis; they must know how to solve their models; they need to be able to program (or at least communicate with programmers); they must understand the policy issues on which they work; they have to know about data sources and all their associated problems; and they have to be conversant with the relevant literature, specially that on elasticities. Not surprisingly, modelers can at times feel a sense of inadequacy when faced with colleagues specializing in just one of these topics. This need to do several things well can also inhibit graduate students from doing thesis work in this area. Perhaps the future direction is teams of modelers, each with different skills, run on the lines of research groups in natural sciences".

We have expanded a well-known – and publicly available – CGE model to include MNEs. This is the GTAP model (Hertel, 1997), which is highly relevant because it is designed to make use of a very rich database of the world economy. We also wanted to introduce MNEs in the model in such a manner that OECD (2007) data on the activities of MNEs could be used, as the latter are absent in the GTAP database. By doing this we overcome the problem of obtaining data for general equilibrium simulations considering MNEs – all of these data are also publicly available –, which has been partly the reason why most applied trade models have not included the role of MNEs during decades.

The model has been applied to the analysis of the impact of MNEs on a host economy, an issue that raises considerable debate. More specifically, the model has been applied to the impact of a higher involvement of MNEs in five sectors of the Czech economy. The sectors are Chemicals, Motor vehicles, Electronics, Trade, and Finance. The short-medium term impact of MNEs (both at a 20-sector-disaggregation as well as the aggregate level) is offered for two types of simulations. The first one focuses on the effects of MNEs on the capital stock available for the production of MNEs in the host country (Chapter 4). The second one combines the impact of the increase in the capital stock available for MNEs with the effect of profit repatriation, i.e., when the MNEs send back to their home country the remuneration of the increased capital stock that their entry brings about (Chapter 5). In other words, in the simulation of Chapter 5, the impact of profit repatriation is added to the effects of MNEs already analysed in the previous chapter. This offers a benchmark with respect to which the effects of profit repatriation can be better analysed. These simulations are performed for each of the sectors above mentioned.

Note, however, that in both simulations, we are not considering a mere increase of the capital stock due to the entry of MNEs. As commented in Chapters 1 and 2, FDI consequences (i.e., the consequences of the capital movements related to the activities of MNEs) go beyond capital stock variations. The most important aspect of FDI is that it is related to a particular type of firm, i.e., the MNE. Therefore, we do not model a general increase in the capital stock, but an increase in the capital available to MNEs. These firms exhibit a specific technology of production different to that of national firms. More precisely, the Czech data suggest that MNEs tend to be, in general, more capital intensive, and to rely more on imported intermediates than national firms (data on cost structures of national firms and MNEs per sector appear in Figure 2 in Chapter 4). So our model considers both the MNEs' specific technology together with the role of FDI inflows.

2) A (Mostly) Unexplored Issue: Profit Repatriation

As noted in Chapter 5, profit repatriation is an effect of MNEs which has been mostly neglected in the literature. The outcomes obtained with our model suggest, however, that its impact may be of great relevance.

In principle, the effects of MNEs on the capital stock, and the corresponding increase in value added and income, lead to rather small increases in GDP and welfare. An aggregate wage increase slightly predominates over a fall in the rental rate of capital. This panorama is changed considerably, however, when there is profit repatriation. The small positive impacts on aggregate variables due to the entry of MNEs are likely to be offset by the negative effects of profit repatriation. We still obtain a decrease in the rental of capital and an increase in the aggregate wage (with the exception of the impact of MNEs in Motor vehicles, where both the wage and the rental rate of capital fall). Nevertheless, with profit repatriation the decrease in the rental rate of capital predominates over the general increase in the aggregate wage. Consequently, there is a fall in GDP and welfare. For the Czech case, in general, profit repatriation beyond 50 and 60 percent of the income generated by the entry of MNEs would result in a fall of GDP and welfare, respectively.

3) The Analysis of the Particular Sectoral Effects of MNEs

At the macro and microeconomic level the model shows the differential impact of MNEs across sectors. We believe this in an essential point in order to address most policy issues, and there is still much scope for this type of analysis, as very few studies have considered economy-wide effects of MNEs acting in different sectors. What is more, those few studies including different sectors have mainly concentrated on manufactures, due to the absence of data on MNEs in services. In this study, we contemplate the impact of MNEs in services sectors, a relevant issue because of the growing importance of these sectors in the world economy and the parallel growth of MNEs' activities in them (Barba Navaretti and Venables, 2004, chapter 1; UNCTAD, 2004).

This differential impact of MNEs across sectors has two relevant aspects. The first one is related to the particular sector in which the entry of MNEs takes place. The second one is related to the different patterns of adjustment to the shock across sectors.

Regarding the first one, our results show that the way in which a higher involvement of MNEs without profit repatriation affects a host economy is rather similar across sectors. But, what about the magnitude of the effects? The magnitude is related to the particular sector in which MNEs enter. The analysis of the Czech case suggests that a higher involvement of MNEs in Motor vehicles will not result in important GDP and welfare increases. Therefore, if the policy-maker considers setting some incentives for MNEs, the other four sectors analysed offer some better perspectives. The simulation of the entry of MNEs with full profit repatriation also suggests that the sector in which MNEs enter matters. While Motor vehicles stands out as the sector where profit repatriation is the most harmful, Electronics yields the least unfavourable outcomes, i.e. the smallest falls in GDP and welfare.

These are interesting nuances regarding particular effects on aggregate variables according to the sector where the entry of MNEs takes place. The second aspect is related to the different sectoral responses to the shock. As mentioned above, we consider a 20-sector level disaggregation of the Czech economy. In this latter regard, our results could have been a story about differences in labour intensities across sectors or across the national and MNEs' part of each sector, i.e., sectors could respond differently to the shock according to whether they are more capital or labour intensive. Production patterns, however, do not seem to be related to relative factor intensities. This makes sense when one realises that intermediates costs account for more than 60 percent of total costs of production in most sectors. Fortunately, a CGE model takes into account this intermediates structure. Intersectoral links are difficult to follow in a 20-sector model, but computational methods allow serious treatment of these relations.

Cost structures (Figure 2 in Chapter 4) have provided some light regarding the evolution of prices of the different varieties, i.e., between the variety of the same good produced either by national firms or by MNEs. Some national parts of sectors seem to charge higher prices because they are more labour intensive (and the wage has risen) after the entry of MNEs without profit repatriation. By contrast, in the simulation with profit repatriation MNEs are in some cases increasing their prices by more than domestic firms. This is due to the greater reliance on imported intermediates of MNEs which harms them in a context where foreign prices become relatively more expensive.

In the end, however, despite their role on prices, sectoral production patterns would have not been determined by intermediates, but by some of the components of final demand. In the Czech case, output responses (and with them labour demands) across sectors vary depending on how the entry of MNEs affects sectoral exports and private consumption. There are two broad patterns. One is for most manufacturing sectors, which are highly responsive to the evolution of their own exports —as most of their production is indeed devoted to exports—. The other pattern applies for most services sectors together with Food and Petroleum, whose production responds to the evolution of private consumption. The use of production in terms of their possible destinations – intermediates, investment, private consumption, public consumption or exports – in each of the 20 sectors of the economy is presented in Figure 1 in Chapter 4.

Thus, profit repatriation is harmful for those sectors more dependent on private consumption. Profit repatriation reduces the amount of income available for private consumption, and therefore, final consumption falls. By contrast, in the simulation considering the entry of MNEs with no profit repatriation these private-consumption-oriented sectors tend to be better off. New MNEs bring capital with them and more capital implies that the remuneration of capital goes to the representative household increasing the income available for private consumption and, also, private consumption itself.

The pattern is quite different for those manufactures more oriented to exports. In the simulation with profit repatriation these sectors are better off because repatriation tends to depress prices in the host economy, thus, enhancing the export competitiveness of these sectors. By contrast, in the simulation of the entry of MNEs without profit repatriation, the sectors in which that entry takes place is determinant for the evolution of prices in the host economy. As a consequence, export competitiveness depends on the sector where the shock originates, and manufacturing sectors may be better or worse off after the entry of MNEs without profit repatriation.

It is interesting, then, that sectoral output responds to how MNEs affect the evolution of some *demand* components. So the general equilibrium nature of the model, which considers the demand side of the economy, provides important information to capture the effects of MNEs.

4) Identification of a Causation Chain in the Results

CGE models have been criticised on the grounds that they provide results which can be, sometimes, difficult to interpret (Böhringer, Rutherford and Wiegard, 2003). We believe, however, that CGE models may provide a lot of information about the impact of the shock analysed. Identifying a clear causation chain in the results will then require careful and time-consuming analysis, but this is precisely due to the rich information obtained. We have tried to identify such a causation chain behind the results.

A number of tables have been presented in the previous chapters, that try to explain in detail the impact of MNEs on the host economy. Putting all the information together, we have identified several patterns of adjustment of sectors in the model as well as the reasons for the differential macroeconomic impact of MNEs entering different sectors.

These patterns have been confirmed by the sensitivity analysis performed. Indeed, the sensitivity analysis shows no variations in the causation chain of adjustments across the economy suggested, nor does it affect the main outcomes. In other words, having simulated MNEs arrivals with extreme values for different elasticities, does not vary neither the aggregate nor sectoral results in a meaningful manner. What is more, changes tend to be very small and, in some cases, non-existent. This gives robustness to the causation chain identified.

2. WHAT IS LEFT?

The CGE model including MNEs presented in this book is a first step of a more ambitious research program. In this section we discuss some possible extensions of the model for future work.

1) A Longer Term Approach Introducing
Dynamics and Capital Accumulation

The GTAP standard version is a static model, which does not include any treatment of time and in which current investment does not augment the productive stock of capital available to firms. This is consistent with the interpretation of the results from this model (and our extension) as a medium-term shock. The panorama offered could well vary in the long run, though. This is, certainly, an interesting area for future analysis. A simple introduction to dynamic CGE models, and their differences with the static ones, is provided in Gómez-Plana (2005); a possible way of including dynamics in our model is given in Gómez-Plana (2007). It should be noted, however, that dynamic models imply more data requirements for the calibration of a higher number of variables, as well as involving a number of assumptions related to the future rate of growth of the economies and their populations, the rate of depreciation, time preference rates, and so on, which are not strictly related to the impact of MNEs.

2) MNEs' Externalities

Chapter 1 offers some Figures about the important relationship of MNEs and R&D activities. This suggests that MNEs may have a relevant role as promoters of technological innovation and progress. A lot of empirical studies, most of which are based on an econometric approach, have tried to find this positive impact of MNEs on host economies. However, as we mentioned in Chapter 2, this empirical literature is fairly inconclusive (Görg and Greenaway, 2004; Barba Navaretti and Venables, 2004, chapter 7). In other words, the evidence on positive spillovers stemming from MNEs is at best mixed.

From a different perspective, spillovers have been recently included in a few CGE models analysing climate policy, but the results are sensible to the way of including spillovers in the model; see Köhler et al. (2006) for a survey. In fact, among the CGE models including MNEs only Bchir et al. (2002) and Gilham (2005) simulate externalities linked to FDI flows. The former obtain an overwhelming impact on welfare that leads the authors to exclude them from the standard version of their model, and Gilham also finds a stronger impact when FDI leads to spillovers.

Extensions along this line are, then, particularly challenging. This issue seems to lack the empirical support necessary to be introduced in a well grounded model of MNEs and FDI. An interesting simulation could deal, however, with the increase in productivity in national firms and/or MNEs necessary to offset the negative effect of profit repatriation. By doing this, it would be possible, then, to evaluate whether the increase in productivity needed seems possible or not. This approach contrasts with the one adopted in the above mentioned CGE models linking FDI with spillovers. The latter assume *ad hoc* differentials in total factor productivity between both types of firms, for which data are difficult to be obtained. The alternative proposed would make this assumption unnecessary.

3) Introducing Imperfect Competition, Heterogeneity and Unemployment

The model, in its current version, incorporates a simple way to differentiate between national firms and MNEs (and their corresponding "varieties" of products). The assumption of sector and type-of-firm capital specificity allows following this approach. Other alternatives introducing either Cournot competition or monopolistic competition seem quite appropriate for the analysis of MNEs, though. In addition, the assumption of full employment can be relaxed. Both extensions can be considered in the immediate future along the lines of some previous work with CGE models not including MNEs; see Bajo-Rubio and Gómez-Plana (2004, 2005). Furthermore, incorporating recent developments on heterogeneous firms (e.g., Helpman et al., 2004), something not included so far into any CGE model of MNEs, could be also of much interest.

The extensions just mentioned would certainly enrich the model presented. Nevertheless, with a later introduction of any of them, one by one, we will be able to isolate their own impact from the effects of MNEs we have already considered. This process has to be taken step by step, otherwise, one may easily get lost among too many forces interacting simultaneously in the host economy. As Markusen (2002, p. 21) puts it: "I have always believed that an effective approach to a topic is to start simple and build up to more complicated and realistic models".

REFERENCES

Agarwal, J. P. (1980) "Determinants of foreign direct investment: A survey", *Weltwirtschaftliches Archiv*, vol. 116, pp. 739-773.

Aitken, B. and Harrison, A. (1999) "Do domestic firms benefit from direct foreign investment? Evidence from Venezuela", *American Economic Review*, vol. 89, pp. 605-618.

Aitken, B., Harrison, A. and Lipsey R. (1996) "Wages and foreign ownership: A comparative study of Mexico, Venezuela and the United States", *Journal of International Economics*, vol. 40, pp. 345-371.

Alfaro, L., Chanda, A., Kalemli-Ozcan, S. and Sayek, S. (2004) "FDI and economic growth, the role of local financial markets", *Journal of International Economics,* vol. 64, pp. 113-134.

Alfaro, L., Chanda, A., Kalemli-Ozcan, S. and Sayek, S. (2006) "How does foreign direct investment promote economic growth? Exploring the effects of financial markets on linkages", Working Paper No. 12522, National Bureau of Economic Research.

Antràs, P. (2003) "Firms, contracts, and trade structure", *Quarterly Journal of Economics*, vol. 118, pp. 1375-1418.

Antràs, P. (2005) "Incomplete contracts and the product cycle" *American Economic Review,* vol. 95, pp. 1054-1073.

Antràs, P. and Helpman, E. (2004) "Global sourcing", *Journal of Political Economy*, vol. 112, pp. 552-580.

Antràs, P. and Helpman, E (2008) "Contractual frictions and global sourcing", forthcoming in Helpman, E., Marin, D. and Verdier, T. (eds.) *The organization of firms in a global economy*, Harvard University Press.

Antràs, P. and Rossi-Hansberg, E. (2008) "Organizations and trade", Working Paper No. 14262, National Bureau of Economic Research.

Armington, P. S. (1969) "A theory of demand for products distinguished by place of production", *International Monetary Fund Staff Papers*, vol. 16, pp. 159-176.

Arrow, K. and Hahn, F. H. (1971) *General competitive analysis*, Holden-Day, San Francisco, CA.

Aw, B. Y. and Lee, Y. (2008) "Firm heterogeneity and location choice of Taiwanese multinationals", *Journal of International Economics*, vol. 75, pp. 167–179.

Bajo-Rubio, O. (1991) *Teorías del comercio internacional*, Antoni Bosch, Barcelona.

Bajo-Rubio, O. and Díaz-Roldán, C. (2002) "Inversión extranjera directa, innovación tecnológica y productividad. Una aplicación a la industria española", *Economía Industrial*, No. 347, pp. 111-124.

Bajo-Rubio, O. and Gómez-Plana, A. G. (2004) "Reducing social contributions for unskilled labor as a way of fighting unemployment: An empirical evaluation for the case of Spain", *FinanzArchiv*, vol. 60, pp. 160-185.

Bajo-Rubio, O. and Gómez-Plana, A. G. (2005) "Simulating the effects of the European Single Market: A CGE analysis for Spain", *Journal of Policy Modeling*, vol. 27, pp. 689-709.

Bajo-Rubio, O. and López-Pueyo, C. (2002) "Foreign direct investment in a process of economic integration: The case of Spanish manufacturing, 1986-1992", *Journal of Economic Integration*, vol. 17, pp. 85-103.

Bajo-Rubio, O. and Montero-Muñoz, M. (2001) "Foreign direct investment and trade: A causality analysis", *Open Economies Review,* vol. 12, pp. 305-323.

Bajo-Rubio, O. and Torres, A. (2001) *The impact of Spain's integration with the EC on trade and foreign investment*, Wydawnictwo Akademii Ekonomicznej im. Oskara Langego we Wrocławiu, Wrocław.

Bajo-Rubio, O., Díaz-Mora, C. and Díaz-Roldán, C. (2008) "Foreign direct investment and regional growth: An analysis of the Spanish case", *Regional Studies*, forthcoming.

Balasubramanyam, V. N., Salisu, M. and Sapsford, D. (1996): "Foreign direct investment and growth in EP and IS countries", *Economic Journal,* vol. 106, pp.92-105.

Baldwin, R. E. and Martin, P. (1999) "Two waves of globalisation: Superficial similarities, fundamental differences", in Siebert, H. (ed.) *Globalisation and labour*, J.C.B. Mohr for Kiel Institute of World Economics, Tübingen, pp. 3-59.

Baldwin, R. E., Forslid, R. and Haaland, J. I. (1996) "Investment creation and diversion in Europe", *The World Economy,* vol. 19, pp. 635-659.

Barba Navaretti, G. and Venables, A. J. (2004) *Multinational firms in the world economy,* Princeton University Press, Princeton.

Barrios, S., Görg, H. and Strobl, E. (2005) "Foreign direct investment, competition and industrial development in the host country", *European Economic Review,* vol. 49, pp. 1761-1784.

Barry, F. and Bradley, J. (1997) "FDI and trade: The Irish host-country experience", *Economic Journal,* vol. 107, pp. 1798-1811.

Bchir, H., Decreux, Y., Guérin, J.-L. and Jean, S. (2002) "MIRAGE, a computable general equilibrium model for trade policy analysis", Working Paper No. 17, Centre d'Études Prospectives et d'Informations Internationales.

Bernard, A. B. and Jensen, B. J. (2007) "Firm structure, multinationals, and manufacturing plant deaths", *Review of Economic and Statistics,* Vol. 89, pp. 103-204.

Bernard, A. B., Eaton, J., Bradford J., and Kortum, S. S. (2003) "Plants and productivity in international trade", *American Economic Review,* 93, pp. 1268–90.

Bernard, A. B., Jensen, B. J., Redding, S. J. and Schott, P. K. (2007a) "Firms in international trade", *Journal of Economic Perspectives,* Vol. 21, pp. 105-130.

Bernard, A. B., Redding, S. J. and Schott, P. K. (2007b) "Comparative advantage and heterogeneous firms", *Review of Economic Studies,* 74, pp. 31–66.

Blomström, M. and Kokko, A. (1997) "How foreign investment affects host countries", Policy Research Working Paper No. 1745, The World Bank.

Blomström, M., Lipsey, R. E. and Zejan, M. (1994) "What explains the growth of developing countries?", in Baumol, W. J., Nelson, R. R. and Wolff, E. N. (eds.): *Convergence of productivity: Cross-national studies and historical evidence,* Oxford University Press, Oxford, pp. 243-259.

Blonigen, B. A. (2001) "In search of substitution between foreign production and exports", *Journal of International Economics,* vol. 53, pp. 81-104.

Blonigen, B. A. (2005) "A review of the empirical literature on FDI determinants", Working Paper No. 11299, National Bureau of Economic Research.

Blonigen, B. A., Davies, R. B. and Head, K. (2003) "Estimating the knowledge-capital model of the multinational enterprise: Comment", *American Economic Review,* vol. 93, pp. 980-994.

Böhringer, C., Boeters, S. and Feil, M. (2005) "Taxation and unemployment: an applied general equilibrium approach", *Economic Modelling*, vol. 22, pp. 81-108.

Böhringer, C., Rutherford, T. F. and Wiegard, W. (2003) "Computable General Equilibrium Analysis: Opening a Black Box", Discussion Paper No. 56, Zentrum für Europäische Wirtschaftsforschung.

Borensztein, E., De Gregorio, J. and Lee, J. W. (1998) "How does foreign direct investment affect economic growth?", *Journal of International Economics*, vol. 45, pp. 115-135.

Bornstein, M. (2001) "Post-privatisation enterprise restructuring", *Post-Communist Economies*, vol. 13, pp. 189-203.

Brainard, S. L. (1993) "A simple theory of multinational corporations and trade with a trade-off between proximity and concentration", Working Paper No. 4269, National Bureau of Economic Research.

Brainard, S. L. (1997) "An empirical assessment of the proximity-concentration trade-off between multinational sales and trade", *American Economic Review,* vol. 87, pp. 520-544.

Brown, D. and Stern, R. (2001) "Measurement and modeling of the economic effects of trade and investment barriers in services," *Review of International Economics* 9, pp.262–286.

Brown, D., Deardorff, A. and Stern, R. (2003) "The effects of multinational production on wages and working conditions in developing countries", Working Paper No. 9669, National Bureau of Economic Research.

Buch, C., Piazolo, D. and Kokta, R. M. (2003) "Foreign direct investment in Europe: Is there redirection from the South to the East?", *Journal of Comparative Economics*, vol. 1, pp. 94-109.

Burfisher, M. E., Robinson, S. and Thierfelder, K. (2001)"The Impact of NAFTA on the United States", *Journal of Economic Perspectives,* vol. 15, pp. 125–144.

Campos, N. F. and Kinoshita, Y. (2002): "Foreign direct investment as technology transferred: Some panel evidence from the transition economies", *The Manchester School*, vol. 70, pp. 398-419.

Carkovic, M. and Levine, R. (2005) "Does foreign direct investment accelerate economic growth?", in Moran, T. H., Graham, E. M. and Blomström, M. (eds.) *Does foreign direct investment promote development?*, Institute for International Economics, Washington, DC, pp. 195-220.

Carr, D. J., Markusen, J. R. and Maskus, K. (2001) "Estimating the knowledge capital model of the multinational enterprise", *American Economic Review*, vol. 91, pp. 693-708.

Carr, D. J., Markusen, J. R. and Maskus, K. (2003) "Estimating the knowledge-capital model of the multinational enterprise: Reply", *American Economic Review*, vol. 93, pp. 995-1001.

Caves, R. E. (2007) *Multinational enterprise and economic analysis* (3rd edition), Cambridge University Press, Cambridge.

Co, C. Y. (2001) "Trade, foreign direct investment and industry performance", *International Journal of Industrial Organization,* vol. 19, pp. 163–183.

Coase, R. H. (1937) "The nature of the firm", *Economica*, vol.4, pp. 386-405.

Conyon, M. J., Girma, S., Thompson, S. and Wright, P. W. (2002) "The productivity and wage effects of foreign acquisitions in the United Kingdom", *Journal of Industrial Economics*, vol. 50, pp. 85-102.

Crespo, N. and Fontoura, M. P. (2007) "Determinant factors of FDI spillovers – What do we really know?", *World Development*, Vol. 35, pp. 410–425.

Czech National Bank (2004) "2001 Foreign direct investment", Annual reports, available at:http://www.cnb.cz/www.cnb.cz/en/statistics.

Damijan, J., Knell, M., Majcen, B. and Rojec, M. (2003) "The role of FDI, R&D accumulation and trade in transferring technology to transition countries: Evidence from firm panel data for eight transition countries", *Economic Systems*, vol. 27, pp. 189-204.

Dawkins, C., Srinivasan, T. N. and Whalley, J. (2001) "Calibration", in Heckman J. J. and Leamer, E. (eds.) *Handbook of Econometrics*, vol. 5, Elsevier, Amsterdam, pp. 3653-3706.

Devarajan, S. and Robinson, S. (2005) "The Influence of computable general equilibrium models on policy", in Kehoe, T. J., Srinivasan, T. N. and Whalley, J. (eds.) *Frontiers in applied general equilibrium modeling: In honor of Herbert Scarf*, Cambridge University Press, Cambridge, pp. 402-428.

Dimaranan, B. V. (ed.) (2007) *Global trade, Assistance, and Production: The GTAP 6 Data Base*, Center for Global Trade Analysis, Purdue University, West Lafayette, IN.

Dixit, A. and Norman, V. (1980) *International Trade Theory*, Cambridge University Press, Cambridge.

Djankov, S and Hoekman, B (2000) "Foreign investment and productivity growth in Czech enterprises", *The World Bank Economic Review*, vol. 14, pp. 49-64.

Doms, M. E. and Jensen, J. B. (1998) "Comparing wages, skills, and productivity between domestically and foreign owned manufacturing establishments in the United States", in Baldwin, R. E, Lipsey, R. E. and Richardson, D. J. (eds.) *The United States: Geography vs. Ownership in*

Economic Accounting, The University of Chicago Press, Chicago, pp. 235-255.

Donaghu, M. and Barff, R. (1990) "Nike just did it: International subcontracting and flexibility in athletic footwear production", *Regional Studies*, vol. 48, pp. 37-70.

Dunning, J. H. (1977a) "Trade, location of economic activity and the MNE: A search for an eclectic approach", in Ohlin, B., Hesselborn, P. O. and Wijkman, P. J. (eds.) *The international allocation of economic activity,* Macmillan, London, pp. 395-431.

Dunning, J. H. (1977b) "The determinants of international production", *Oxford Economic Papers*, vol. 25, pp. 289-330.

Dunning, J. H. (1979) "Explaining changing patterns of international production: In defence of the eclectic theory", *Oxford Bulletin of Economics and Statistics*, vol. 41, pp. 269-295.

Dunning, J. H. (1981) "Explaining the international direct investment position of countries: Towards a dynamic or developmental approach", *Weltwirtschaftliches Archiv*, vol. 122, pp. 667-677.

Dunning, J. H. (2000) "The eclectic paradigm as an envelope for economic and business theories of MNE activity", *International Business Review*, vol. 9, pp. 163-190.

Dunning, J. H. and Narula, R. (1998) "The investment development path revisited: Some emerging issues", in Dunning, J. H. and Narula, R. (eds.) *Foreign direct investment and governments: Catalysts for economic restructuring,* Routledge, London, pp. 1-41.

EBRD (2001) *Transition Report*, European Bank for Reconstruction and Development.

Ekholm, K., Forslid, R. and Markusen, J.R. (2007) "Export-Platform foreign firect investment", *Journal of the European Economic Association*, Vol. 5, pp. 776-795.

Ethier, W. (1986) "The multinational firm", *Quarterly Journal of Economics*, vol. 101, pp. 805-833.

Ethier, W. and Markusen, J. R. (1996) "Multinational firms, technology diffusion and trade", *Journal of International Economics*, vol. 41, pp. 1-28.

Eurostat, (2009a) *Statistics on foreign control of enterprises - all activities (FATs)*, available at: http://epp.eurostat.ec.europa.eu/portal/page/portal/european_business/data/database

Eurostat, (2009b) *European Union Foreign Affiliates Statistics (Outward FATS)*, available at: http://epp.eurostat.ec.europa.eu/portal/

page/ portal/ balance_of_payments/data/database

Evenett, S. J. and Voicu, A. (2001) "Picking winners or creating them? Revisiting the benefits of FDI in the Czech Republic", mimeo, The World Bank.

Fajnzylber, F. and Martínez Tarragó, T. (1976) Las empresas trasnacionales: Expansión a nivel mundial y proyección en la industria mexicana, Fondo de Cultura Económica, México.

Feenstra, R. C. (1998) "Integration of trade and disintegration of production in the global economy", *Journal of Economic Perspectives*, vol. 12, pp. 31-50.

Feenstra, R. C. (2004) "Multinationals and organization of the firm", in Feenstra, R. *Advanced international trade: Theory and evidence*, Princeton University Press, Princeton, pp. 371-409.

Feenstra, R. C. and Hanson, G. H. (1996) "Foreign investment, outsourcing, and relative wages", in Feenstra, R. C., Grossman, G. M. and Irwin, D. A. (eds.) *Political Economy of Trade Policy: Essays in honor of Jagdish Bhagwati*, The MIT Press, Cambridge, MA, pp. 89-127.

Feldstein, M. (1995) "The effect of outbound foreign direct investment on the domestic capital stock", in Feldstein, M., Hines, J. and Hubbard, R. G. (eds.) *The effects of international taxation on multinationals corporations*, University of Chicago Press, Chicago, pp. 43-66.

Feliciano, Z. and Lipsey, R. E. (1999) "Foreign ownership and wages in the United States, 1987-1992", Working Paper No. 6923, National Bureau of Economic Research.

Fernández-Otheo, C. M. and Myro, R. (2003) "Desinversión de capital extranjero en la industria española, 1993-2002", *Estudios sobre la Economía Española*, No. 168, FEDEA.

Fernández-Otheo, C. M., Martín, D. and Myro, R. (2004) "Desinversión y deslocalización de capital extranjero en España", *Ekonomiaz*, No. 55, pp. 106-129.

Ferrett, B. (2004) "Foreign direct investment and productivity growth: A survey of theory", GEP Research Paper 2004/15, Leverhulme Centre for Research on Globalisation and Economic Policy, University of Nottingham.

Fosfuri, A., Motta, M. and Ronde, T. (2001) "Foreign Direct Investment and Spillovers through Workers' Mobility," *Journal of International Economics,* vol. 53, pp. 205-222.

Gilham, J. (2005) "The economic interrelationships of tourism: A computable general equilibrium analysis", PhD Dissertation, University of Nottingham.

Goldberg, L. and Klein, M. (1999) "International trade and factor mobility: An empirical investigation", Working Paper No. 7196, National Bureau of Economic Research.

Gómez-Plana, A. G. (2005) "Simulación de políticas económicas: Los modelos de equilibrio general aplicado", *Cuadernos Económicos de ICE*, No. 69, pp. 198-217.

Gómez-Plana, A. G. (2007) "Política medioambiental y sustitución tecnológica entre inputs", *Hacienda Pública Española/Revista de Economía Pública,* No. 181, pp. 9-28.

Görg, H. and Greenaway, D. (2004) "Much ado about nothing? Do domestic firms really benefit from foreign direct investment?", *The World Bank Research Observer*, vol. 19, pp. 171-197.

Graham, E. W. (1992) "Los determinantes de la inversión extranjera: Teorías alternativas y evidencia internacional", *Moneda y Crédito*, No. 194, pp. 13-55.

Greenaway, D. and Kneller, R. (2007) "Firm heterogeneity, exporting and foreign direct investment", *Economic Journal*, vol. 117, pp. 134-161.

Grossman, S. J., and Hart, O. D. (1986) "The costs and benefits of ownership: A theory of vertical and lateral integration", *Journal of Political Economy*, vol. 94, pp. 691-719.

Grossman, G. M. and Helpman, E. (2002) "Integration vs. outsourcing in industry equilibrium", *Quarterly Journal of Economics*, vol. 117, pp. 85-120.

Grossman, G., Helpman, E. and Szeidl, A. (2006) "Optimal integration strategies for the multinational firm", *Journal of International Economics*, vol. 70, pp. 216-238.

Grubert, H. and Mutti J. (1991) "Taxes, tariffs and transfer pricing in multinational corporate decision making", *Review of Economics and Statistics*, vol. 73, pp. 285-293.

Hanslow, K., Phamduc, T. and Verikios, G. (1999) *The Structure of the FTAP Model,* Research Memorandum MC-58, Productivity Commission, Canberra.

Hanson, G., Malatoni, R. and Slaughter, M. (2005) "Vertical production networks in multinational firms", *Review of Economics and Statistics*, vol. 87, pp. 664-678.

Harrison, G. W., Jones, R., Kimbell, L. J. and Wigle, R. (1993) "How robust is applied general equilibrium analysis?", *Journal of Policy Modeling*, vol. 15, pp. 99-115.

Haskel, J. E., Pereira, S. and Slaughter, M. (2002) "Does inward foreign direct investment boost the productivity of domestic firms?", Working Paper No. 8724, National Bureau of Economic Research.

Head, K. and Ries, J. (2001) "Overseas investment and firm exports" *Review of International Economics*, vol. 9, pp. 108-22.

Helpman, E. (1981) "International trade in the presence of product differentiation, economies of scale, and monopolistic competition: A Chamberlin-Heckscher-Ohlin approach", *Journal of International Economics*, vol. 11, pp. 305-340.

Helpman, E. (1984) "A simple theory of international trade with multinational corporations", *Journal or Political Economy*, vol. 92, p. 451-471.

Helpman, E. (2006) "Trade, FDI, and the organization of firms", *Journal of Economic Literature*, vol. 44, pp. 589-630.

Helpman, E., Melitz, M. J. and Yeaple, S. R. (2004) "Exports versus FDI with heterogeneous firms", *American Economic Review*, vol. 94, pp. 300-316.

Helpman, E, Melitz, M. and Rubinstein, Y. (2007) "Estimating trade flows: trading partners and trading volumes", Working Paper No. 12927, National Bureau of Economic Research.

Hertel, T. W. (ed.) (1997) *Global trade analysis. Modelling and applications*, Cambridge University Press, Cambridge.

Hertel, T. W., Hummels, D. L., Ivanic, M., and Keeney, R. (2007) "How confident can we be of CGE-based assessments of Free Trade Agreements?", *Economic Modelling*, vol. 24, pp. 611-635.

Hirsch, S. (1976) "An international trade and investment theory of the firm", *Oxford Economic Papers*, vol. 28, pp. 258-270.

Huttunen, K. (2007) "The effect of foreign acquisition on employment and wages: Evidence from Finnish establishments", *Review of Economics and Statistics,* vol. 89, pp. 497-509.

Hymer, S. H. (1976) The international operations of national firms: A study of direct foreign investment, The MIT Press, Cambridge, MA.

Ietto-Gillies, G. (2000) "Profits from foreign direct investment", in Chesnais, F., Ietto-Gillies, G. and Simonetti, R. (eds.) *European Integration and Global Corporate Strategies*, Routledge, London, pp. 71-91.

Ihrig, J. (2000) "Multinationals' response to repatriation restrictions", *Journal of Economic Dynamics and Control*, vol. 24, pp. 1345-1379.

IMF (1993) *IMF Balance of Payments Manual*, 5th edition, available at: http://www.imf.org/external/np/sta/bop/BOPman.pdf.

Jansen, K. (1995) "The macroeconomic effects of direct foreign investment: the case of Thailand", *World Development*, vol. 23, pp. 193-210.

Jensen, J., Rutherford, T. and Tarr, D. (2007) "The impact of liberalizing barriers", *Review of Development Economics*, vol. 11, pp. 482-506.

Jones, R. W. (1971) "A three-factor model in theory, trade and history", in Bhagwati, J. N., Jones, R.W., Mundell, R. A. and Vanek, J. (eds.) *Trade, balance of payments and growth: Papers in International Economics in honor of Charles P. Kindleberger*, North-Holland, Amsterdam, pp. 3-21.

Jones, R. W. (2000) *Globalisation and the theory of input trade*, The MIT Press, Cambridge, MA.

Jones, R. W. (2002) "Trade theory and factor intensities: An interpretative essay", *Review of International Economics*, vol. 10, pp. 581-603.

Jorgenson, D. (1984) "Econometric methods for applied general equilibrium analysis", in Scarf, H. E. and Shoven, J. B. (eds.) *Applied general equilibrium analysis*, Cambridge University Press, Cambridge, pp. 139-203.

Kalotay, K. and Hunya, G. (2000) "Privatization and FDI in Central and Eastern Europe", *Transnational Corporations*, vol. 9, pp. 39-66.

Kehoe, T. J. (2005) "An evaluation of the performance of applied general equilibrium models on the impact of NAFTA", in Kehoe, T. J., Srinivasan, T. N. and Whalley, J. (eds.) *Frontiers in Applied General Equilibrium Modeling: In Honor of Herbert Scarf*, Cambridge University Press, Cambridge, pp. 341-377.

Kehoe, T. J., Polo, C. and Sancho, F. (1995) "An Evaluation of the Performance of an Applied General Equilibrium Model of the Spanish Economy," *Economic Theory*, vol. 6, pp. 115-141.

Kinoshita, Y. (2001) "R&D and technology spillovers through FDI: Innovation and absorptive capacity", Discussion Paper No. 2775, Centre for Economic Policy Research.

Köhler, J., Grubb, M., Popp, D. and Edenhofer, O. (2006): "The transition to endogenous technical change in climate-economy models: A technical overview to the Innovation Modeling Comparison Project", *Energy Journal*, Special Issue: Endogenous Technological Change and the Economics of Atmospheric Stabilisation, pp. 17-55.

Konings, J. (2001) "The effects of foreign direct investment on domestic firms: Evidence from firm-level panel data in emerging economies", *Economics of Transition*, vol. 9, pp. 619-633.

Krkoska, L. (2001a) "Assessing macroeconomic vulnerability in Central Europe", *Post-Communist Economies*, vol. 13, pp. 41-55.

Krkoska, L. (2001b) "Foreign direct investment financing of capital formation in Central and Eastern Europe", Working Paper No. 67, European Bank for Reconstruction and Development.

Krugman, P. (1979) "Increasing returns, monopolistic competition, and international trade", *Journal of International Economics*, vol. 9, pp. 469-480.

Krugman, P. (1980) "Scale economies, product differentiation, and the pattern of trade", *American Economic Review*, vol. 70, pp. 950-959.

Krugman, P. (1995) "Increasing returns, imperfect competition and the positive theory of international trade", in Grossman, G. and Rogoff, K. (eds.) *Handbook of International Economics* (vol. III), North-Holland, Amsterdam, pp. 1243-1277.

Latorre, C. (2002) "La inversión directa en los países del Este Europeo: Una valoración de su naturaleza y volumen", *Economía Industrial*, No. 345, pp. 67-78.

Latorre, C. (2004): "Nota crítica: Modelos de comercio que incorporan multinacionales: ¿Es posible? Una visión de las aportaciones que James R. Markusen reúne en su libro "Multinational firms and the theory of international trade", *Información Comercial Española*, No. 817, pp.230-235.

Latorre, C. (2009) "The economic analysis of multinationals and foreign direct investment: A review", *Hacienda Pública Española*, vol. 191, pp. 97-126.

Latorre, C., Bajo-Rubio, O. and Gómez-Plana, A. G. (2009) "The effects of MNES on host economies: A CGE approach", *Economic Modelling*, vol. 26, pp. 851-864.

Lee, H and van der Mensbrugghe, D. (2001) "A general equilibrium analysis of the interplay between foreign direct investment and trade adjustments", Working Paper No. 119, Research Institute for Economics and Business Administration, Kobe University.

Lipsey, R. E. (1999) "The role of foreign direct investment in international capital flows", in Feldstein, M. (ed.) *International Capital Flows*, The University of Chicago Press, Chicago, pp. 307-330.

Lipsey, R. E. (2002) "Home and host country effects of FDI", Working Paper No. 9293, National Bureau of Economic Research.

Lipsey, R. E. (2003) "Foreign direct investment and the operations of multinational firms: Concepts, history and data", in Choi, E. K. and

Harrigan, J. (eds.), *Handbook of International Trade*, Blackwell, Oxford, pp. 287-319.

Lipsey, R. E. and Sjoholm, F. (2003) "Foreign firms and Indonesian manufacturing wages: An analysis with panel data", Working Paper No. 9417, National Bureau of Economic Research.

Lipsey, R. E. and Sjoholm, F. (2004) "Foreign direct investment, education and wages in Indonesian manufacturing", *Journal of Development Economics*, vol. 73, pp. 415-422.

Lipsey, R. E. and Weiss, M. Y. (1981) "Foreign production and exports in manufacturing industries", *Review of Economics and Statistics*, vol. 63, pp. 488-94.

Lipsey, R. E. and Weiss, M. Y. (1984) "Foreign production and exports of individual firms", *Review of Economics and Statistics*, vol. 66, pp. 304-07.

Lizal, L. and Svegnar, J. (2002) "Investment, credit rationing, and the soft budget constraint: Evidence from Czech panel data", *Review of Economics and Statistics*, vol. 84, pp. 353-370.

Lorentowicz, A., Marin, D. and Raubold, A. (2002) "Ownership, capital or outsourcing: What drives German investment to Eastern Europe?", Discussion Paper No. 3515, Centre for Economic Policy Research.

Lucas, R. (1990) "Why doesn't Capital Flow from Rich to Poor Countries?", *American Economic Review*, vol. 80, pp. 92–96.

MacDougall, G. D. A. (1960) "The benefits and costs of private investment from abroad: A theoretical approach", *Economic Record*, Special Issue, pp. 13-35.

Marin, D. (2004) "A nation of poets and thinkers –less so with Eastern enlargement? Austria and Germany", Discussion Paper No. 4358, Centre for Economic Policy Research.

Markusen, J. R. (1984) "Multinational, multi-plant economies, and the gains from trade", *Journal of International Economics*, vol. 16, pp. 205-226.

Markusen, J. R. (1995) "The boundaries of multinational enterprises and the theory of international trade", *Journal of Economic Perspectives*, vol. 9, pp. 169-189.

Markusen, J. R. (1997) "Trade versus investment liberalisation", Working Paper No. 6231, National Bureau of Economic Research.

Markusen, J. R. (2002) Multinational Firms and the Theory of International Trade, The MIT Press, Cambridge, MA.

Markusen, J. R. and Venables, A. J. (1998) "Multinational firms and the new trade theory", *Journal of International Economics*, vol. 46, pp. 183-203.

Markusen, J. R. and Venables, A. J. (2000) "The theory of endowment, intra-industry trade and multinational trade", *Journal of International Economics*, vol. 52, pp. 209-234.

Markusen, J. R., Rutherford, T. and Tarr, D. (2005) "Trade and direct investment in producer services and the domestic market for expertise", *Canadian Journal of Economics*, vol. 38, pp. 758- 777.

Martínez González-Tablas, A. (1979) *Capitalismo extranjero en España*, Cupsa, Madrid.

Mathiesen, L. (1985) "Computation of Economic Equilibria by a Sequence of Linear Complementarity Problems", *Mathematical Programming Study*, vol. 23, pp. 144-162.

McKitrick, R. R. (1998) "The econometric critique of computable general equilibrium modeling: The role of functional forms", *Economic Modelling*, vol. 15, pp. 543–573.

McLaren, J. (2000) "Globalization and vertical structure", *American Economic Review,* vol. 90, pp.1239-1254.

Melitz, M. J. (2003) "The impact of trade on intra-industry reallocations and aggregate industry productivity", *Econometrica*, vol. 71, pp. 1695-1725.

Molero, J. (2000) "Multinationals, domestic firms and the internationalization of technology: Spain as an intermediate case", in Chesnais, F., Ietto-Gillies, G. and Simonetti, R. (eds.) *European integration and global corporate strategies*, Routledge, London, pp. 192-221.

Molero, J. and Álvarez, I. (2003) "The technological strategies of multinational enterprises: Their implications for national systems of innovation", in Cantwell, J. and Molero, J. (eds.) *Multinational enterprises, innovative strategies and systems of innovation*, Edward Elgar, Cheltenham, pp. 177-205.

Molero, J. and Buesa, M. (1993) "Multinational companies and technological change: Basic traits and taxonomy of German industrial companies in Spain", *Research Policy*, vol. 22, pp. 265-278.

Molero, J., Buesa, M. and Casado, M. (1995) "Technological strategies of MNCs in intermediate countries: The case of Spain", in Molero, J. (ed.) *Technological innovation, multinational corporations and new international competitiveness: The case of intermediate countries*, Harwood Academic Publishers, Reading, pp. 265-291.

Mundell, R. A. (1957) "International trade and factor mobility", *American Economic Review*, vol. 47, pp. 321-335.

Muñoz, J., Roldán, S. and Serrano, A. (1978) *La internacionalización del capital en España 1959-1977*, Cuadernos para el Diálogo, Madrid.

Mussa, M. (1974) "Tariffs and the distribution of income: The importance of factor specificity, substitutability, and intensity in the short and long run", *Journal of Political Economy*, vol. 82, pp. 1191-1203.

Neary, J. P. (1978) "Short-run capital specificity and the pure theory of international trade", *Economic Journal*, vol. 88, pp. 488-510.

Nocke, V. and Yeaple, S. (2007) "Cross-border mergers and acquisitions vs. greenfield foreign direct investment: The role of firm heterogeneity", *Journal of International Economics*, vol. 72, pp. 336–365.

OECD (2001) Reviews of foreign direct investment: Czech Republic, Paris.

OECD (2004) *Science and technology statistical compendium*, available at: http://www.oecd.org/document/8/0,2340,en_2649_33703_23654472_1_1_1_1,00.html.

OECD (2005) *Measuring globalisation: OECD Handbook on economic globalisation indicators*, Paris.

OECD (2007) *Measuring globalisation: Activities of multinationals*, Volume 1, Manufacturing 2000-2004, Paris.

OECD (2009a) *Globalisation: Activities of multinationals*, available at: http://stats.oecd.org/index.aspx?r=983789

OECD (2009b) *Globalisation: Foreign direct investment statistics*, available at: http://stats.oecd.org/index.aspx?r=983789

O'Rourke, K. (1995) "Computable general equilibrium models and Economic History", mimeo, available at: http://www.gams.com/solvers/mpsge/orourke.htm.

Petri, P. A. (1997) "Foreign direct investment in a computable general equilibrium framework", paper presented at the Brandeis-Keio Conference on "Making APEC work: Economic challenges and Policy Alternatives", Keio University, Tokyo, March 13-14.

Rauch, J. E. and Trindade, V. (2003) "Information, international substitutability and globalisation", *American Economic Review*, vol. 93, pp. 755-791.

Romer, P. M. (1993) "Idea gaps and object gaps in economic development", *Journal of Monetary Economics*, vol. 32, pp. 543-573.

Rutherford, T. F. (2005) "GTAP6inGAMS: The dataset and static model", prepared for the workshop "Applied general equilibrium modeling for trade policy analysis in Russia and the CIS", Moscow, December 1-9.

Rutherford, T. F. and Paltsev, S. V. (2000) "GTAPinGAMS and GTAP-EG: Global datasets for economic research and illustrative models", Working Paper, Department of Economics, University of Colorado, September.

Rutherford, T. F. and Tarr, D. G. (2008) "Poverty effects of Russia's WTO accession: Modeling "real" households with endogenous productivity effects", *Journal of International Economics,* vol. 75, pp. 131–150.

Sanna-Randaccio, F. and Veugelers, R. (2003) "Global innovation strategies of MNEs: Implications for host economies", in Cantwell, J. and Molero, J. (eds.) *Multinational enterprises, innovative strategies and systems of innovation,* Edward Elgar, Cheltenham, pp. 17-46.

Sanna-Randaccio, F. and Veugelers, R. (2007) "Multinational knowledge spillovers with decentralised R&D: A game theoretic approach", *Journal of International Business Studies,* vol. 38, pp. 47-63.

Scarf, H. E. and Shoven, J. B. (eds.) (1984) *Applied general equilibrium analysis,* Cambridge University Press, Cambridge.

Schöllmann, W. (2001) "Foreign participation in privatisation: What does it mean? Empirical evidence from the Czech Republic, Hungary and Poland", *Post-Communist Economies,* vol. 13, pp. 373-387.

Seabra, F. and Flach, L. (2005) "Foreign direct investment and profit outflows: A causality analysis for the Brazilian economy", *Economics Bulletin,* vol. 6, pp. 1-5.

Sembenelli, A. and Siotis, G. (2005) "Foreign direct investment, competitive pressure and spillovers. An empirical analysis of Spanish firm-level data", Discussion Paper no. 4903, Centre for Economic Policy Research.

Shoven, J. B. and Whalley, J. (1984) "Applied general-equilibrium models of taxation and international trade: An introduction and survey", *Journal of Economic Literature,* vol. 22, pp. 1007-1051.

Shoven, J. B. and Whalley, J. (1992) *Applying General Equilibrium,* Cambridge University Press, Cambridge.

Smarzynska, B. (2004) "Does foreign direct investment increase the productivity of domestic firms? In search of spillovers through backward linkages", *American Economic Review,* vol. 94, pp. 605-627.

Swenson, D. L. (2003) "Overseas assembly and country sourcing choices", Working Paper No. 10697, National Bureau of Economic Research.

Swenson, D. L. (2004) "Foreign investment and mediation of trade flows", *Review of International Economics,* vol. 12, pp. 609-29.

UNCTAD (several years) *World Investment Report,* United Nations, New York and Geneva.

Vaitsos, C. (1974) Intercountry income distribution and transnational Enterprises, Clarendon Press, Oxford.

Vaitsos, C. (1975) "Las relaciones económicas entre el Norte y el Sur: Análisis de las inversiones y las técnicas productivas", *El Trimestre Económico*, vol. 42, pp. 143-167.

Verikios, G. and Zhang, X-G. (2001a) "The FTAP2 model: Theory and data", Research Memorandum MC-61, Productivity Commission, Canberra.

Verikios, G. and Zhang, X-G. (2001b) "Global gains from liberalising trade in telecommunications and financial services", Productivity Commission Staff Research Paper, Ausinfo, Canberra.

Vernon, R. (1966) "International investment and international trade in the product cycle", *Quarterly Journal of Economics*, vol. 80, pp. 190-207.

WIIW (several years) *Handbook of Statistics: Countries in transition*, Wiener Institut für Internationale Wirtschaftsvergleiche, Vienna.

Williamson, O. E. (1975) "Markets and hierarchies: Analysis and antitrust implications. A study in the economics of internal organisation", Free Press, New York.

Williamson, O. E. (1985) "The Economic Institutions of Capitalism: firms, markets, relational contracting", Free Presss, New York, Chapters 1-3.

Yeaple, S. (2003a) "The role of skill endowments in the structure of U.S outward FDI", *Review of Economics and Statistics*, vol. 85, pp. 726-734.

Yeaple, S. (2003b) "The complex integration strategies of multinationals and cross country dependencies in the structure of FDI" *Journal of International Economics*, vol. 60, pp. 293-314.

Zhai, F. (2008) "Armington meets Melitz: Introducing firm heterogeneity in a global CGE model of trade", *Journal of Economic Integration*, 23, pp. 575-604.

Zhang, K. H. and Markusen, J. R. (1999) "Vertical multinationals and host-country characteristics", *Journal of Development Economics*, vol. 59, pp. 233-252.

INDEX